14.50

Making IT work for you

(Information Technology across the Primary Curriculum)

Valsa Koshy and Pat Dodds

First published in 1995 by:

Stanley Thornes (Publishers) Ltd
Ellenborough House
Wellington Street
CHELTENHAM GL50 1YD

A catalogue record for this book is available from the British Library.

ISBN 0 7487 2096 0

Designed and typeset in Buckingham by Can Do Design
Printed in Great Britain by Redwood Books, Trowbridge

Acknowledgements

We would like to thank the following people:

- The children whose enjoyment and enthusiasm for using IT inspired us to take on this challenging task.
- All the teachers on in-service courses who shared their thoughts with us.
- Our initial training students whose confidence in their use of IT grew through the sensitive support we trust this book reflects.
- Hounslow Town Primary School in the London Borough of Hounslow and their IT co-ordinator Sarah Cooper who has demonstrated to us what can actually be achieved in a well co-ordinated IT environment.

Contents

Preface

The Impact Project (1993), which evaluated the 'impact' of Information Technology (IT) on children's achievements, based on a study involving 2300 pupils and 19 LEAs in the UK, outlined the following as the benefits of IT for learning:

- computers were found to be motivators which heightened pupils' interest and enjoyment of subjects
- children's involvement in activities was sustained over quite lengthy periods
- IT offered a focus for collaborative and group activities and contributed to the development of a range of process skills
- some open-ended work offered in IT enabled pupils to become involved in more complex and challenging learning situations than normal, which were then carried over into more traditional learning settings.

These results are consistent with our own findings through years of working with children and from experiences related to us as initial and in-service trainers.

We believe that IT, with its speed, power and versatility, offers a unique resource in teaching and learning. How to make the best use of that resource is the theme of this book. The focus is on how IT can enhance teaching and learning. The book gives many practical ideas on how to explore the potential of IT for learning.

Introduction

Information Technology (IT) is concerned with any machine which can store and process information. Tape recorders, video recorders, cameras, fax machines, calculators and computers are everywhere and they play an important part in our daily lives. Careful planning and consideration can help teachers to make optimum use of these machines to enrich children's learning.

Why use IT?

1 Good practice in teaching and learning can be achieved through using IT.

2 The speed and versatility of IT creates powerful learning opportunities which cannot always be achieved through books and pencil and paper tasks.

3 Experience and research have shown that using IT can increase children's motivation.

4 IT is part of the National Curriculum, in England and Wales, and of the Scottish guidelines and curriculum guidelines in Northern Ireland.

What does this book offer?

This book offers a positive contribution to the use of IT for effective teaching and learning. The book:

- is based on experiences and examples from real classrooms
- identifies links with the National Curriculum and applications of IT to other subjects
- presents ideas for planning and assessing activities for both Key Stages 1 and 2
- provides users with advice on how to get the maximum benefit from a range of resources
- demystifies jargon associated with IT, especially relating to computers
- offers a list of resources and support agencies.

THINK ABOUT IT!

Before you read any further take a few minutes to reflect on your personal needs to ensure effective use of IT in your classroom. You may want to write them down.

Making effective use of IT

A hundred teachers were asked to list the questions they would most like to ask about the use of IT. The most frequently asked questions are listed overleaf. As you work your way through the book you should find answers to these concerns.

How early can you introduce children to IT?

What are databases?

What kind of things can you do in IT with younger children?

How do I organise the use of IT in my classroom?

Which machine is best?

What are the different parts of a computer?

How do I assess children's IT capability and keep a record of their experiences?

How do you select software?

How do you organise your hardware and software?

What do you do when the machine refuses to work?

Where do I find out more about the jargon and what it all means?

When I plan my lessons, how do I decide which specific program to use?

How do I group children for IT?

How do I make sure that I have covered all the National Curriculum statements relating to IT?

I have taken on the role of IT co-ordinator and have to review the school policy – help!

THINK ABOUT IT!

Do you have a question that is not included in this list?
Write it down and see if you can find a page reference to help you.

About this book

Whether you plan your teaching in subject areas, through cross-curricular themes or using some style of organisation between the two, the ideas in this book will offer you support for the on-going cycle of planning, teaching and assessing as illustrated in the diagram.

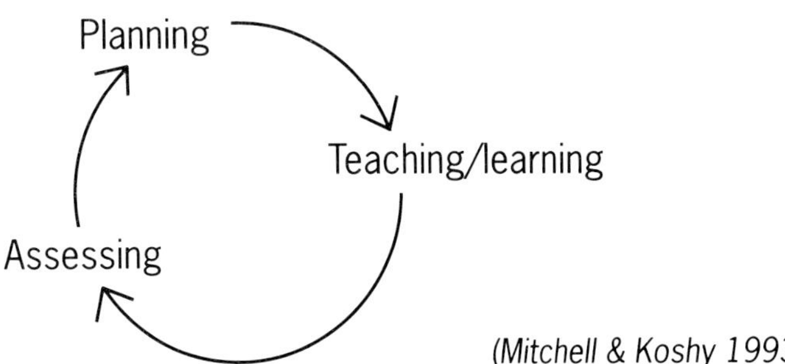

(Mitchell & Koshy 1993)

It is intended that children will develop competence in IT through your overall curriculum plan which sets all activities in a meaningful context.

The introductory part of this book addresses the broader issues of using IT in a primary school. A range of specific activities and ideas to help, plan, teach and assess IT capability are then provided.

First, we have focused on the role of the three core curriculum subjects – Mathematics, English and Science. Then we have attempted to show how teaching IT can be integrated into cross-curricular themes.

Most of the activities in the book focus on the use of the computer, because our survey of a hundred teachers has shown that this is the area of IT where most help was requested.

It is impossible to include and anticipate all IT developments. It is hoped that you, the reader, will add to the book and up-date it in the spaces provided in the resources section.

THINK ABOUT IT!

Review your current curriculum planning. Look at planning documents and mark in pencil all references to using IT. Are there plenty of references to IT?

Information Technology in the National Curriculum

Information Technology in the National Curriculum identifies two strands of IT capability. Trying to understand what each of the strands is about should assist you in relating them to classroom lessons and choosing from the resources available. Such understanding should also help you to make the maximum use of the potential offered by IT to enhance children's learning.

The two strands are:

- communicating and handling information
- controlling, monitoring and modelling.

Communicating and handling information

Communicating information involves children in using words, pictures and sounds to communicate their ideas and information as effectively as possible to others. This involves them in talking to people, tape-recording, drafting and redrafting their ideas and also presenting the ideas in different formats to suit different audiences.

Useful IT resources:

Concept keyboards
Tape recorders
Video recorders
Word processors
Desk-top publishing packages
Electronic mail
Graphics packages
Music packages

Handling information encourages children to ask questions and seek explanations of the world around them. IT resources, such as data handling packages, enable children to collect, store, retrieve and analyse data to be used for a variety of purposes. With the built-in facility of obtaining tables and graphs and instant print-outs of analysed information, data can be presented in a variety of formats to suit each purpose and audience.

Useful IT resources:

Databases
Spreadsheets
Teletext
Electronic mail
Interactive videos
CD-ROMs
Multi-media

Controlling, monitoring and modelling

We live in a world surrounded by many applications of IT. Children need to appreciate how all the appliances around them affect their lives and to reflect on the extent to which their lives are dependent on them.

Examples are:

- the travel agent can check availability of your Caribbean holiday in seconds
- some cars are completely built by robots
- teletext gives you weather, news and traffic reports
- most banking can be done at the cash point
- sending a fax can be cheaper than a phone call
- newspaper reporters gather last minute news items and they can be printed in your daily newspaper.

With so many examples of IT in our environment, it makes sense to have your classroom reflect this.

A useful starting point with any group would be to engage the children in an activity which investigates the use and application of IT in their own lives.

Children can be involved in programming toys and robots to make them carry out specific tasks. Using roamers, floor turtles and Logo they can learn to control, predict and describe the effects of their decisions.

Through computer simulations and adventure games children are encouraged to handle different situations and to find the best solutions possible by making the best decisions available to them. Whether the situations involve a fantasy world, such as building traffic lights in a 'gnome development', or building a school tuckshop, IT packages offer opportunities to develop problem-solving processes. 'What would happen if ...' becomes a meaningful situation where alternative solutions need to be sought.

Useful IT resources:

Roamers
Floor turtles
Logo
Control Logo
Datalogging
Sensors
Adventure games
Simulations
Mathematical investigations
Spreadsheets

Information Technology and learning

Motivation can undoubtedly affect learning. As teachers, we have all experienced children saying things such as:

'This is the best lesson in the world!'

'Oh! that was good!'

'Can I stay in at playtime and do some more?'

Such comments are often overheard when children are working with computers. It is fair to assume that this level of motivation leads to purposeful learning.

Collaborative work often leads to effective learning provided it is well planned and focused. Co-operative working is a sound educational process but it is hard to implement. A careful match is required between the setting of the group and the way the task is given to the pupils. It is important that the process and the outcome require genuine co-operation, otherwise the group setting will break down. IT offers a purposeful context for children to work together (see also *Grouping children* on p. 20).

Problem solving encourages children to develop processes needed to investigate and persevere with a task. Many content-free programs, such as Logo, databases, adventures and simulations, are designed to encourage problem-solving strategies.

Whilst working on a piece of problem-solving software, children are encouraged to:

- ask questions
- sort information
- clarify ideas
- make and test hypotheses
- see mistakes as part of the learning process
- ask 'what would happen if ...'
- make decisions.

In addition, at a social level, children are trained to:

- take turns
- listen
- discuss
- accept other people's opinions
- be challenged
- give and accept criticism.

Developing children's IT capability

Children need to appreciate the use of IT outside the classroom and in offices and shops.

They need to develop increasing confidence in the use of IT.

They should be able to select and use suitable software for tasks.

By reflection and discussion they should be able to evaluate the effectiveness of their IT projects and the role of IT in their daily lives.

It is never too early for children to be IT users. Well selected programs can enhance the learning process of all children of any age.

Using IT not only encourages children to learn new facts and skills, but it also encourages processes which help them to be authors, mathematicians, scientists, designers, artists and historians etc. in the future.

Making friends with your computer

The world of IT is constantly developing, which offers a challenge to both experienced and novice users. We have to make sure we get to know new hardware and software.

Comments which are often made by new users are:

'It will take me ages to learn how a computer works.'

'I have so much else to do with my time.'

'If only someone would give me just enough information to make a start.'

These are very genuine concerns. The purpose of the following few pages is to help all those teachers who want to know that 'little bit' so that they can make a start. These pages may also help to highlight, for an experienced IT co-ordinator, what anxieties are felt by the less experienced teachers.

Obviously, a complete mastery of all computing techniques may take a long time to acquire, but you do not need to be an expert to make a start. An analogy with driving is quite helpful. In order to start to learn to drive, you do not need to know how all the parts under the bonnet work. Once you start driving you increase your familiarity with the car. You get used to the noises it makes, how it behaves and then you may want to study more about how the inside of the car works.

Just by putting the disks into the disk drive, or following the instructions for the hard-disk, many educational programs can be used.

There is an abundant supply of software available to choose from. These programs can be classified into two categories: **structured software** and **content-free software**.

Structured programs are easier to use as they are ready-made to be followed in a specific way. All the outcomes have been decided previously by the designer.

Content-free software packages such as data handling, Logo, and word processing are more open-ended in their uses. These can be used according to the needs and purpose of the user – they offer more flexibility and allow for differentiation. You will need to spend a little more time to use content-free programs to get used to their layout and appreciate the potential they offer for effective learning.

Hardware

The computer hardware consists of the main system unit, which includes the monitor and the keyboard, and the peripheral equipment, such as the printer, the mouse and other tools.

By reading the instruction manual and connecting the right cables into the sockets (most machines have very few cables to connect these days), you can make a start.

Software

The programs stored on floppy disks are called software. Other programs are pre-loaded into the computer. These are also part of the software.

More explanations of technical terms are given in the section on *Demystifying the IT jargon* on pp. 99–100.

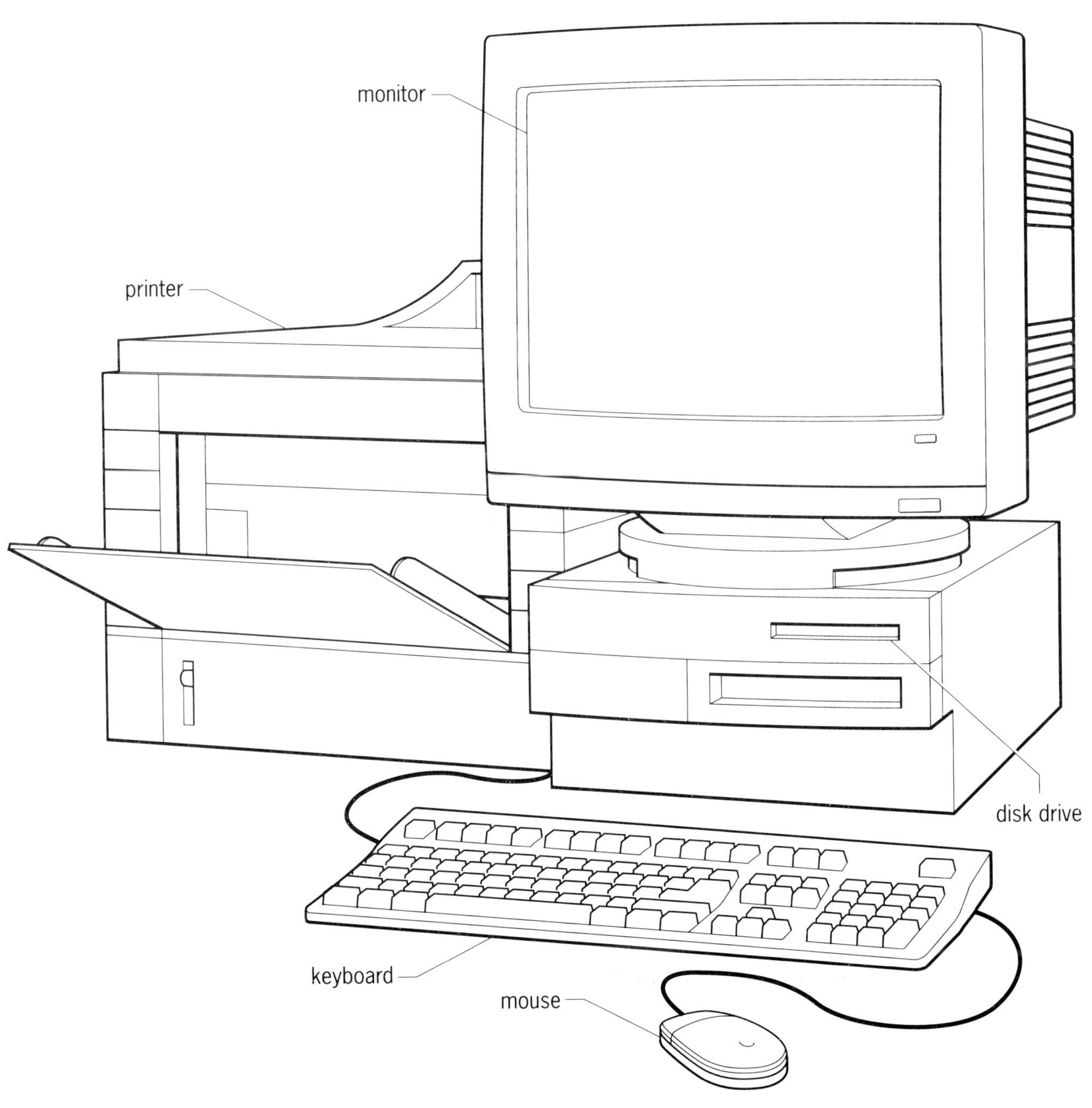

Organisational issues

A close look at the questions teachers often ask (p. 7) about the use of IT shows that many of them are to do with organisational matters, specifically related to the use of computers.

How do you know which computer to buy?

Where do you have the computer in the classroom?

How do I choose appropriate software?

How do I store the software?

How do you organise thirty children to use IT when you have only one computer?

How many children should make up a group for computer work?

To address the above issues effectively, the school needs a co-ordinator and a clear policy for IT throughout the school.

The role of the IT co-ordinator is:
- to lead the development and periodic review of the school policy for IT, including budget implications
- to have an overview of the place of IT in the school development plan
- to keep up-to-date with IT developments
- to co-ordinate the hardware and software availability in the school
- to co-ordinate review of software
- to support the school staff in the use and application of IT
- to provide and facilitate appropriate training to suit staff needs and school developments.

A school policy

This book provides information that will assist in the setting up or reviewing of a school IT policy.

The THINK ABOUT IT! sections will provide you with a framework.

THINK ABOUT IT!

Is there an IT co-ordinator in your school? If so, what is his/her role?
Do you have a comprehensive hardware and software guide for your school?
What training do you think *you* would like?

Buying hardware

The most important point to remember here is that when buying new hardware for your school you need to consider the most appropriate make for the needs of the children and teachers in your school. You need to take into account the children's age and educational needs. The newspapers are full of bargain offers from the manufacturers and the post is flooded with mail order discount offers. Before you commit yourself to ordering anything you need to ask yourself:

- is the machine easy for the children and staff to operate?
- is there a good supply of suitable educational software available for this machine?
- do other schools in the neighbourhood/LEA use these machines? This is important because more and more schools have shared in-service training days. It is also important that any LEA support is available for that particular machine.

Managing hardware

Having made the choice of what machinery you have available or are going to purchase, here are some helpful suggestions for the effective management of the hardware.

In an ideal situation you should be working towards at least one computer system per classroom. Two would be a great improvement, allowing more children to have access.

Consider other areas in the school where a computer could be used, such as the library and rooms in which group work takes place. If each classroom cannot have a computer, then you need to think about the best way computer access can be time-tabled. Think about whether it is better to have a computer in the classroom all the time for one week per term or to have it for a half-day every week.

Supplementary hardware, such as joysticks, concept keyboards and roamers, needs to be available in a central store.

Colour coding plugs and sockets enables teachers, helpers, adult assistants and children to set up the hardware with the least difficulty. It is also helpful to have the basic information about the particular system, i.e. loading, running, saving and other instructions, placed near the computer. A 'trouble shooter' guide (see p. 18) would be extremely useful, as sometimes only a minor adjustment is needed to put the machine back into action.

Each teacher needs to find a place in the classroom for the computer which fits in with the teaching style and the pattern of work of the class.

THINK ABOUT IT!

How is the use of hardware organised in your school?
What are the positive and negative aspects of this organisation?

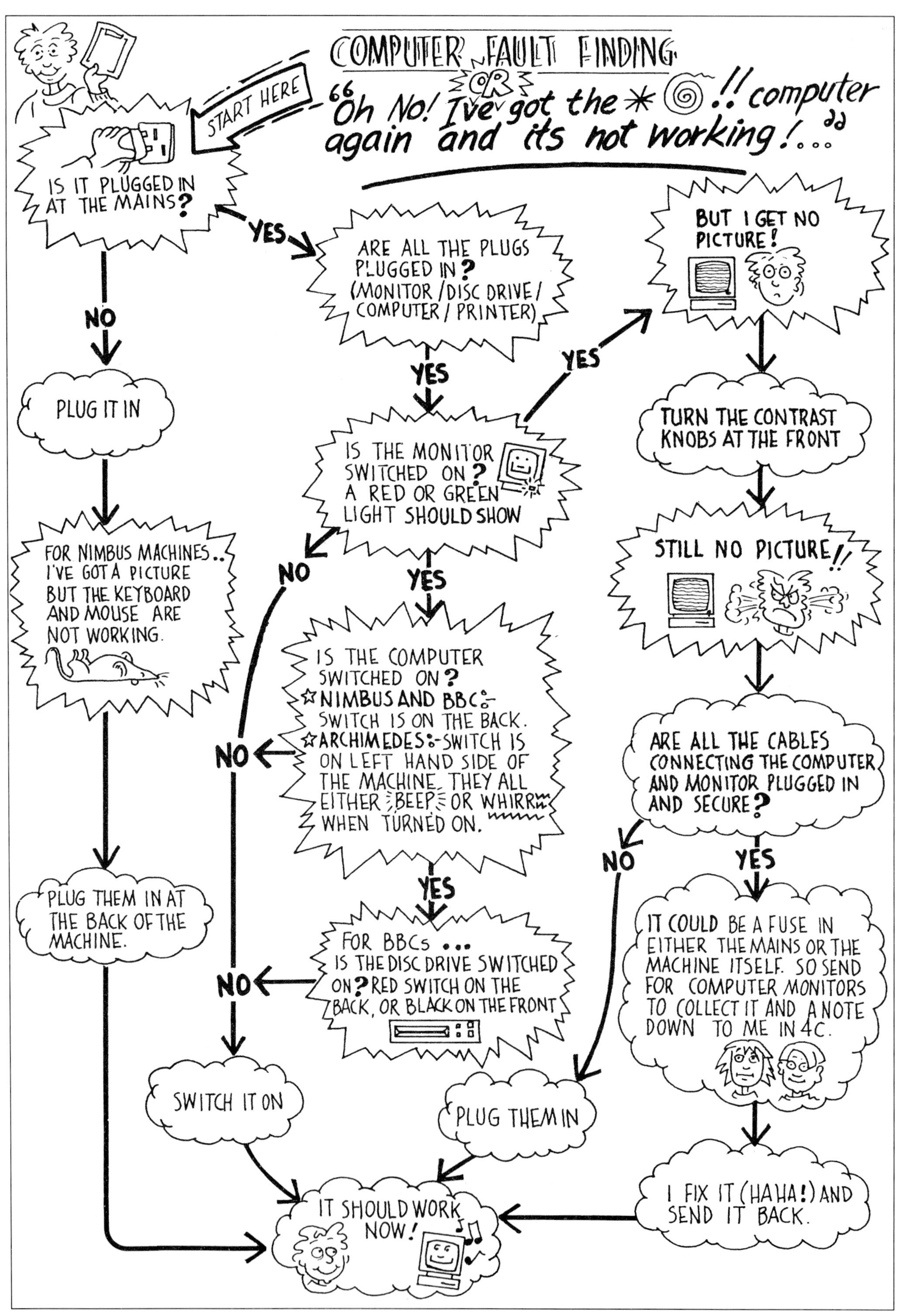

This is an example used in a school where they have Nimbus, BBC and Archimedes computers. The fault finding chart will obviously need to relate to the computers in your own school.

NEW COMPUTER MAINTENANCE.

- ♦Do not place the system where it will have prolonged exposure to direct sunlight, or to very hot or cold conditions.
- ♦Clean the system regularly.
- ♦No drinks or food should be kept or consumed near the computer.
- ♦Do not attempt to take apart any of your system components.
- ♦Any disks used on systems at home etc should first be checked by the IT Co-ordinator for viruses.
- ♦On the back of every PC there is a small fan. This should be cleaned regularly, and should never be blocked as this can cause the machine to over heat.
- ♦If anything goes wrong, or is not working correctly, then report it to the IT Co-ordinator.
- ♦Always shutdown the system before you move it.
- ♦If something goes wrong DO NOT PANIC and ALWAYS ASK if you want help or advice-----OK?

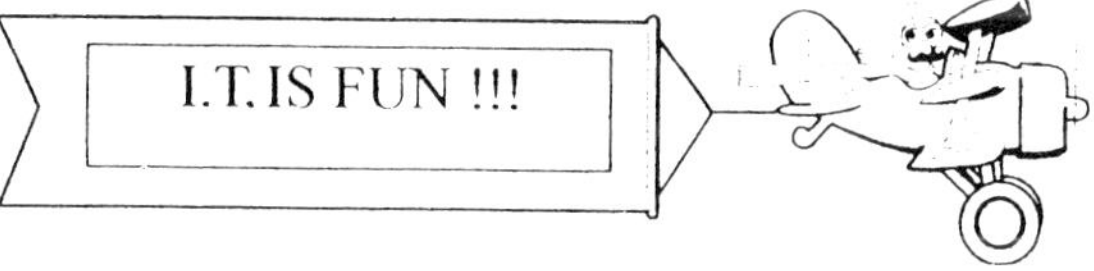

IT Co-ordinator's checklist for the staff

Selecting and managing software

The following questions may assist you when considering buying software:

- Does the program enrich children's learning?
- Does this piece of software enhance the existing curriculum framework?
- Is the program suitable for the age group of the children?
- Are there good back-up notes in the manual?
- Is there a good balance of structured and content-free software available in our school?
- Does the level of language match the concepts offered in the program?

Time spent reviewing and evaluating software is time well spent.

Software packages need careful and efficient management. Software is part of the communal resources of the school and in order to achieve the most efficient and maximum use, it needs to be catalogued and made easily accessible.

Some useful suggestions

All software should have back-up copies made for regular use and the master copy should be locked away. This not only enables you to feel secure that the original is always available if something goes wrong, it also enables teachers and children to save and manipulate files on their own disks.

Software should be listed and copies of the list issued to all staff. It would be most useful to circulate a grid indicating the type of program and the suggested age range.

Storing working copies of disks and copies of manuals in plastic zipped see-through wallets has been found very useful in many schools. These wallets could also contain any useful ideas which have worked successfully for the staff.

Providing the IT experience in your school

Each school should have an individual record of what programs they use and when. An example is shown opposite.

THINK ABOUT IT!

Which software packages do you use in your classroom? Can you classify them according to curriculum areas?

Grouping children

Groups of three seem a good number for children to interact with each other and to have hands-on experience. Larger groups with one keyboard may lead to frustration and children becoming disinterested. However, this does not exclude the computer being avialable for larger groups who are collecting and inputting data or producing a class magazine or newspaper.

Group work – taking turns at the keyboard while working collaboratively on a project

	R/Yr 1	Yr 2	Yr 3	Yr 4	Yr 5	Yr 6
Communicating and handling information	Window,	Folio, Prompt Writer →		Caxton →		
				Oxfordshire Write →		
					Aldus Pagemaker →	
	Concept Keyboard		Touch Explorer →			
		List Explorer →				
		Infant Tray →		Tray →		
				Junior Pinpoint		
	Data Show →		CD-ROM	Grass →	Grasshopper	
		Our Facts →		Key	Excel	
Controlling, monitoring and modelling	Jumbo →					
	Roamers →					
	Floor Turtles →					
		Logo → →				
					Control Logo →	
	Adventures → →					
	Teddy Bears' Picnic →					
			Nature →			
			Sensors →		Datalogging →	

Providing IT experiences – this is an example of the way one school records which programs they use.

It is useful to have both mixed and single sex groups working on the computer to counteract any domination of a particular sex. It may also be a good idea to have different types of groups working together at different times. Some groupings may have to be made according to the needs of the task. For example, a group of children working on a structured program dealing with operations with large numbers on the screen may need to be of similar ability and competence, whereas designing a newspaper or a pattern could be managed by a group of children of mixed ability who have different roles allocated to them.

Whatever groupings you use they should be carefully planned. The children should be clear about their own role within the group. Group roles could be rotated on a basis designed to suit the task. This gives each child the opportunity to learn and develop a variety of 'hands on' skills and experiences.

Group work needs to be organised so that the number of groups is manageable. It requires careful time planning to allow the teacher to work purposefully with each group.

THINK ABOUT IT!

Consider your own classroom:

a How do you allocate children to working groups, e.g. ability, friendship?

b If you use a variety of grouping formats, note down why you do this. For each curriculum area note which grouping strategy you use.

Getting the children started

With good preparation and organisation children can learn to use computers quickly. It is surprising how easily they become independent and take responsibility for the hardware and software. Quite often teachers comment that the children remember instructions and procedures much more easily than they do themselves.

Children need to be told the safety aspects of using computers. They should be made aware of electrical power connections and the need to keep the hardware and software dry.

They could also be given some operational explanations at the start, such as 'the computer only remembers what has been done when it is switched on, unless your work was saved'.

A list of basic functions and names of the important parts could be presented on a chart in the computer area of your classroom or on the computer trolley.

An introductory list could include:

cursor
shift
delete
return (enter)
arrows
save

THINK ABOUT IT!

Review provision for children to be independent users of the computer in your school/class.
What information could be provided in the computer areas?
Devise a user chart for the computer you have in your classroom.

Children's computer notebooks

It is a very good idea to give children special notebooks to help them with their computer work. Children, at every level, can start using their computer notebook from an early stage to personalise their experience with computers. Such a notebook can show the child's increasing competence and development in using computers and can serve as a self-assessment record. It can also be part of a record of achievement.

A computer notebook can be used by children for a variety of purposes:

- to keep instructions on how to use a program
- to jot down points they need to remember whilst working through a program
- to work things out to help them to enter information into the computer
- to draw plans and maps
- to keep a note of options used to avoid repetition
- to keep reminders of where they are up to, if they are engaged in an extended program of writing or solving an adventure.

The notebooks can be used by both children and teachers to evaluate what has been done and to assess what they have learnt and can do.

CD-ROM print-outs stuck in the computer notebook facilitating research and discovery

The learning cycle

The diagram shows clearly the stages of the teaching and learning process.

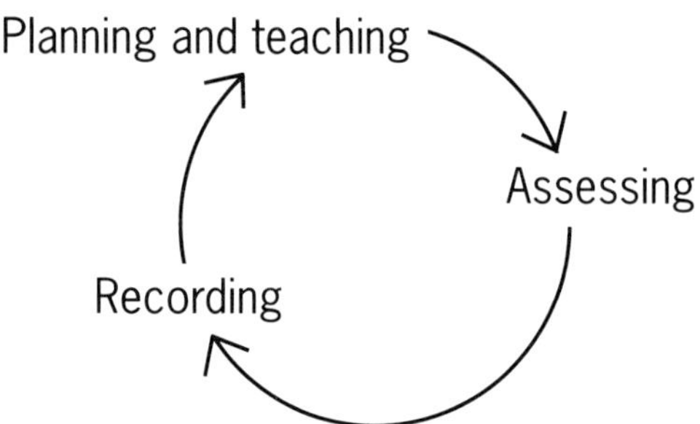

Planning

There are two main ways of planning the curriculum – **theme based** or **subject based**. Sometimes a mixed approach operates.

Example of theme-based planning

Class: 3P Age: 7–8 years	Theme: Ourselves Word-process poems on ourselves, families, autobiographies, favourite things, pets, books, etc.
Strand 1	
Communicating and handling information	Use DTP – family tree, newspaper page, e.g. from your date of birth (Times Newspaper CD-ROM, see p. 103) Tape recorder – family interviews Video – drama workshop on family life CD-ROM – newspaper from a recent birthday Graphics – to illustrate writing Databases – personal statistics, family statistics, favourite things, e.g. food, TV programs, hobbies Decision trees – personal identification tree Spreadsheets – personal finances (pocket money)
Strand 2	
Controlling, monitoring and modelling	Moving house Adventure games Concept keyboards Logo – design a personal logo

Example of subject-based planning

Subject: Maths Theme: Shape and space Class: 3P Age: 7–8 years

- Use turtles and roamers to draw shapes.
- Make polygons using Logo.
- Design symmetrical patterns.
- Tessellate shapes.
- Draw maps.
- Produce spirals.
- Use 'New Tile' program to design wallpaper.

Assessing children's IT capabilities

We assess children's learning generally by:

- listening to what they say
- observing what they do and
- analysing what they record.

This is no different for IT.

Whilst planning an activity the possible learning outcomes for the child should be listed. During the time the children are engaged in the activity, the teacher can make notes (or tapes) on what happened. These will help in the filling in of records.

An example of a sample formative assessment record kept by a teacher is shown overleaf. Careful targeting of the activity can ensure effective collecting of assessment information. As you can see, an activity can assess a child's level of attainment in different subject areas. Tangible outcomes, such as print-outs and word-processed sheets, can be kept as evidence.

This formative assessment arose from an investigation with a Year Three class.

A blank photocopiable version of this grid is provided on p. 110.

Recording IT capability

A profile based on the teacher's ongoing observations of a child is an effective record. It is important to record a child's achievement based on different pieces of software and in different contexts and at intervals.

The grid on p. 27 (which may be photocopied) presents one possible model to start you thinking about recording experiences.

It can be used to make a record of programs used by each child with dates and comments. Remember it is only a model to help you start thinking about your own system.

Formative assessment record

Name: Sunita Patel Date: 7/94

Activity: Smarties

Planned outcomes	What happened	Future action
– Sort and classify according to colour	Used 2 criteria to sort – good use of vocabulary.	
– Make up a data-collection sheet	In a group, devised an excellent sheet – trialled it and refined it.	
– Collect data Input data into database	Followed instructions	I must give Sunita a more complex enquiry
– Interrogate – 2 questions	In turn, asked questions – very original enquiry.	
– Print out graphs and interpret them	Very skilled use of keyboard and printing instructions.	I must have a chat with her, praise her achievement and ask her to do a self-assessment sheet.
– Word-process 10 discoveries about the contents of a Smarties tube	Made up an impressive display, used dictionary while editing.	
– Design a 'good' container for 100 Smarties	Got into a muddle with flaps, but made it.	Talk to Sunita about making boxes.

Comments: I will show Sunita how to use a spell-check on the word-processing package.

She does enjoy working with computers.

IT experience record

Name: Class:

Skill	Dates and programs used			
Use a concept keyboard				
Use a word-processing package				
Use a structured program by following instructions				
Use graphics and sound with IT package				
Use a DTP package and a variety of fonts				
Use a tape recorder, camera, video recorder				
Store, retrieve and interpret information using a database				
Use a spreadsheet				
Follow an adventure game				
Use a simulation				
Use programmable toys				
Logo/Control Logo				
Make a decision tree				
Set up a datalogging program				

Children's self-assessment

Children can also keep a record of IT packages they have used and learnt in a personal portfolio. Their own comments can greatly motivate the children to challenge themselves further. Children's computer notebooks also can be part of the ongoing record, as already stated.

The best program I used this week is 'Arounts the world in 80 days. The best bit was typing the co-ordinates of the hazards like Shipwrecks and contaching the police. I am good at Geography so it was exciting to be tested. I learnt that some eskimos are called Inuits and kill seals for clothing. They live in Canada.

Name Fahanah **Class** 4R
IT package Database

Date 23.11.94

What have I learnt from it?

I have learnt to input data
I know how to save the data
I can ask questions and get some answers
I can draw a pictogram, pie chart and a bar chart and put numbers on the axis
I am still stuck on scattergraphs or is it scattergrams ! , I don't really understand them
I am going to

Children's portfolios, computer notebooks and their self-assessment records can greatly assist the teacher to communicate with parents about their children's IT learning experiences.

Using IT to teach Mathematics

This section looks at the ways in which IT, particularly computers, can support the teaching and learning of mathematics. Using IT as a resource you can develop both content and processes. Specifically, IT offers the following support:

Programming languages, such as *Logo*, help children to design and create geometric and number patterns. Logo is also a very powerful problem-solving tool.

Structured programs, such as mathematical games, can help children to develop mathematical concepts, acquire skills and learn facts. These programs also offer opportunities for practice and reinforcement. They offer a more effective and motivating alternative to repeating the same kind of 'sums' from a text book for practice and are likely to produce better results. The computer also takes part of the role of the teacher, marking work by offering instant feedback to the children. Quite often we find children are happier to accept correction on a computer screen than in their Mathematics notebook.

Some specially designed software helps to introduce *investigations* which encourage children to use and apply the mathematics they have learnt.

Content-free software, such as *databases* and *spreadsheets*, can help children to collect, store, sort, analyse and interpret data and produce tables, graphs and charts.

Adventure games, and simulations can involve children in drawing maps, learning about directions and developing problem-solving strategies.

The following pages give some examples of how different types of programs can support the teaching and learning of mathematics.

Roamers and floor turtles

Roamers and floor turtles are increasingly used in primary classrooms to provide children with experiences of programming and controlling machines. Working with turtles is a very enjoyable activity for both very young and older children. The floor turtles can be programmed to move forward and backward and to turn left and right. Roamers can be programmed to play music. These facilities provide children with the pleasure of controlling robotic machines by giving them sequenced instructions.

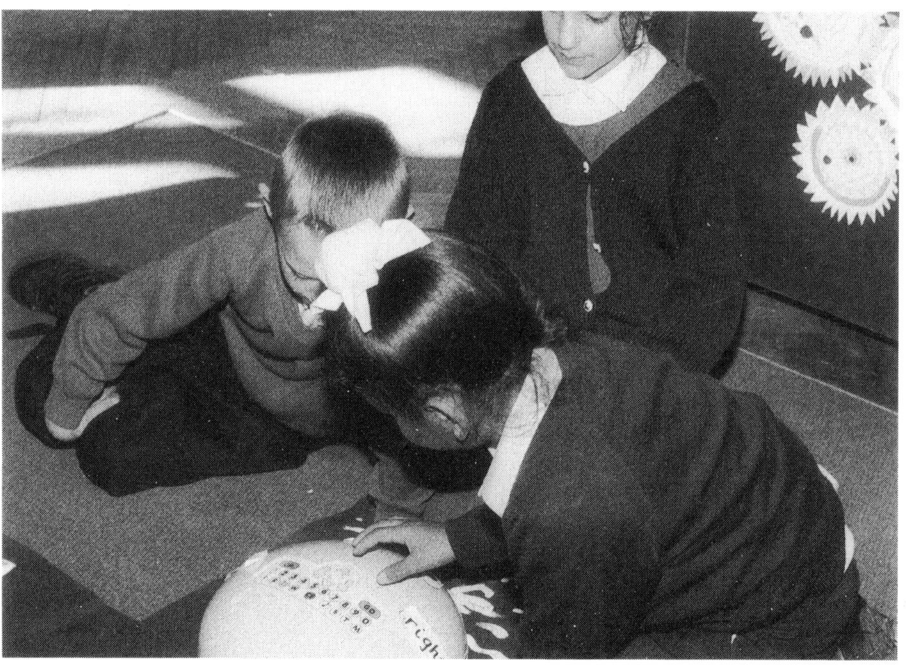

Talking about distances and angles, wondering 'What if...', estimating and enjoying communicating in mathematical language

Ordinary classroom activities can often provide contexts for 'turtle-play'. PE and drama also provide opportunities for movements.

Pre-turtle activity

Child A gives Child B instructions to produce a picture or pattern using everyday language, e.g.:

'Go forward 6 finger spaces'

'Turn a square corner... '

Can the turtle go shopping? Can it deliver letters?

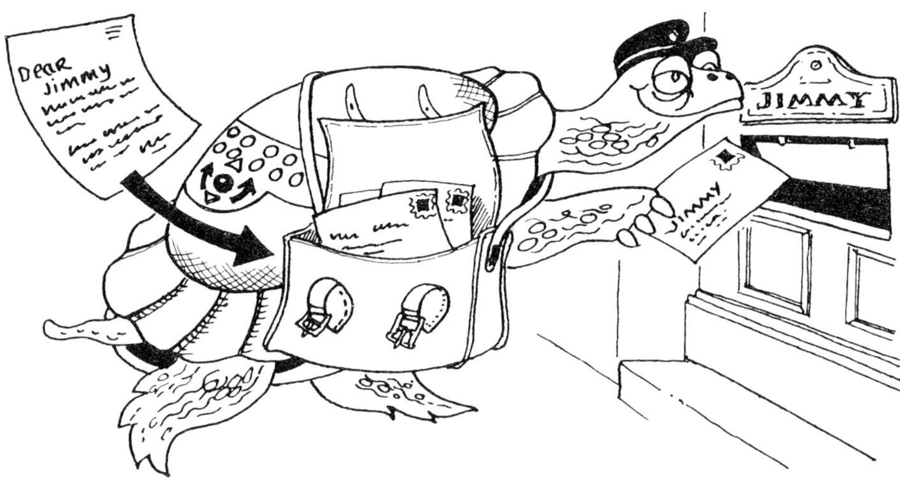

In the hall or in the playground set up obstacles and a child, who is blind-folded, is given instructions to get to a destination to collect a mystery prize.

An English activity designed to develop children's speaking and listening skills and drama can use turtles and roamers in a meaningful way. For example, ask the children to program the turtles to act out the story of Little Red Riding Hood. They may want to dress up the turtles for the roles they are playing.

Can you get the roamer to write your name?

Logo

Logo is a programming language which offers children a powerful tool for problem solving. It originated in the USA where Seymour Papert offered Logo as a simulated micro-world of problem solving for children to explore, discover and form concepts.

Logo offers children an environment which encourages them to experiment, make mistakes in a non-threatening way and refine their ideas to achieve more elegant outcomes. It also helps them to set their own goals and extend their thinking.

Working with Logo helps children to develop an awareness of angles and distances and a feel for shape and space. It also helps to develop processes such as:

- estimating
- breaking down problems into manageable parts
- planning
- refining ideas
- hypothesising – 'what if... '
- being systematic.

Watch the turtle move:

Forward	20
Left	60
FD	30
RT	60
FD	60

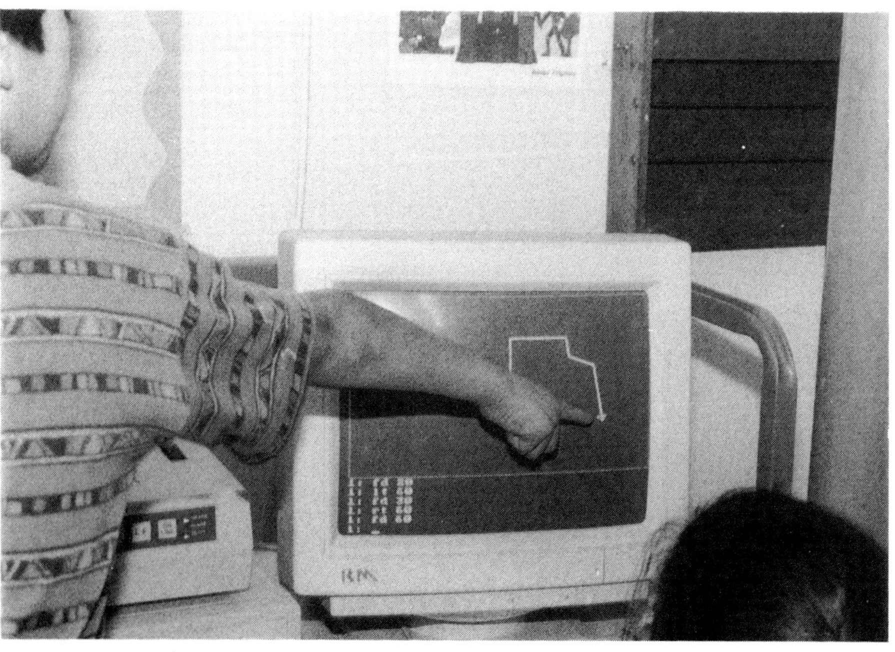

Playing with the turtle and giving commands in direct drive (where you can actually see the movements) gives children the experience of programming and learning about distance and direction.

Turtle games on the screen

You can put an acetate sheet with a picture of a maze on the computer screen and try to get the turtle 'home'.

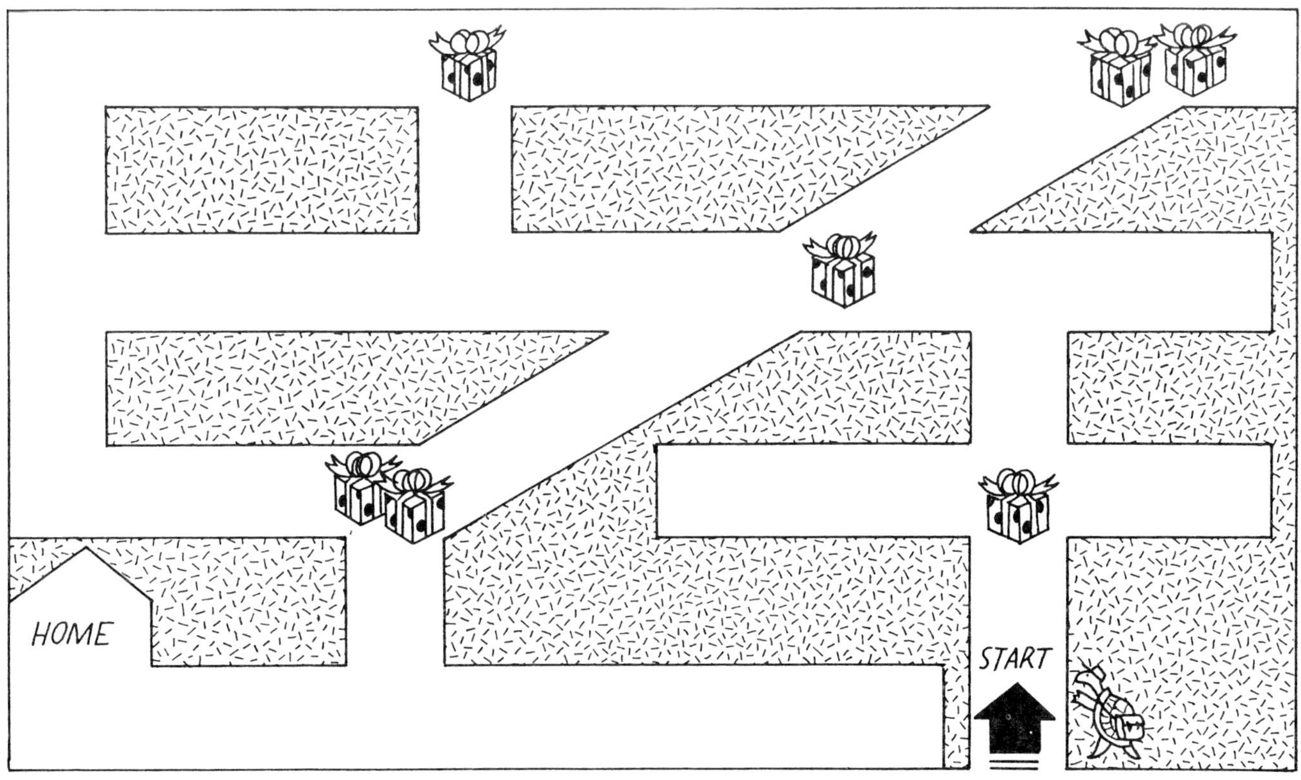

How can the turtle get home collecting the largest number of presents? (A large photocopiable version of this is provided on p. 111.)

Or stick a toffee or sweet on the screen with blue-tack. The idea is to take turns to hit the toffee by moving the turtle, inputting distances and turns. Later on, a competition element can be introduced to hit the target in as few moves as possible. This activity will help children to estimate angles and distances.

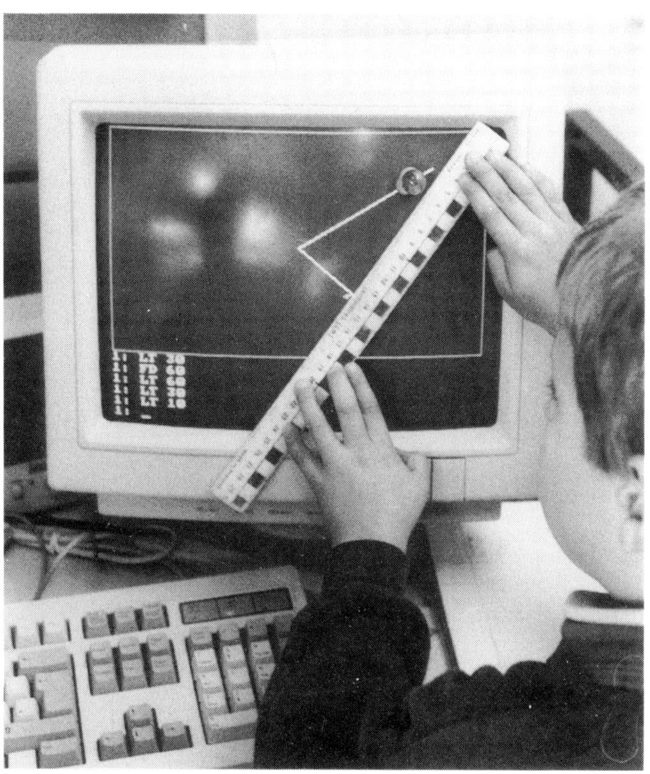

Play the 'turtle ball' game using an acetate sheet stuck to the screen. The aim is to make the turtle hit a number by programming it to move in any direction and using Logo commands. Once a number has been hit, that number cannot be hit again. Each player is allowed a specific number of moves for each round. Take turns and see how high a score you can get after six rounds.

An acetate sheet with this picture can be stuck to the screen (A large photocopiable version is provided on p. 112.)

Making polygons

After the initial experience of moving the turtle around, children can be asked to make regular polygons. Children may need help with the size of angles. The angle for a pentagon is $\frac{360}{5} = 72$ degrees.

Draw a square, a pentagon, a hexagon and an octagon.

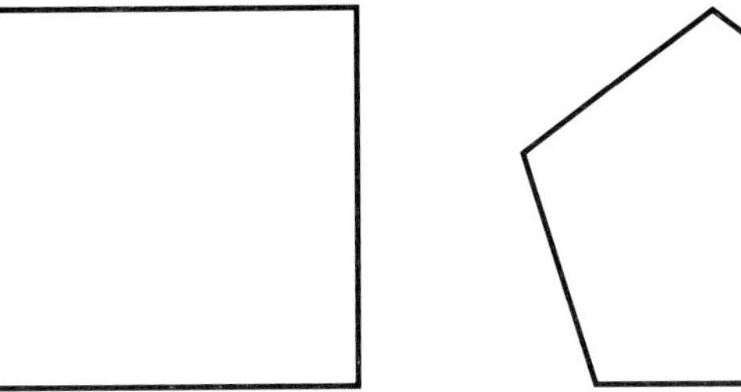
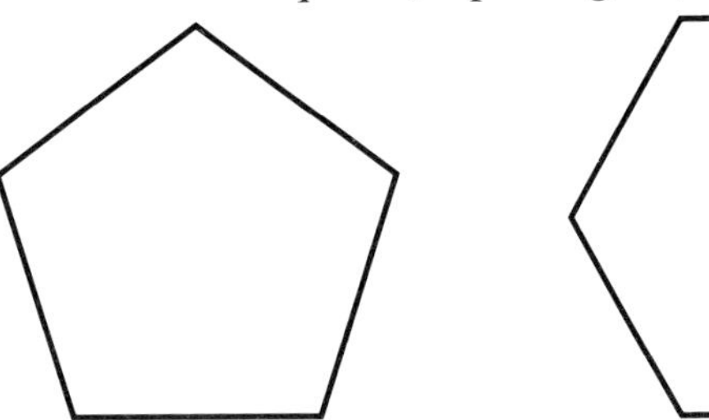
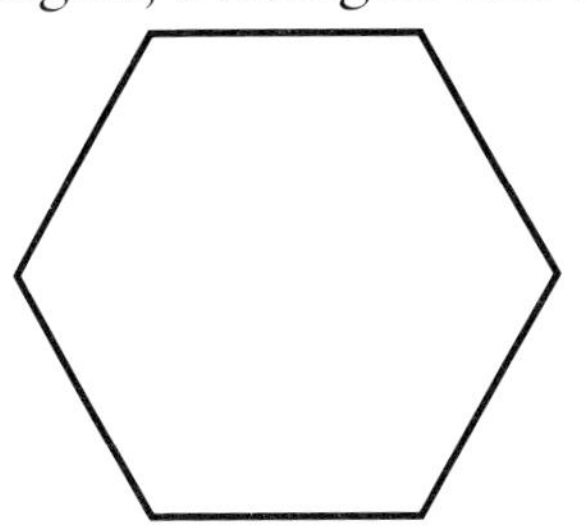
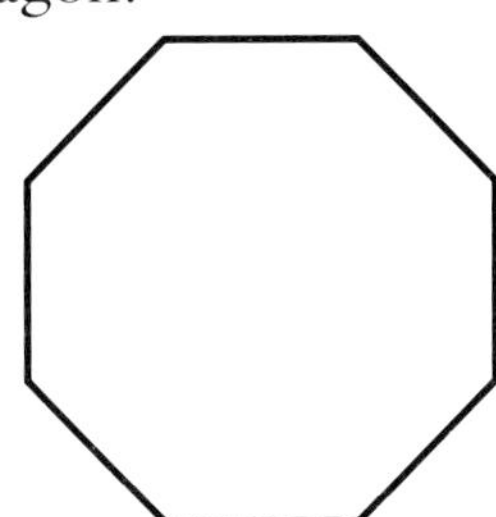

Using the REPEAT command you can draw these faster.

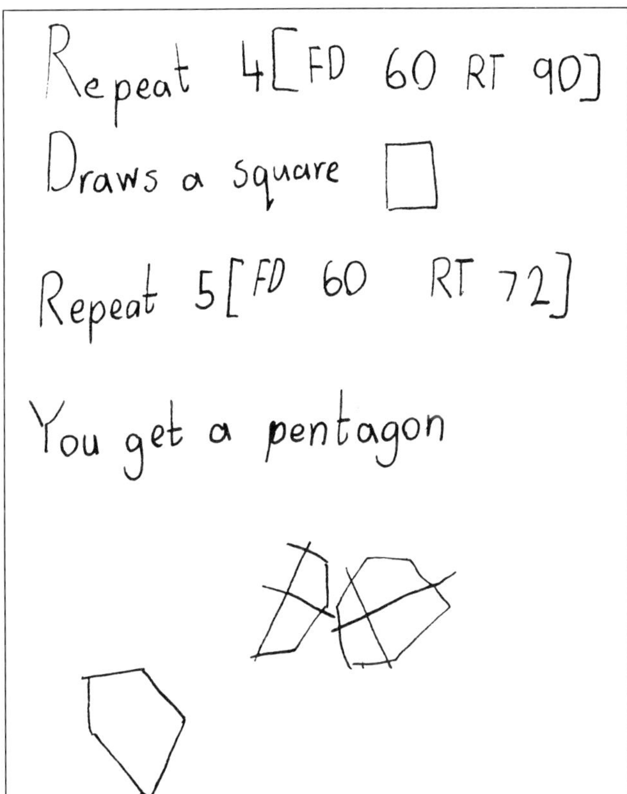

Want to draw a face? The PEN UP and PEN DOWN commands help.

or LIFT — or DROP

Triangle

rt 120
fd 50
rt 120
fd 50
rt 120
fd 50

repeat 3[rt 120 fd 50]

Circle

rt repeat 360 [rt 1 fd 1]

Right First Time!!!

Hexagon

fd 15
fd 10
rt 45
fd 25
rt 45

fd 25
rt 45
fd 25
rt 45
fd 25

rt 45
fd 25
rt 25
rt 20
fd 25

rt 45
fd 25

We made an Octogan!!

Square

We are going to try rt, 50

Not enough!

rt, 30

Bit more!

rt 5 rt 5
50 altogether 90

fd 50
rt 90
fd 50
rt 90
fd 50
rt 90
fd 50

Finished Square

now we've been shown how to use reapeat

repeat 4 [rt 90 fd 50]

Hexagon 2nd Try

the angle for an octogan is 45°degrees
the angle for a square is 90°
So we think the hexagon is between 90° or 45°

Well try 60°

repeat 6 [rt 60 fd 40]

Yes Got it!!

Pentagon

We are going to try 72°

repeat 5 [rt 72 fd 24]

We got it right again!!

Shape	Sides	Angle
Triangle	3	120
Square	4	90
Pentagon	5	72
Hexagon	6	60
Octagon	8	45
Circle		360

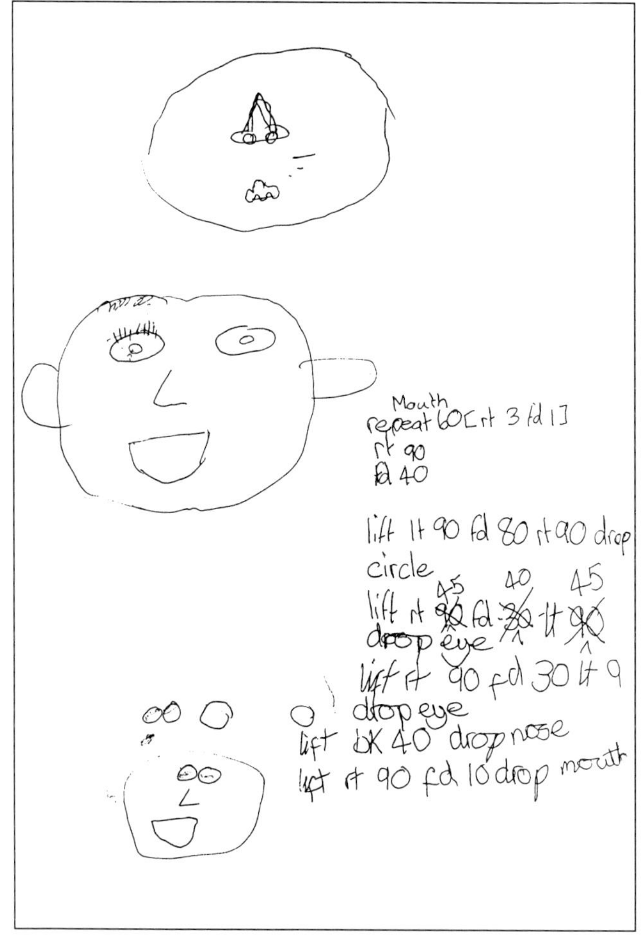

Building procedures

Do you want to teach Logo to remember commands?

Teaching the turtle to add one more word to its memory, like FORWARD or RIGHT, tells it to do something.

Do you want to build a procedure to make a star? You can use FD and RT.

You can type in:

Build 'star

Repeat 5[FD 20 RT 144]

Every time you type in `star` a star appears. By moving the turtle to different positions you can make a sky full of stars.

You can build a procedure to rotate shapes.

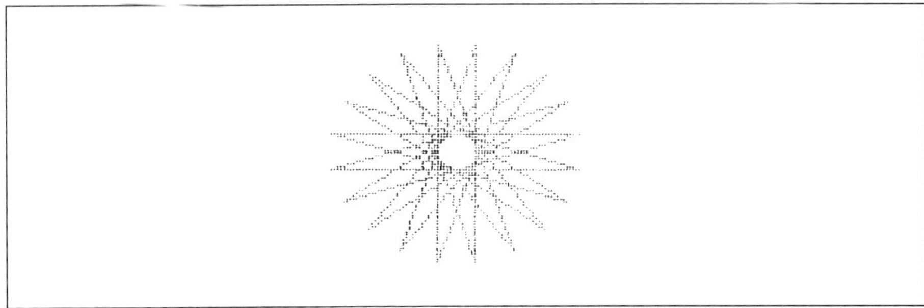

Can you make this rocket?

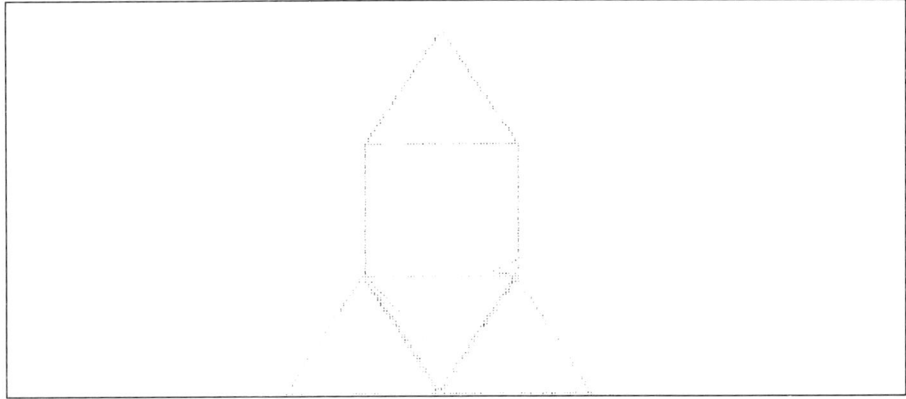

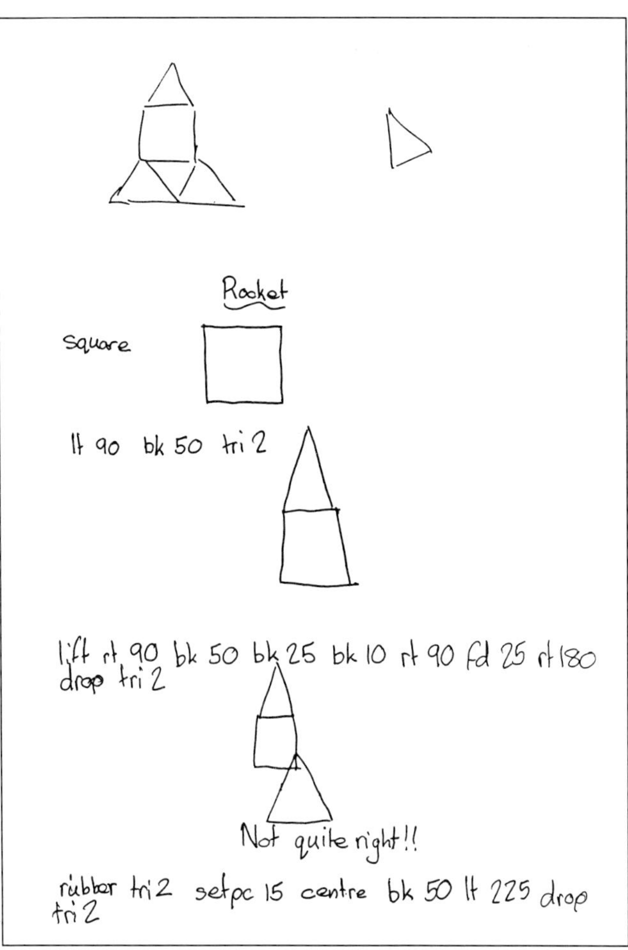

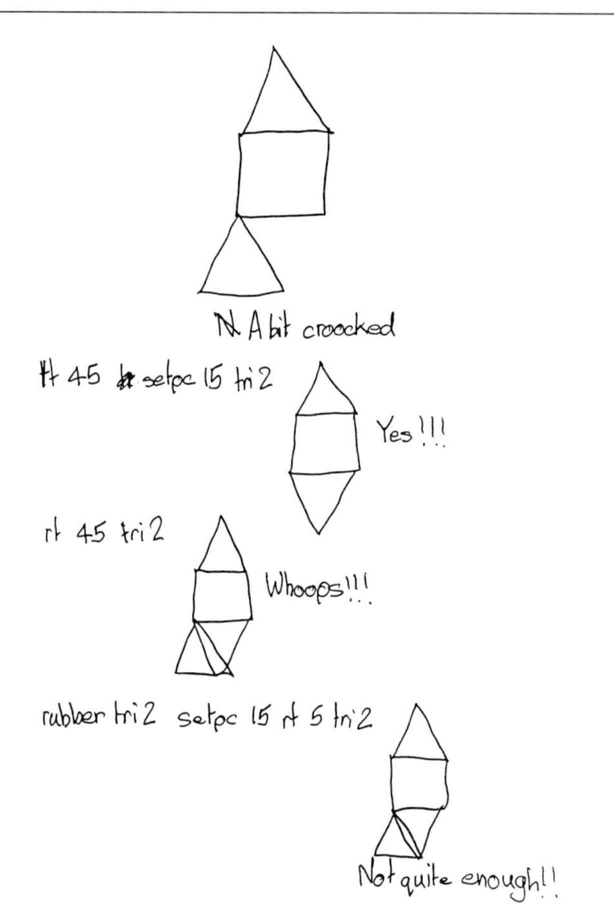

rubber tri2 setpc 15 rt 10 tri2.

One to go!!

lift lt 60 fd 50 rt 60 drop tri 2

Done it at last!!!

How to draw the rocket

At last I have drawn the rocket. Miss Watson asked me to write down what advice I would give someone else who is trying to draw the rocket for the first time.

Well, I would tell them not to get upset when your picture looks different to what you hope it is going to look like. Miss told us that the mistakes we make in the program are called `bugs'. You must keep trying and not let the bugs get you down.

After trying different ways ,I now think to draw the rocket , you could first make a procedure called `tri' to draw a triangle and then make another procedure called `sq ' to make a square. The rocket has really only got these two shapes.

I think you should first draw the square. Then by asking the turtle to move `forward', `back', `right' and `left' you must try to draw the top triangle and the bottom triangles in the right positions. If you have `bugs' in your program then you can rub it out. I used the `rubber' command to do this. I felt really excited when I built the rocket in the end. It took me two lessons and one dinner time to do it.

When you have drawn one rocket, you can make the rocket into a procedure and draw lots of rockets quite easily.

Can your Logo program use colour? Look in the manual.

Logo challenges

Say you want to create a garden scene. Children may take responsibility for different parts of the picture and create their own bits. This involves creating sub-procedures within procedures and coping with the bugs (mistakes) to get to the final picture. Through collective problem solving children make sense of the movements and actions of the turtle, learning about angles and properties of shapes – all a lot more interesting than reading about or being told how shapes behave. Children become mathematicians rather than just hearing about mathematics.

A useful activity to encourage problem solving and extend children's thinking is to ask them to choose a pattern or design they want to create. This may be something they have seen in a book or picture, or it may be something they want to design themselves. In their computer notebook, they draw or stick a copy of the picture they want to make and systematically work to achieve their goal. This journey towards achieving their goal can be a very fascinating and satisfying experience. Getting stuck and unstuck during their journey not only provides many mathematical learning opportunities, but a rewarding experience too.

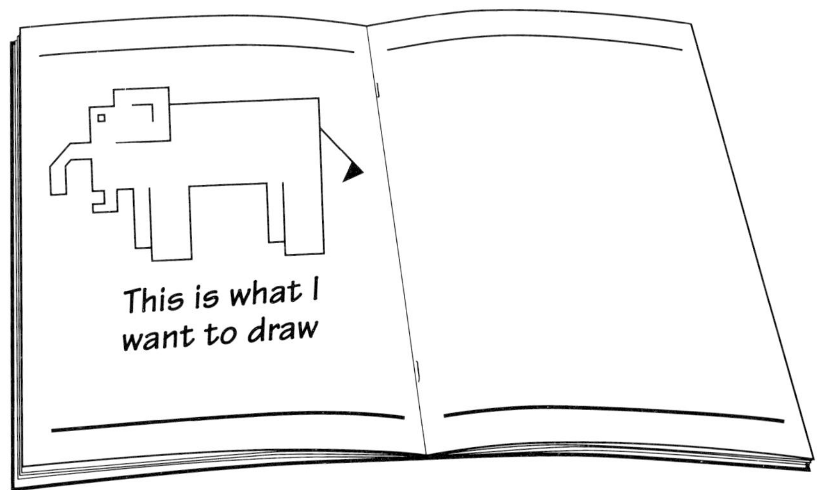

Computer simulations

Computer simulations such as 'Angle 90' and 'Take Half' (Smile programs) help to demonstrate to children the concepts of angles and fractions in a very stimulating way.

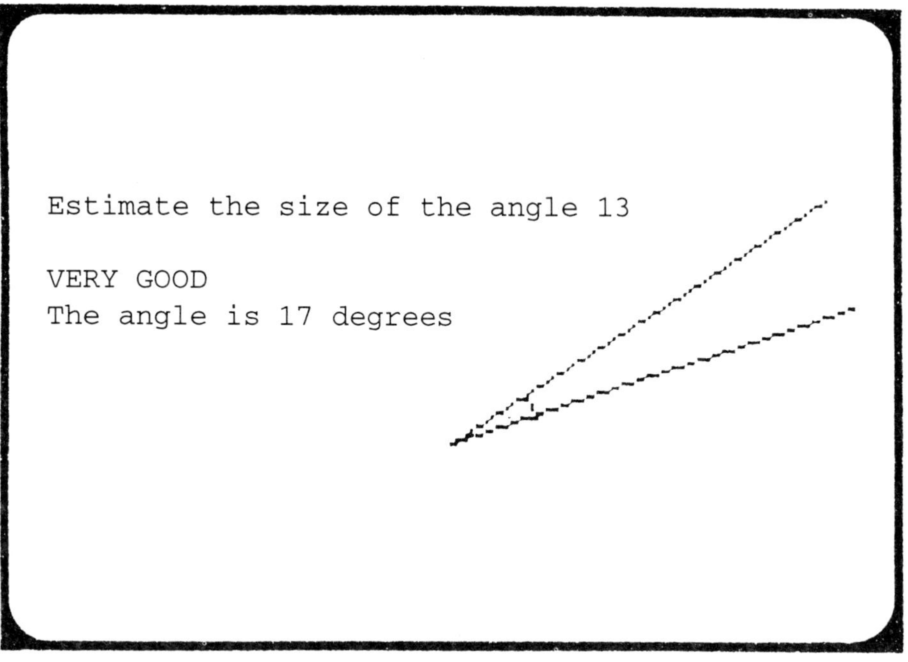

Angle 90 helps children to estimate sizes of acute angles, prior to pencil and paper trials

A program such as 'Guess' (Smile) can often help children to develop number concepts.

A group of children, guessing the number the computer has chosen, may sit around the computer with a number line to help them to master the order in which numbers appear on a number line and to enable them to extend that knowledge to larger numbers.

Not only does this program help children in ordering numbers, it also helps them to appreciate how numbers are written, the role of the zero and so on.

A teacher listening to the children's conversation can assess their knowledge of different aspects of number effectively, as they are likely to be working in a relaxed state.

Practising skills and developing concepts

Computer programs, if carefully selected, can be very helpful for children to practise skills and think about mathematical concepts. For example, 'Toy Shop' (Number Games) is a game for two or more players. The objective is to pay amounts of money, in turn, for toys which appear on the screen and the person who pays the last coin to make up the cost of a particular toy wins that toy.

Many concepts, facts and skills are developed through playing this game. Children need to appreciate the value of the coins, carry out additions and subtractions as well as think of good strategies which enable them to win the toys.

Children can be asked to make a version of 'Toy Shop' using cards and plastic money.

As 'Toy Shop' is a group activity, it encourages children to be engaged in mathematical discussions.

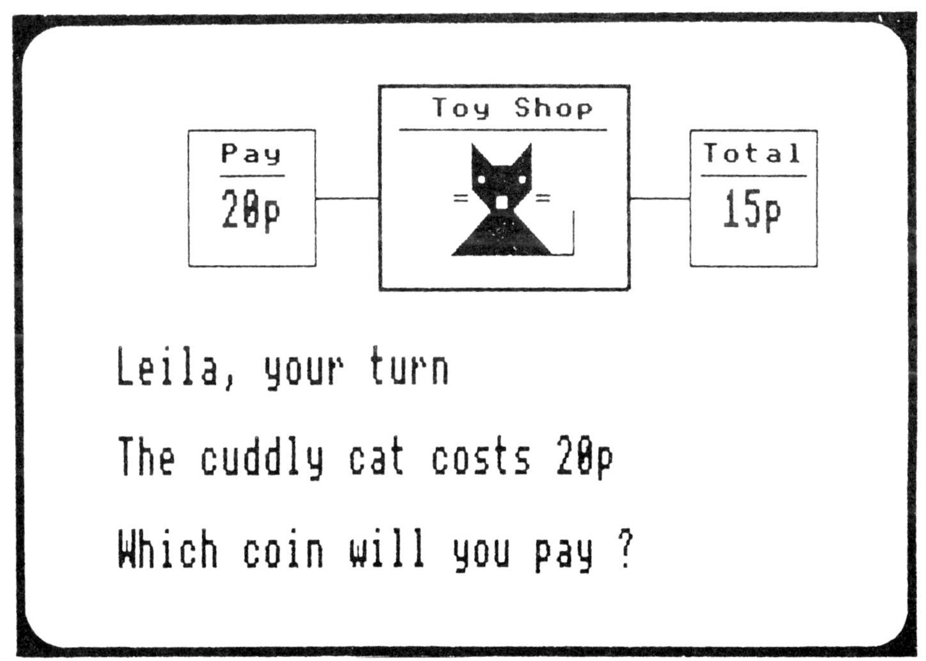

The total so far is 15p. Which coin must Leila choose to win?

Supporting investigations

Using software which has embedded investigations, children can be encouraged to ask questions and develop mathematical processes. Such programs offer children many opportunities to apply the mathematics they know and to develop the following processes:

- looking for patterns
- predicting
- generalising
- conjecturing
- classifying
- asking questions
- hypothesising
- refining and reflecting on their mathematical strategies which are part of 'Using and Applying Mathematics' (Mathematics NC).

An investigation on 'Polygons' (Mathematical Investigations) asks the children: *How many diagonals are there for a 7-sided shape?*

The program helps the children to learn about diagonals. When an answer is offered, the computer demonstrates the correct answer by drawing the correct number of diagonals.

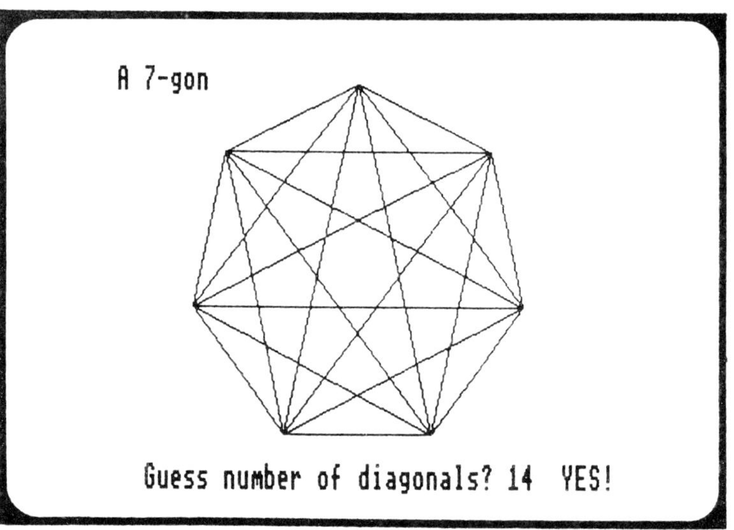

Programs like this encourage children to think mathematically and work out the answers away from the computer, returning to the computer only to test their hypotheses or to look at the tables of results.

The advantage of using the computer for such an investigation is that the computer can demonstrate how many diagonals can be drawn for a 32-sided shape in a few seconds – something which cannot be done by the teacher or the children so easily on paper. Valuable thinking time is, therefore, saved.

Also a computer can take on one of the roles of the teacher and encourage the children to make predictions, refine their theories and work towards generalising their findings.

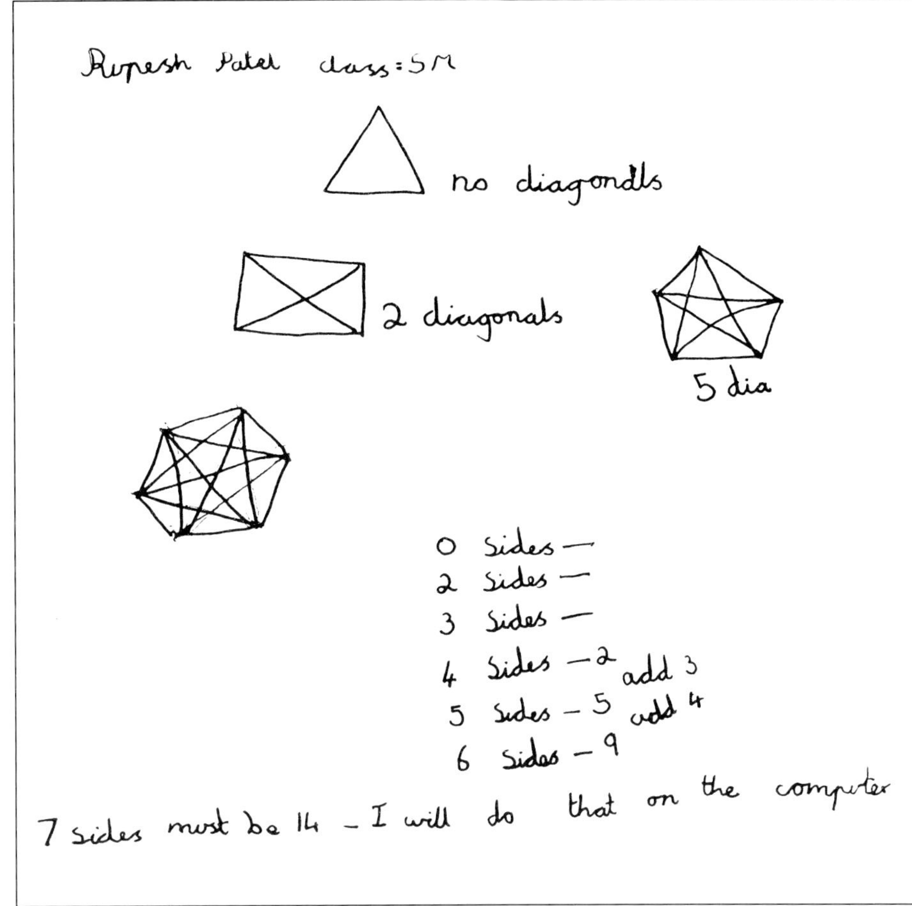

Working out the formula for finding out how many diagonals there are for an *n*-sided shape, $\frac{n(n-3)}{2}$, becomes great fun.

Polygons Investigation

I enjoyed working out how many diagonals there are for a 15- sided shape with the computer. First I tried some of my guesses , soon I realised that I was way out. I then drew out some polygons and their diagonals and tested my ideas on the computer. The great thing about having the computer was that I couldn't draw so fast and correctly. Computer is a whizz when it comes to drawing. It drew a 39 -sided shape and all its diagonals in less than a minute!

I discovered that when you draw diagonals in a polygon you can only draw diagonals to the sides 3 less than the total number of sides. Say you are point A on a polygon , you don't draw a diagonal to that point or to the two points next to it.

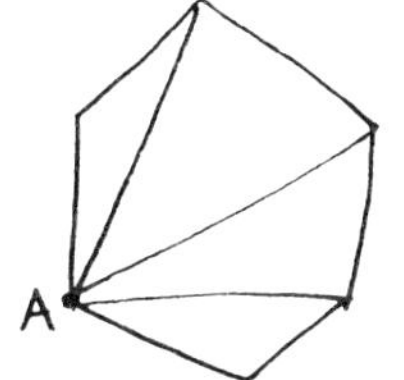

6 Sided Polygon

The computer helped me to see this and come up with a formula :

For a polygon with n - sides you can work out the number of diagonals by going n(n-3) divided by 2

Using a word-processing package the findings of an investigation can be presented to others in an attractive format. Recording their methods of working thus becomes purposeful and not a 'chore'!

Using databases for handling data

Databases are software packages which store information as files. They can be compared to filing cabinets. As you store information on index cards as records and put them in a filing cabinet, you can use a database to store a large number of records all set in a uniform way. Each of the records has some headings called 'fields' and the records can be stored in 'files'.

All the information in this filing cabinet can be stored on a 3" disc

Name: Valerie Symons
Age: Nine
Hobbies: Swimming, violin
Favourite food: Fish and beans

Example of a record

Besides storing information, database packages offer an information processing facility; you can ask to order data alphabetically or numerically, or ask specific questions about aspects. Charts, graphs and tables can be printed out.

In a classroom, using databases encourages children to sort and classify information in different ways, to ask questions, to make and test hypotheses, to look for patterns and to analyse information.

Two examples of how databases can be used to teach and learn mathematics are presented on the following pages.

Favourite sweets

Age range
5–7 years.

Ways of working
Whole class, pairs and groups.

Resources
A simple database package, paper, pencil, flip chart.

Starting points
With a flip chart, ask the children what they think the favourite sweet of the class is. The teacher writes down all the names of sweets suggested. Together they discuss a data collection sheet and data is either entered by the teacher (if using this with young children) or by the children themselves. Then the teacher introduces the children to a database program and shows them how they can enter the information.

After all the data is entered, children are shown how to ask questions and how they can produce graphs and charts.

A display can be mounted using children's data sheets and print-outs which will encourage further thinking and discussion.

No.	Name of sweet	Number of children
1	Flying Saucers	1
2	Smarties	2
3	Flumps	1
4	Cola Bottles	3
5	Polos	4
6	Chewing Gum	11
7	Jelly Babies	0
8	Jelly Tots	0
9	Fizzy Chews	0

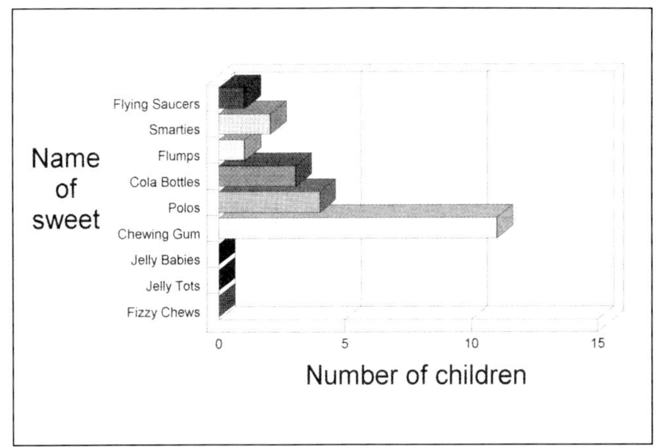

Extensions and more ideas

- Popular birthdays.
- Popular pets.

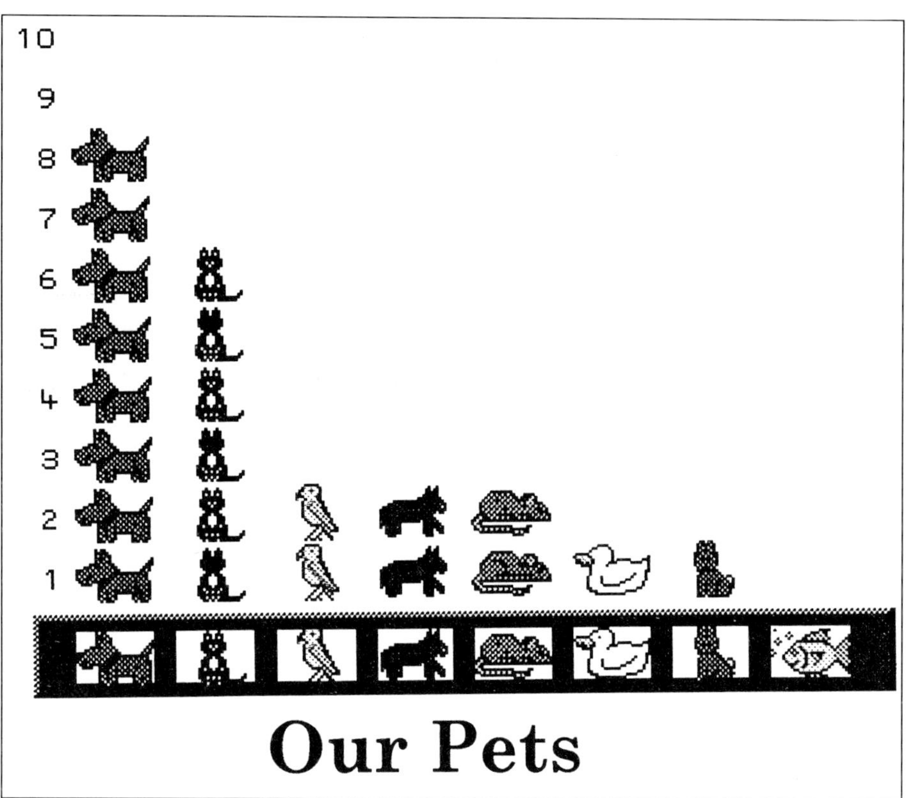

Setting up a shop in school

Age range

8–11 years.

Ways of working

A class task with children working in small groups collecting, putting in and interrogating and analysing data.

Resources

A suitable database.

Starting points

The teacher can set this task for all the children and discuss with the class various ways in which they can collect data. Names of fields which are relevant can be discussed in the whole group. A data sheet is then compiled.

The teacher then introduces the children to the database package program and explains how to input the data and how to interrogate and obtain print-outs for analysis.

Extensions and more ideas

- Analyse print-outs of tables and graphs to help with ideas for the shop.
- Display all information and conclusions for everyone to see.
- Class discussion.

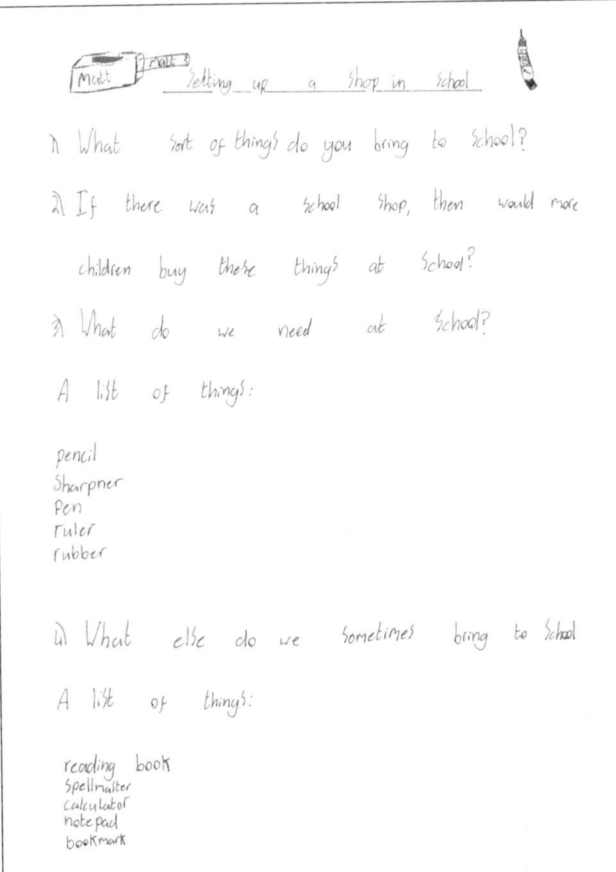

Setting up a shop in School

1) What sort of things do you bring to School?

2) If there was a school shop, then would more children buy these things at School?

3) What do we need at School?

A list of things:

pencil
Sharpner
Pen
ruler
rubber

4) What else do we sometimes bring to School

A list of things:

reading book
Spellmaster
Calculator
note pad
bookmark

Our Survey

We asked 8 children from our class about:-
1. The different things that they bring to school - Database = SHOP
2. If they would buy these things from a school shop - Database = SHOP1

Here are our results.

If there was a school shop, then more people would have things like pens, pencils and rubbers because they would save up and buy them from the shop.

The school shop would also sell important things like fountain pens and staplers because they would sell the most.

Before we set up a shop we would have to do lots of research:-

1. Prices.
2. Cheapest but most trendy looking pens.
3. Pencil cases that would sell.
4. Extras - things like staplers that would sell because we would like to have our own.

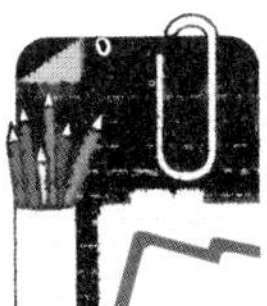

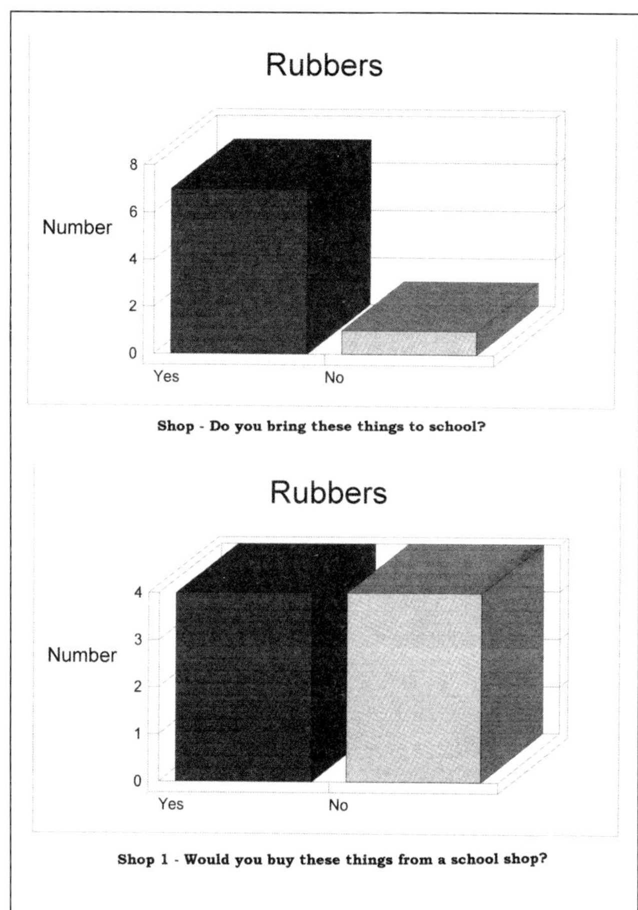

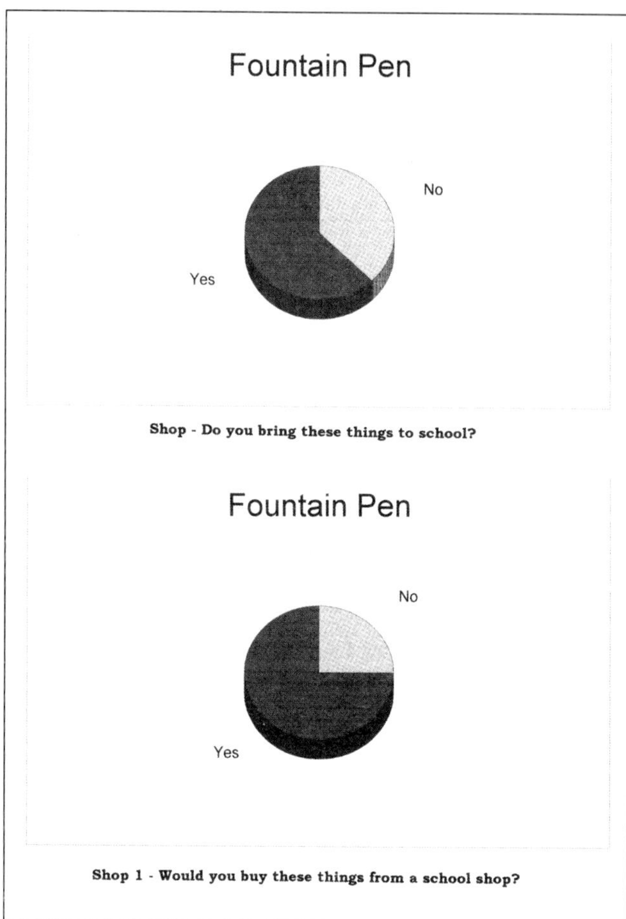

STATIONERY SHOP

**Really low prices for good quality stationery for school.
You can order for things with one of our order forms, these are in our leaflets.
We sell perfect pencils, rubbers, sharpeners and engrave them free of charge.**

Stegasaurus Stationery.

The School Shop.

We sell stationery at low low prices.
We will let you have a free try outs with the stationery at our shop.
Buy something get something free

We sell cheap but good quality stationery.
You can order stationery from our weekly leaflets.
Letters will be going out to tell you when we will have our grand opening.
Plenty of displays to show you what we will be selling.

Be there or be square.
Save money, and have cool, cheap stationery.

Using spreadsheets

A spreadsheet is an electronic sheet of paper which is set out with a number of boxes called 'cells' and a grid of 'rows' and 'columns'. It is a powerful tool because of its facility to manipulate numbers. It can perform number operations and work out averages.

A spreadsheet looks like this:

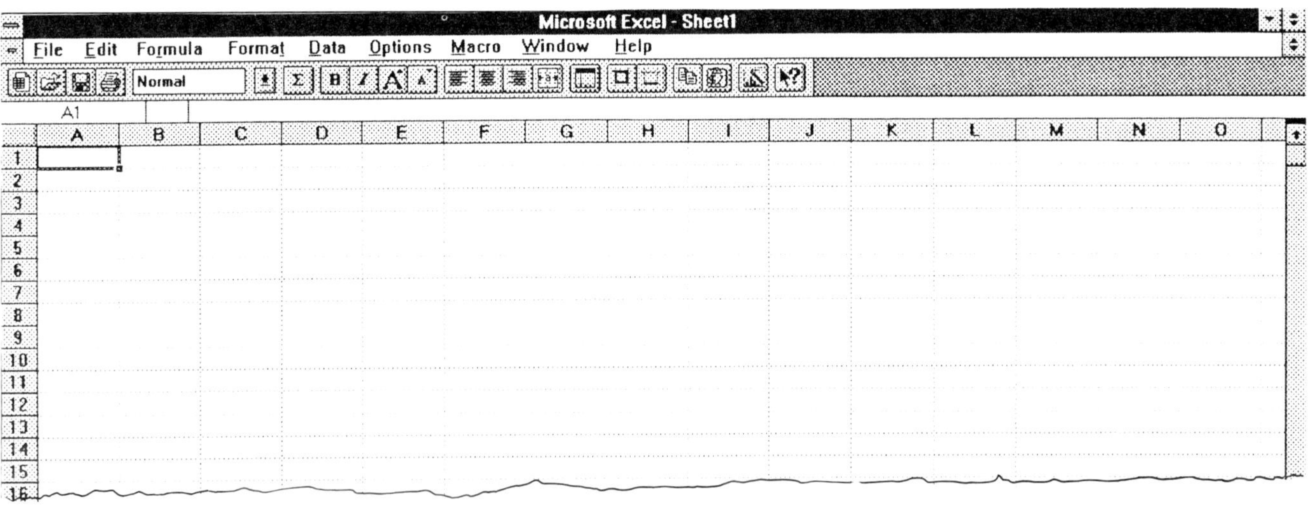

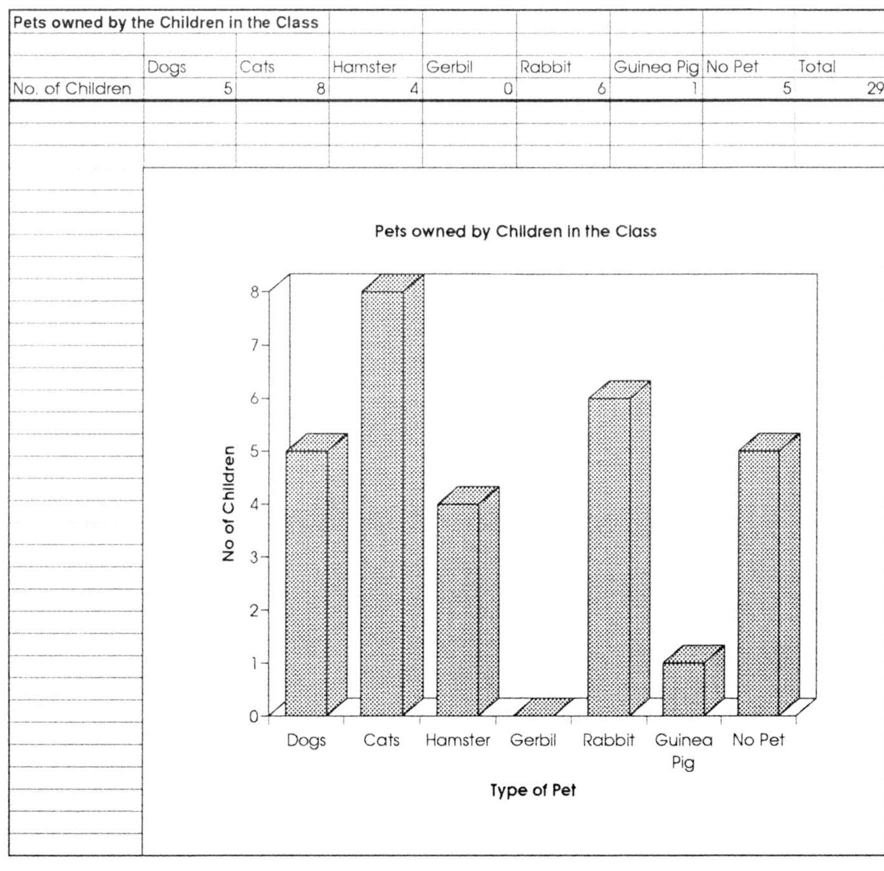

Pets owned by the Children in the Class								
	Dogs	Cats	Hamster	Gerbil	Rabbit	Guinea Pig	No Pet	Total
No. of Children	5	8	4	0	6	1	5	29

The numerical data held in the computer's memory can be manipulated in many different ways. The data is inter-related, so if one number is altered, the other data is re-presented. By using formulas it is possible to solve problems and analyse results. The general principles involved in problem solving using spreadsheets are the same whichever package is used. Specific instructions are provided with the software packs.

Times tables

Age range 8–11 years

Ways of working Teacher explaining to a small group or whole class first, then working in small groups.

Resources A spreadsheet.

Starting points The teacher shows the class how a spreadsheet works. She explains the relationship between rows and grids and how calculations are made. She can then ask a group of children to carry out the task. Print-outs can be used for displays and for further exploration of how a spreadsheet is used.

Extensions and more ideas A spreadsheet can be used to investigate sales in a school tuck-shop, to find the maximum size box which can be made from a given piece of cardboard or to investigate any numerical problems which involve large amounts of tables and figures.

	A	B	C	D	E	F	G	H	I	J	K	L	M	N
1	GRID SHOWING THE TIMES TABLE UP TO 12													
2														
3		1	2	3	4	5	6	7	8	9	10	11	12	
4		2	4	6	8	10	12	14	16	18	20	22	24	
5		3	6	9	12	15	18	21	24	27	30	33	36	
6		4	8	12	16	20	24	28	32	36	40	44	48	
7		5	10	15	20	25	30	35	40	45	50	55	60	
8		6	12	18	24	30	36	42	48	54	60	66	72	
9		7	14	21	28	35	42	49	56	63	70	77	84	
10		8	16	24	32	40	48	56	64	72	80	88	96	
11		9	18	27	36	45	54	63	72	81	90	99	108	
12		10	20	30	40	50	60	70	80	90	100	110	120	
13		11	22	33	44	55	66	77	88	99	110	121	132	
14		12	24	36	48	60	72	84	96	108	120	132	144	
15														
16														
17														

Grannie Annie's problem

Age range

10–11 years. Children need to be familiar with spreadsheets and working out formulas in order to take on this challenge.

Ways of working

In small groups.

Resources

A spreadsheet such as 'Grasshopper' or 'Excel'.

Starting points

The teacher introduces the problem to the children, reads out the letter below and asks the children to solve the problem in their small groups and get a print-out.

Grannie Annie received a letter from her grand-daughter Mary telling her that she would like a bicycle which costs £400.00 for next Christmas. It was only the beginning of January!

Grannie Annie wrote back to Mary:

Dear Mary,

You know I like you to think and plan ahead. So here is a proposition. I will give you some money regularly to save so that you can buy the bicycle yourself. Here are three options. Think about them and let me know which option you would like to use.

Option 1
£2.00 this month, £4.00 next month, £6.00 in month three and so on for 12 months.

Option 2
£1.00 now, £2.00 next month, £4.00 the month after and so on for 12 months.

Option 3
£60.00 now, £55.00 next month, £50.00 the month after and so on for 12 months.

Write and let me know. Give me the reason for your choice of option.

Love,
Grannie Annie

After several groups have attempted the task, it would be useful to compare methods and results.

Extensions and more ideas

Children can be asked to set problems, like Grannie Annie's, to solve for themselves.

A mathematical adventure

Age range 8–11 years.

Ways of working In small groups, for about 40 minutes to 1 hour.

Resources Computer notebook, 'Martello Tower' program, calculator, copy of grid below, map (available with the computer package).

Starting points Introduce the context of the adventure. Explain to the children that the challenge is to find the way around a coastal fort and escape to the sea. There are mathematical puzzles to solve on the way. The children need to be told that there are useful objects which they can pick up on the way, which may help them to escape. They should keep a record of these objects on a copy of the grid provided.

It is useful to tell children that the adventure can take a long time and that they need to keep notes about their progress. Although a map is provided, children will benefit from drawing their own maps.

Extensions and more ideas Children can be encouraged to make up games, models and stories based on the adventure at the Martello Tower.

Collecting objects to use on your adventure

Object offered	Where found	Where used	What happened

Tiling

Age range 6–11 years.

Ways of working After the initial introduction, in small groups.

Resources 'New Tiles' program and instructions.

Starting points The teacher can introduce the program to the whole class, then set a task of making a pattern to small groups. Setting a context, such as designing a wallpaper pattern or tile pattern for a purpose (perhaps related to the class topic), would encourage children to try more creative and challenging ideas.

Extensions and more ideas Can you make a bigger tile using four small tiles? Get a print-out of the pattern you have made and display it.

Using IT to teach English

Using IT to teach and develop the four aspects of primary English – speaking, listening, reading and writing – increases the requirement for literacy rather than reducing it. Using IT brings communication alive unlike some paper and pencil tasks which children are involved in.

Working at the computer generates *talk* within the group. The nature and quality of the talk will obviously depend upon the task and way it is set. IT, such as a tape recorder and a video camera (or stills camera), captures sound and action which is otherwise transient, whilst also providing an alternative to writing. Children for whom English is a second language can also benefit greatly by working with other children around the computer. The purposeful talk, linked to the visual forms on the screen, encourages the making of connections between the first language and the equivalent expressions used in English. Collaborating within an IT-led activity provides a genuine focus for discussion, makes listening necessary and encourages interaction, decision making and reflection.

Language permeates every aspect of the learning process. The challenge for the primary teacher is to develop a child's language competence, making it an effective tool in dealing with all aspects of the curriculum.

Word-processing

Word-processing is probably the aspect of IT which has had the greatest impact on English teaching and on our everyday lives. By using the word-processing facility a teacher can achieve very effective ways of developing children's writing.

Word-processing packages are developing all the time with ever-increasing enhancements for preparation and presentation.

Although using a computer does not automatically produce good writers, it has been found that with clear guidelines given by the teacher the quality of children's writing does often improve.

What does a word-processor offer children?

- The ability to convey ideas on screen where they can be read clearly.
- The facility to edit the text to correct spelling and punctuation, insert and delete text giving them the opportunity to use their energy to be more creative.
- The facility to save and retrieve text over a period of time.
- The chance to print out text in a variety of styles and formats.

- It does not let poor handwriting detract from the content, thus equalising children's work.
- It often results in a rise in children's self-esteem.

Word-processing is often a slow task for children and this could be demotivating. Lack of computer availability can often lead to children waiting some time if long pieces of text are being produced. Starting with short writing tasks gives satisfaction and builds keyboard skills. Limit the size of the task to make maximum use of your resources.

The flexibility provided by the **concept keyboard** should not be underestimated. It is not only applicable in the early years or with special needs pupils. In the upper primary stage a concept keyboard can be used for specific English skills, to access a database and to link with work in many curriculum areas using, for example, maps and pictures.

There are many excellent software packages that can be used imaginatively to teach explicit language skills. They are especially useful for tackling 'knowledge about language' in a contextual way.

Resources for word-processing

The school should build up a range of resources that offer plenty of scope for children to be effective communicators to a wide range of audiences for a variety of purposes.

A primary school should aim to have:

- a range of word-processing and desk-top publishing packages that increase the facilities offered
- a range of software, which is well organised and accessible, to support the English curriculum
- tape recorders with good microphone and counter facilities
- video recorder
- stills camera with flash
- electronic mail and fax machine
- CD-ROM.

Some examples of how children can use word-processing in the classroom are given on the following pages.

That's my name

Age range Nursery/Reception.

Resources Computer with either conventional or concept keyboard.

Starting points Builds on the importance to each child of his or her name. This is often the first word that the children practise writing and a word that they usually have a lot of exposure to. Using children's names can form the basis of many early literacy tasks.

Typing their names provides the children with a manageable task through which to become familiar with the keyboard. The alphabet on a concept keyboard overlay provides an active way in which children can become aware of the alphabet and its order.

Always provide the children with reasons for writing their names, such as:

- to name a coat peg
- to label a picture or model
- a place name
- to contribute to a survey chart, e.g. favourite colours, food, pets, colour of eyes, hair, etc.
- to reserve a book to take home
- the lunch list
- birthday chart
- letter awareness, e.g. names beginning with 'D', names ending in 'y', names containing an 'a'
- to label work folders.

Extensions and more ideas

- Children can produce name labels of different sizes and use different fonts which are appropriate to the use of the label.
- Keeping a name list for the class on the computer makes classroom administration and display more efficient.
- From name labels, children can then move on to captions.

Book reviews

Age range 6–11 years.

Ways of working In small groups or individually.

Resources Word-processing package plus graphics package or DTP package, computer notebook.

Starting points With the whole class discuss the purpose and common format for book reviews (with young children discuss a suggested format in the first instance).

Decide on the font and font size for headings and sub-headings.

Practice of the review format should be carried out orally to introduce the activity, as appropriate to the experience and/or age range of your class.

Explain that computer notebooks could be used for planning and drafting prior to computer time.

Jurassic Park

by

Michael Crighton

Jurassic Park is a very good book which along with the Steven Spielberg film, set off a craze in dinosaurs.

The book is mainly about two archaeologists, Alan and Ellie. They go to an island where scientists have recreated dinosaurs by starting off with dinosaur DNA preserved in fossilized mosquitos and completing the code. When the dinosaurs are hatched they keep them in 10,000 volt fenced paddocks but soon they escape.

My favourite part is when the Velociraptors escape and attack Tim and Lex in the kitchen but luckily they escape too and lock the Velociraptors in the kitchen.

I would recommend this for people who like claws, Jaws, Dinosaurs and are aged 10+.

Ben Pring
Age 10

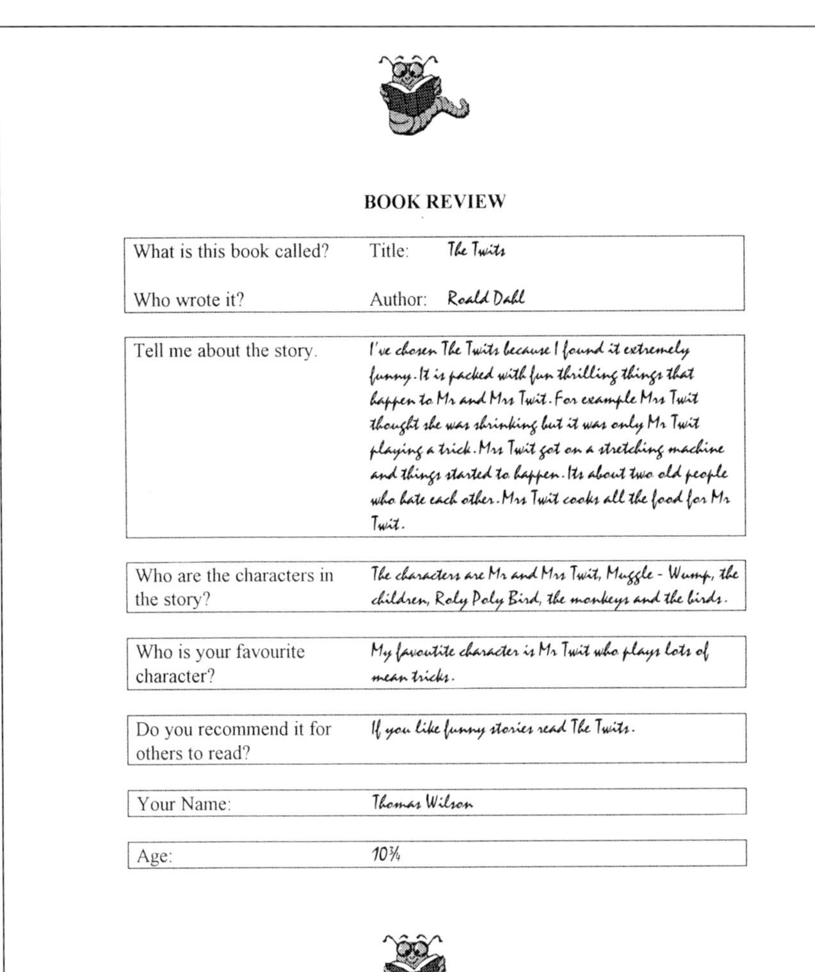

BOOK REVIEW

What is this book called?	Title: The Twits
Who wrote it?	Author: Roald Dahl
Tell me about the story.	I've chosen The Twits because I found it extremely funny. It is packed with fun thrilling things that happen to Mr and Mrs Twit. For example Mrs Twit thought she was shrinking but it was only Mr Twit playing a trick. Mrs Twit got on a stretching machine and things started to happen. Its about two old people who hate each other. Mrs Twit cooks all the food for Mr Twit.
Who are the characters in the story?	The characters are Mr and Mrs Twit, Muggle - Wump, the children, Roly Poly Bird, the monkeys and the birds.
Who is your favourite character?	My favoutite character is Mr Twit who plays lots of mean tricks.
Do you recommend it for others to read?	If you like funny stories read The Twits.
Your Name:	Thomas Wilson
Age:	10¾

Extensions and more ideas

- Work as a group to write a review of a shared book.
- Individual work at the computer is appropriate for this task but children could be paired for peer group support, or to discuss and help with word-processing.
- Use DTP graphics or a graphics package as appropriate for the review.
- Print-outs can form a catalogue of reviews for class reference or to be kept in the library.
- The data stored in the computer can be accessed as an on-screen databank.
- As children become more able readers, make sure that the sections of the review require responses at a number of levels and are not just literal comprehension and simple comments. Think about prediction, characterisation, alternative happenings, relating the story to own experience, reasons for recommendation, etc.
- Prepare a concept keyboard overlay with sentence beginnings such as 'I liked this book because ... ', 'My favourite character was ... ', 'I didn't like the story because ... '. The children then choose to finish the sentence from a list of options, e.g. 'It was frightening', 'It was exciting'.
- Cloze procedure programs can also form the basis for a book review. The teacher or children can input and store the framework for the review. The children can then add their personal opinions.

Note: specially formatted 'Book Review' software is available.

For sale

Age range 7–11 years.

Ways of working Pairs or small groups.

Resources Word-processing package and/or DTP package, range of newspaper small adverts, calculator, computer notebook.

Starting points With the class, look at 'small ad' pages from newspapers.

Using a flip chart, brainstorm the characteristics of these adverts.

Set a budget for the advert to be produced.

Either give out a card with an item 'For Sale' to each group or let them choose what they want to sell.

Let one group start immediately to compose on screen, while other groups plan their adverts in their computer notebooks.

Several versions may be necessary to get the best advert within the set budget (calculators could be used).

Groups take turns to input their adverts.

If you have a DTP package, the adverts can be formatted in columns as a newspaper page. Otherwise use 'cut and paste' on a large sheet of paper.

Extensions and more ideas

- Extend the category for the small ad to items such as cars, household items, favourite toys.
- Unwanted school equipment could be another category.

```
Problem: We were asked to advertise a car and a piano in the local
paper with a budget of £30.
The rates for cars were: Bargain Box with a maximum of 20 words.
                         For one week £18 including VAT
                         For two weeks £25 including VAT
                         Lineage Entry with a maximum of 12 words.
                         For two weeks £14 including VAT
The rates for other entries were:
       Display Box
       For one week £23 + VAT
       Lineage with a maximum of 10 words (85p + VAT for any
        extra word thereafter).
       For one week £8.50 + VAT
We decided to put the car advertisement in a Bargain Box to make
it show up.
We decided to have only one week otherwise we could not afford
another advertisement.
That left us with £12 to buy the other advertisement.
We could only afford the lineage. We then worked out the VAT on
£8.50 (17.5% of £8.50).
We worked this out to be £1.49. On the extra words the VAT was 15p.
We could afford 12 words altogether.
First 10 words £8.50 + £1.49 = £9.99    2 more words cost £2.
We've done it with 1p to spare !!!
```

FORD GRANADA
* H reg
* Low mileage
* Electric windows
* Automatic
* Central locking
* Regularly serviced
* 1 year MOT
* £2,999

Tel. 0695 484305

PIANO:
Upright Yamaha, overstrung, 6 years old, light wood, £4,999
0682 369578

Let's write letters

Letter writing has discreet rules which vary according to the purpose of the letter. Composing a letter requires the writer to be aware of different styles and to make appropriate choices about language and/or presentation.

Suitable types of letters to produce could be:

- to friends
- to penfriends
- to children in another school
- to seek information or advice
- thank you letters
- invitations
- to lobby on important issues.

Email and fax can be incorporated into these activities, if available.

Try using word-processing and desk top publishing packages to create a range of stationery, e.g. headed note paper, cards, compliment slips, invitations, menu cards, certificates. This could be part of a class/school enterprise project.

Carol Smith

Please come to my 6th Birthday Party
on Saturday 15 October
from 3.00pm until 6.00pm.

I live at 2 The Drive.

Please let me know if you can come.

Spring Street Junior School
Spring Street
Preston
Lancs

Dear Rosita

My name is Helen. I go to Spring Street Junior School. What is your school like? My teacher, Miss Hodson, told us about your country. Do you watch television? My Favourite programme is Hopme and Away.

At school my favourite subject is History. Miss Hodson took us all to a museum to look at Roman things for our topic. The best topic we did was about Henry the eighth.

I have a brother called Tony. He is 10 and I am 8. My brother teases me and he won't let me go to watch the football on Saturday.

When you write back tell me about your family.

Love from

Helen

Joke: What's yellow and dangerous?

Shark infested custard!

Appleby Primary School
The Avenue
Bristol
BS9 4EU

Dear Sir/Madam

Our class have been doing a local study. Outside our school there is a very grassy area. It is very flat and uninteresting. We have done a survey on its use and have done a litter count. We think that one reason that people drop litter and let their dogs use it as a toilet is because it is not attractive.

Our teacher suggested that we draw some plans to improve the grassy area. All the plans are displayed in our school entrance hall.

I am writing toi invite someone from the planning office to come to the school to look at our plans and to talk to my class about your job. Other children are writing to the local councillor and to the Residents Association to invite them to school.

We look forward to hearing from you. We are here everyday except Wednesday morning when we go swimming.

Yours faithfully

Darren Millar
Age 9

Word-processing around the classroom

Word-processed material surrounds us in our daily lives. Children need to see this carried over into their classroom environment. Let the children produce:

Displays

The Seasons of the Year

Spring

Summer

Autumn

Winter

Word banks

Words beginning with "th"

the

there

that

them

those

Information

WEEKLY INFORMATION SHEET

- P.E. KIT — Remember your P.E. Kit on Monday and Wednesday.
- RECORDER GROUPS — Tuesday in the music room at 12.30pm.
- THINGS TO COLLECT — cotton reels, coloured foil paper, card tubes, textured material
- BIRTHDAYS — Monday - Susan, Wednesday - Gary, Saturday - Ben

Lists

Days of the Week

Sunday

Monday

Tuesday

Wednesday

Thursday

Friday

Saturday

Labels

Scissors

PENCILS

PAPER

Guides

Writing Corner

Science Work Area

Mathematics Puzzles

Task sheets

Name of Pupil	Number Level 1		
	Count numbers to 10	Read numbers to 10	Write numbers to 10
William Andrews	✓	✓	✓
Susan Barnard	✓		
Rachel Clark	✓	✓	

On tape

Age range 4–11 years.

Ways of working Small groups.

Resources Tape recorders with good microphone facilities, listening centre.

Starting points *Ideas:*

All the activities below can be adapted to the age range you are teaching.

Interview:

- each other for personal news instead of a written diary
- younger/older children about books and other interests
- parents, helpers and other members of the community as part of curriculum research
- each other in role, e.g. as Henry VIII, an explorer, owner of a shop, a character from a book, song or poem.

Simulate a radio programme:

- a class news bulletin
- a radio play
- a quiz programme
- sports round-up.

Collaborative learning:

- groups tape-record their planning discussion. This saves taking notes and can be replayed as required
- presents opportunities as a format for final presentation of group work, e.g. a taped commentary on a wall display
- a dramatic reconstruction following research.

Writing poems, stories and books

Producing poems, stories, books and accounts are possibly the ways in which word-processing is most used in the classroom. Practice is now moving away from using word-processing as a vehicle for providing a neat, corrected copy of work which was written away from the computer. This is sometimes found to be laborious and demotivating for children. Ideas can be brainstormed and developed either straight on to the computer, the tape recorder or jotted down in the computer notebook. Planning could also be in the form of a story board or map. All these methods ensure that children do not just 'copy up'.

Ideas

- Complete a story partly written and stored on disk.
- Some programs provide pictures as a stimulus for stories or poems.
- A picture library helps children to fashion a story appropriate to the style of the picture, e.g. a fairy tale.
- Incorporate other aspects of IT into story writing:
  - children take photos which become the illustrations for a text
  - use a tape recorder for planning and brainstorming
  - video tape a drama activity as a stimulus for writing.
- Photographs or video tape taken on a class outing can provide the basis of a factual book for the class or school library.
- Develop the use of spell-checkers.
- Branching stories can be created either by using specialist software or by reference to different pages.
- Writing instructions and explanations provides a good context for developing text manipulation skills on the computer.

Desk top publishing (DTP)

Producing a newspaper, magazine or newsletter combines the whole range of writing formats – factual, fiction, letters, stories, poems, jokes/riddles/puzzles. This allows all children to contribute and to feel proud of the outcomes.

Children should review and discuss real examples of DTP and have an understanding of how and why they are produced in everyday life.

A newspaper or magazine can either be for a wide audience, including a range of material, or can have a very specific purpose.

Ideas

- A newsletter to parents or for younger children.
- An information sheet for children about to enter the school.
- Fact sheets about the class theme, e.g. 'Good Health'.
- Follow-up to an outing.
- Give information on new books in the library as notices.
- An alternative format for the class 'Weekly News'.
- Fact sheets for mathematics and science projects.

MATHS PUZZLES FOR THE WEEK

Monday	*Can you make all the numbers 1 to 20 using only 4's and any symbols?*
Tuesday	*How many squares are there on an 8 by 8 chessboard? It is not the obvious 64!!*
Wednesday	*The answer is 36. Think of the most challenging 10 questions which will give you that answer.*
Thursday	*Who invented zeros? Write a paragraph about it and display it on the wall.*
Friday	*1991 was a special number in our calendar. When will another number like that happen next? What is a number like this called?*

JUST ARRIVED IN THE LIBRARY

(I) 'Mutiny at Crossbones Bay' by Usborne.
If you like adventure and suspense you will like this book. We have 5 copies, but don't leave it too long.

(II) New set of 'Encyclopaedia of Team Games'

This book tells you the story of team games.

YOUR GUIDE TO GOOD HEALTH

BIG BREAKFAST IS BAD NEWS FOR CLASS 6V

Class 6v has been conducting a survey on children's health habits.

We found out:

- Many of us lead a sedentary life.
- 50% of 6Y children eat vegetables.
- Two thirds of our class are reluctant breakfast eaters.
- Most of the children either eat fish or meat every day.

Try This Quiz ...
and find out if you are food-wise!

1. Name a fruit which gives you vitamin C?
2. What does aerobics exercise?
3. Which helps you most with growth and repairing your body?
   a.) carbohydrates
   b.) proteins
   c.) fats

The concept keyboard and the development of literacy

Using a concept keyboard as a word-processor is quicker for children who are unfamiliar with the QWERTY keyboard, who lack manual dexterity or who are at the early stages of literacy development. However, with all children the versatility and application of the concept keyboard offers exciting potential. Maps, pictures and data are ideal contexts for overlays.

Many word-processing packages include the facility to make overlays for the concept keyboard.

Developing literacy

The concept keyboard can be used in the same way as the 'Breakthrough to Literacy' material.

Ideas for overlays

- Word matching
- Sentence building
- Picture/word matching
- Sequencing
- Cloze procedure
- Spelling/the alphabet

home	mum	dad	television		bed	nan	baby	am	is	are	was	were	be	will	can
brother	sister	boy	girl	friend	mate	day		have	has	come	go	play	came	went	watch
birthday		present		shop	car	park	a	see	saw	want	got	get	like	help	walk
the	and	some	all	this	my	you	me	yes	no	there	what	when	with	after	but
it	we	our	he	him	I	they		for	to	in	out	of	happy	sad	
his	her	she	good	bad	all	lot		es	s	ed	ing	?		not	n't
autumn	winter	Christmas	cold	dark	wet	frosty	foggy					CAPITAL	RETURN	←	→
												SPACE	DELETE	↑	↓

Concept keyboard published overlay

Picture/word matching

For assessment

An overlay allows a teacher to assess a child's knowledge and understanding in a way which is not hindered by lack of appropriate literacy development.

Get interactive with multi-media

'Multi-media' means many communications. Having a multi-media system in the classroom allows you to combine words, pictures, sound and graphics on one computer.

The main advantage is that all the processes can be carried out just by clicking the computer mouse. Multi-media is an exciting way for children to process and create language.

Reading fiction

Some of the best children's literature is becoming available as multi-media packages, motivating children to learn and practise reading. 'Living Books' allows children to join in with the text. By clicking the mouse they can make characters talk, move, sing or dance. The text is read aloud; phrases and lines can be highlighted for the computer to read. A click on the mouse checks a word, moves backwards and forwards within the text and can even change the language from English. Working in a small group, these packages generate story language and awareness making a genuine focus for group reading.

He is eating hot dogs. His Mum cleaned them.

Creating a presentation

A special authoring program can be used so that children can develop their own multi-media presentations. The program brings together all the material that you want to include – such as video, still photographs, graphics, text and sound.

Ideas for multi-media presentations

- An alternative version of a well-known story.
- A factual presentation as the end product of a class theme.
- A school brochure for visitors.
- A local study.
- Personal profiles of each child in the class.

Work based on the CD-ROM 'Living Books'

He got on the bus.
He was tired.

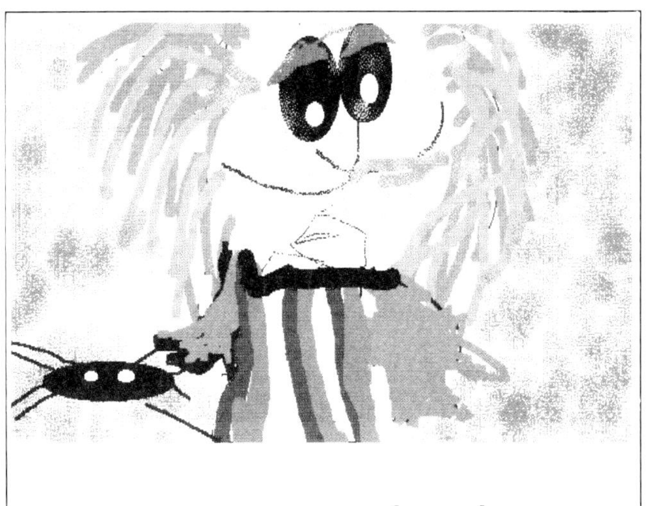

Work based on the CD-ROM 'Living Books'

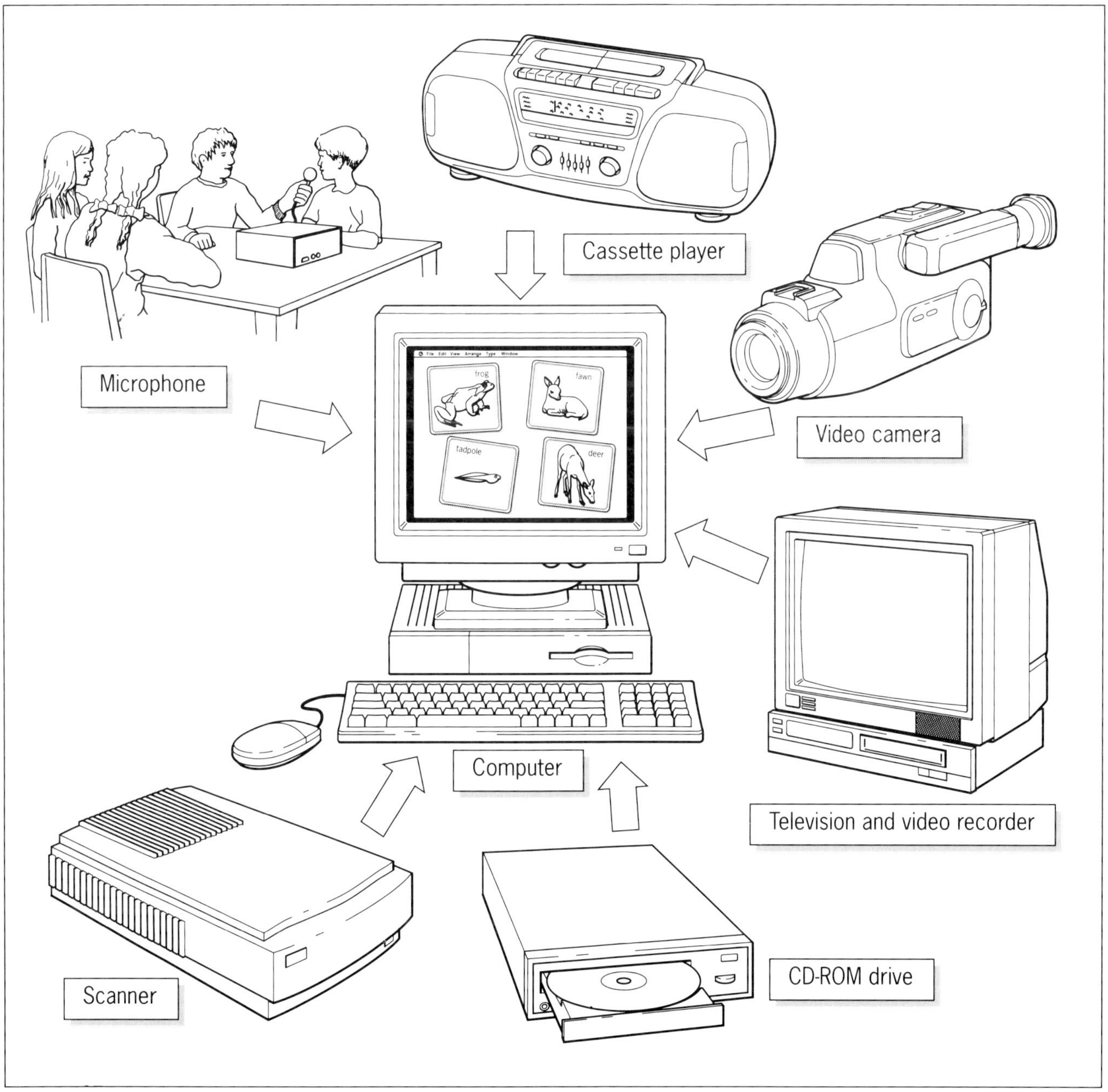
Cassette player
Microphone
Video camera
frog
fawn
tadpole
deer
Computer
Television and video recorder
Scanner
CD-ROM drive

Multi-media system

Using IT to teach Science

Information technology can enhance young children's learning in Science by encouraging them to develop the scientific processes of:

- observing and classifying
- prediction
- planning investigations
- communicating
- recording.

Content-free programs such as databases help the children to collect, sort, analyse and interpret scientific data. They can use a CD-ROM to interrogate and retrieve data.

Using sensors, children can measure temperature, light and sound and monitor the environment.

By using programmable toys and robots, switches and buzzers, they can control devices such as door bells, alarms and traffic lights. Adventure programs and simulations provide children with meaningful contexts for enquiry into many aspects of Science.

Children can also use IT to enhance the presentation of their work. They can use a word-processing or desk top publishing package to present their findings in the form of posters, stories or news items. Using graphics programs they can illustrate their work more effectively.

Children can also be encouraged to be aware of the use of IT in their everyday lives, such as lifts, bar-codes and card operated telephones.

The potential for using IT to teach Science is limitless. Some examples are provided on the following pages.

Using a branching database

Age range 6–11 years (using an appropriate topic for investigation).

Ways of working Whole class, small groups.

Resources A collection of pictures of 'minibeasts', animal cards or appropriate pictures and a 'branching' database.

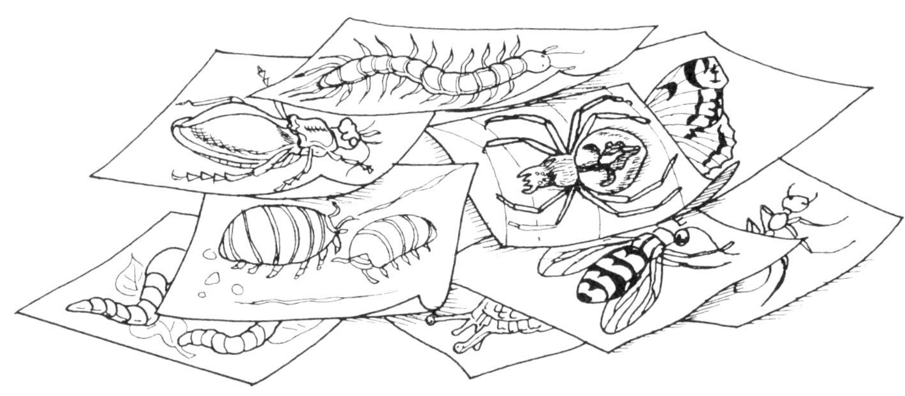

Starting points

Show children which computer program is to be used. Let them work through an existing branching program stored in the computer and become familiar with its structure.

Ask children to sort their pictures into groups. Let them explain their reasons for grouping them. Take two items to the database and ask the children to think of a question which would help to distinguish one item from the other.

Take one card at a time and work through the database. When the database is complete let others try it.

Extensions and more ideas

Children can use a branching database to identify flowers, plants, fruits, etc.

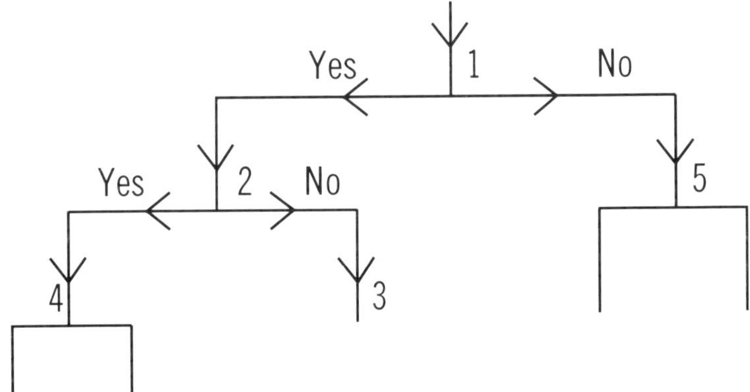

1 Does it have legs?
If yes, go to 2.
If no, go to 5.

2 Does it have 6 legs?
If yes, ...

A buzzer for the sweets box

Age range 8–11 years.

Ways of working In groups.

Resources 'Control' equipment, pressure pads or sensors.

Starting points The teacher sets the challenge: build a 'buzzer' which rings when someone touches the sweets box. Think about how it can be tested for the 'best' buzzer.

By discussion and experiment, the children use 'control' equipment to make a program or procedure that sets off the buzzer when someone is about to open the sweets box.

Extensions and more ideas Can you design:

- a buzzer which lights up the bulbs in the dark?
- a buzzer which goes when the temperature drops below 0° C?
- a buzzer which goes when the teacher's desk drawer is opened?

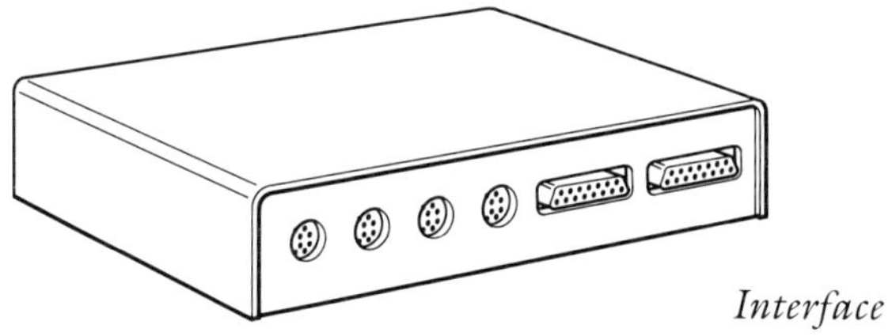

Interface

Rebecca and I took on the challenge of building a buzzer for our sweet box. We used control technology to build a warning device for our sweet box. The bits of equipment we used were a computer, buzzer, pressure pads, disk and an interface. First we had to think about how we would let the computer know that someone was approaching the sweet box. Then we had to make a program for the buzzer to go, a bit like in Logo. It was n't really very difficult but you just had to think about each of the steps carefully .

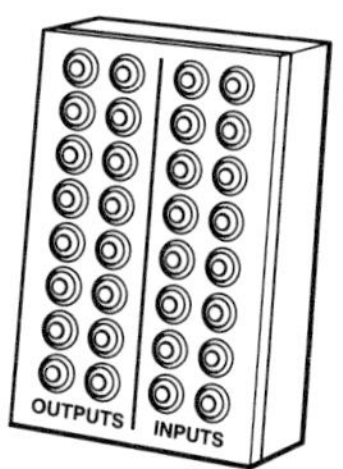

Control box

Bright spots for reading

Age range 7–11 years.

Ways of working Whole class for explanations, then small groups.

Resources A light sensor.

Starting points Tell the children they are going to investigate the light in the classroom to find the brightest spot for reading. Explain and demonstrate how the sensor is set up. Let different groups of children take responsibility for recording the findings. Make up a table of records.

Collect and display print-outs and graphs.

Extensions and more ideas

- Which is the warmest spot in the classroom? Is it near the radiator? Or near the window? Use a datalogging program to find out.
- Which is the warmest time of day in the window box?
- Design a sleeping area for the hamster. A reasonably warm place is needed. What kind of bedding would be best? Can you design an experiment to find out?
- Use a temperature sensor to measure whether or not your body temperature changes when you exercise.

Finding the best spot for reading.

The best spot for reading is where you get the best amount of light. In our classroom we predicted that the most amount of light is where the painting corner is . We did an experiment using a light sensor and a computer. We measured the amount of light in different places in the class. We were wrong . The most amount of light was near the teacher's desk in the front. The next brightest place was the painting corner. We have since decided to move our reading corner to that spot.

Sharon, Alison and David

Simulations

Simulations and adventures such as 'Pond Life' and 'Teddy Bears Picnic' offer children motivating contexts for scientific discussions and investigations.

CD-ROMs are increasingly becoming available, providing limitless possibilities for research and investigations.

CD-ROM holds a large amount of information, much more than is stored on floppy and hard disks. One CD-ROM disc can hold more information than a whole set of encyclopaedias.

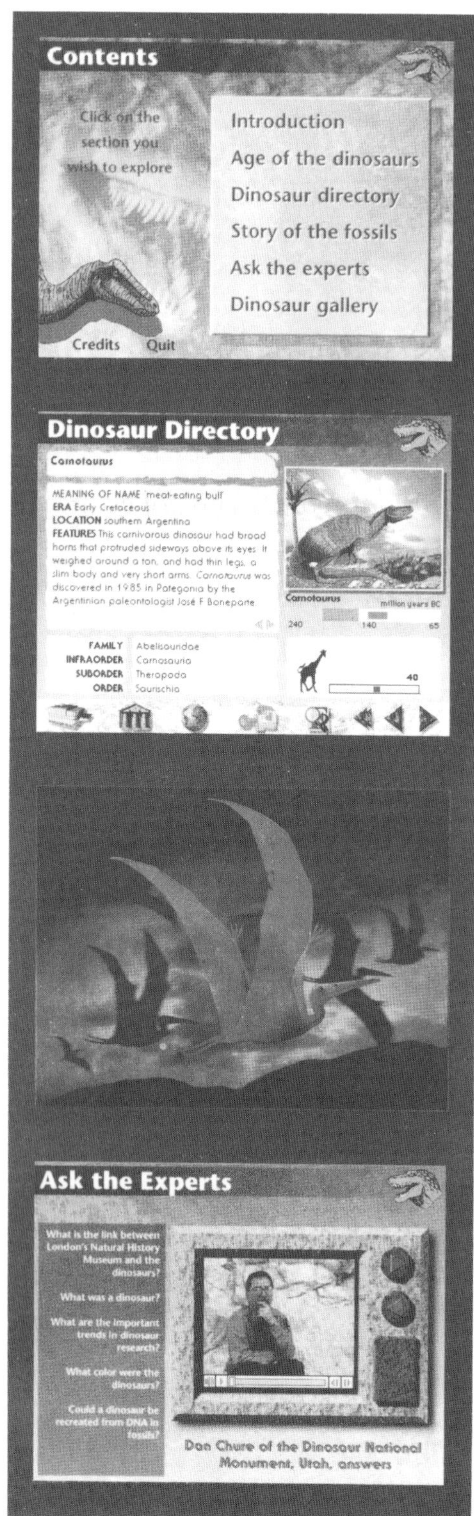

Ourselves

Age range

7–11 years.

Ways of working

Whole class to start, then in small groups.

Resources

Tape measures, rulers, pencils, paper and a spreadsheet.

Starting points

Discuss with the children questions they are interested in finding answers to.

'Who is the tallest in the class?'

'Who has the longest arm?'

'Is there a connection between how tall you are and how fast you can run?'

Encourage the children to make hypotheses.

'The tallest person jumps the highest.'

'Three times your head span is equal to your height.'

'Girls in the class are taller than boys.'

'The tallest person has the largest shoe size.'

Decide what data you need to collect and collect it. Set up a spreadsheet and enter the data.

Nisha Patel 5R/M 3/11/94

RECORDS

FIELDNAMES										
Name	Mariam	Namrata	Anita	Sadia	Parneet	Daniel	Neil	Rahul	Mark	Sean
Height (cm)	1.38 cm	1.34 cm	136 cm	1.28 cm	134 cm	1.45 cm	1.35 cm	1.44 cm	138 cm	1.35 [illegible]
waist (cm)	43 cm	67 cm	65 cm	45 cm	55 cm	64 cm	56 cm	59 cm	66 cm	[illegible]
Shoe size	4	3	4	13	1	5	4	6	2	2
Hair colour	Dark brown	Brown	Black	Dark Brown	Dark Brown	Black	Dark Brown	Dark Brown	Fair	[illegible]
eye colour	Greenish Brown	Hazel	Dark Brown	Dark Brown	Dark Brown	Dark brown	Dark Brown	Brown	Brown	Blue
colour of eyebrows	Dark Brown	Brown	Black	Dark Brown	Dark Brown	Black	Dark Brown	Dark Brown	Fair	Blond.
Speed	10 sec	11 sec	12 sec	13 sec	10 sec	11 sec	11 sec	11 sec	10sec	12 sec

Once the data has been collected, you can obtain graphs and demonstrate answers to some of your questions.

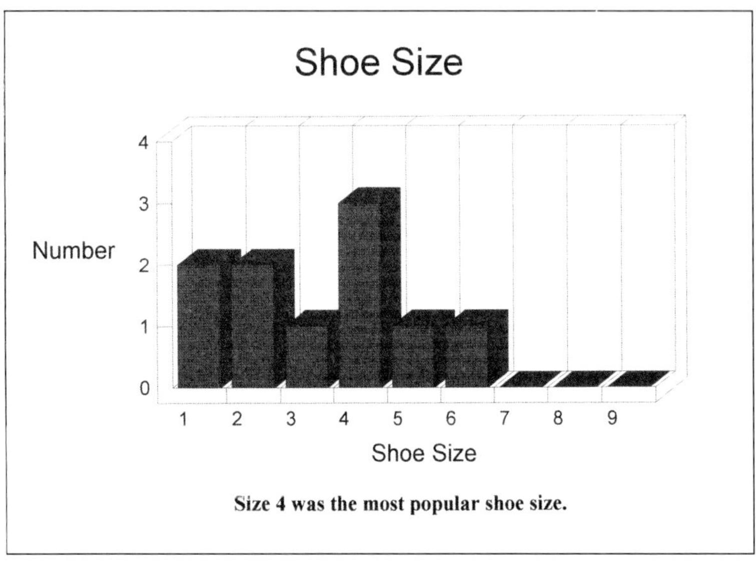

Size 4 was the most popular shoe size.

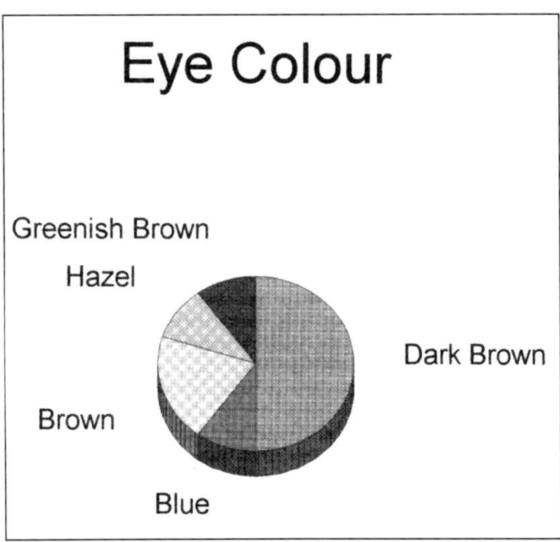

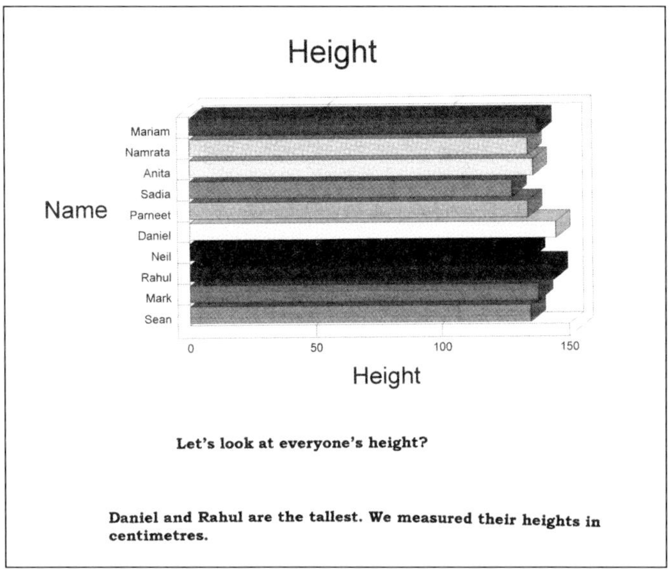

Let's look at everyone's height?

Daniel and Rahul are the tallest. We measured their heights in centimetres.

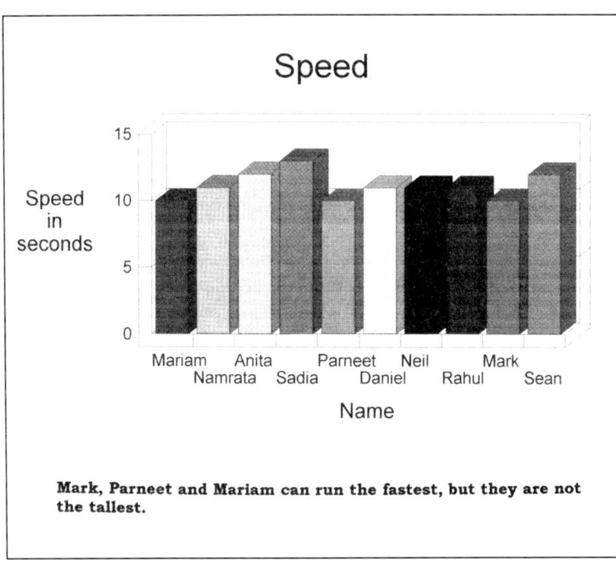

Mark, Parneet and Mariam can run the fastest, but they are not the tallest.

Extensions and more ideas

- Ask a wider variety of questions and carry out more sophisticated searches. The graphs and the results of the investigations can be displayed as posters using word-processing and desk top publishing packages for others to see and pose new questions.
- Using spreadsheets the children can investigate the nutritional content of cereals. Collect labels from empty food packets to set up the spreadsheet.

  'Which cereal gives you the most energy?'

  'Which cereal has the most protein?'

  'Which is the best buy?'

  Display the findings on a poster.

How can IT support a bird project?

Watching birds and making a study of them are very pleasurable activities and make a popular project for children. IT can make a very positive contribution to enhance the quality of this kind of project. Examples of how IT is integrated into this project are given below.

Collect lots of information about birds.

Ask some questions:

- What do different types of birds look like, so that we can identify them?
- What different types of birds visit the school playground?
- Do they come at special times during the day? early morning? lunch times? afternoons?
- Do they have favourite foods?
- Do they make special sounds?
- Are some birds more aggressive?
- Do they come alone or in groups?

Use this information to set up a database.

Think of headings, e.g.

Colour:
Time of visit:
Favourite food:
and so on.

Using a CD-ROM database on birds you can find out more information on birds.

Tape record or video record bird movements and habits.

You can listen to the sounds they make and watch their different types of movement and particular characteristics.

With the information collected, using word-processing and DTP packages, children can make up crosswords, wordsearches, newspapers or a magazine about birds. These require children to apply the information in a purposeful way for a variety of audiences.

BIRD WORDSEARCH

I	O	S	T	R	I	C	H	A	U
P	L	W	V	B	M	K	M	U	B
M	K	I	L	E	N	B	E	T	M
A	R	O	X	H	E	R	O	N	A
G	J	T	P	N	A	C	R	I	G
S	E	H	I	I	G	L	R	B	P
T	F	B	R	O	L	I	J	E	I
W	O	C	E	P	E	R	A	I	E
R	D	R	H	E	A	G	Y	F	L
E	Z	S	P	A	R	R	O	W	P

OWL OSTRICH HERON
EAGLE ROBIN JAY
SPARROW
MAGPIE

Word-processing in Science

Word-processing packages can support learning in Science.

Ideas

Working collaboratively, children can write stories based on scientific ideas, following investigations. They can compose stories at the keyboard.

The day a new chemical was discovered ...

I was sitting at my desk, staring out of the classroom window, when I suddenly noticed that the floor was getting very wet. My experiment was leaking out all over the tiles. I looked round to see if anyone else had noticed, but I was the only one not working hard. I looked again at the floor, how was I going to clear the mess up without Miss Owen noticing that there was something wrong? I glanced up at her, it was all right, she was talking to Kevin.

In my desk I had my P.E. kit, it was the only cloth near by so it had to be sacrificed to the job of cleaning the floor. How I was going to explain it to Mum I didn't know.

I carefully slid my hand into the desk and got my t-shirt out. I managed to drop it on the floor and with my foot started to mop up the mess. My foot just slipped! The liquid on the floor had turned into a very slippery polish that looked as smooth as ice. My experiment must have somehow turned into a floor polish, the combination of wax and everything else ...

Children can use secondary sources to research into astronomy and present their findings on a poster.

Using the 'cut' and 'paste' facilities, they can produce life-cycles of insects.

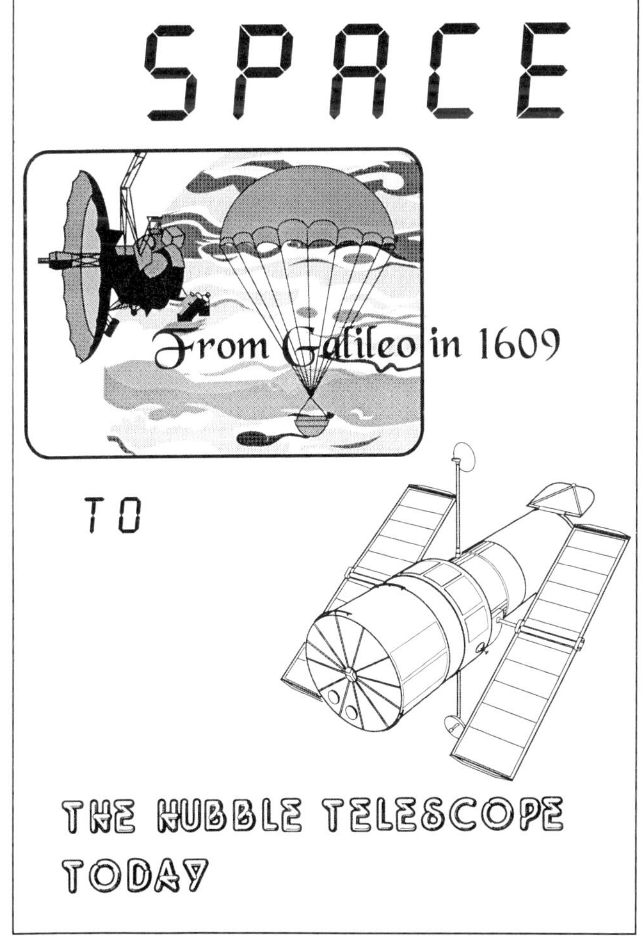

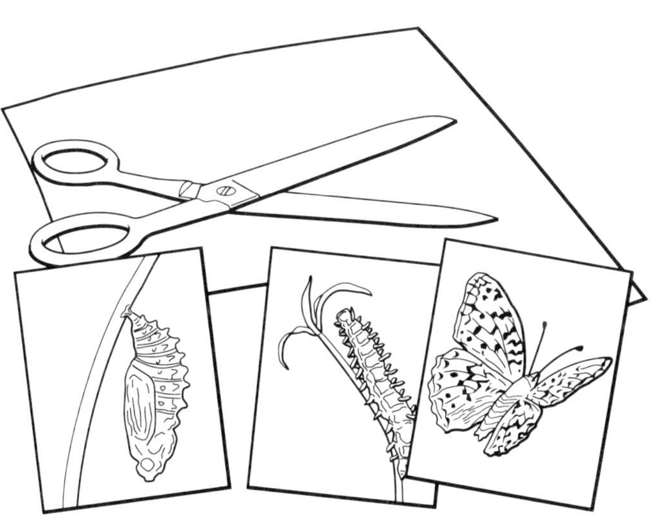

Class newspapers and magazines on scientific themes can be designed and produced.

The 'cut' and 'paste' facilities enable even very young children to undertake sequencing activities such as:

Put tea into the tea pot | Collect water | Drink tea | Boil water | Making tea | Pour boiling water into the tea pot | Get the tea pot ready | Add milk and/or sugar | Pour tea into the cup

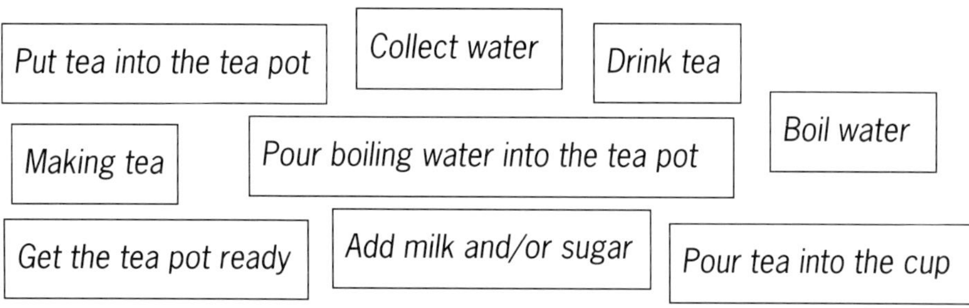

Cards such as these can be made into sets and given jumbled up to other children to put into order. The activity promotes discussion and decision making.

Incorporating computer graphics, the presentation can be made even more impressive.

For example, you can make up a puzzle with labels for different parts of the body to be placed in their proper positions.

Or match animal babies to their mothers.

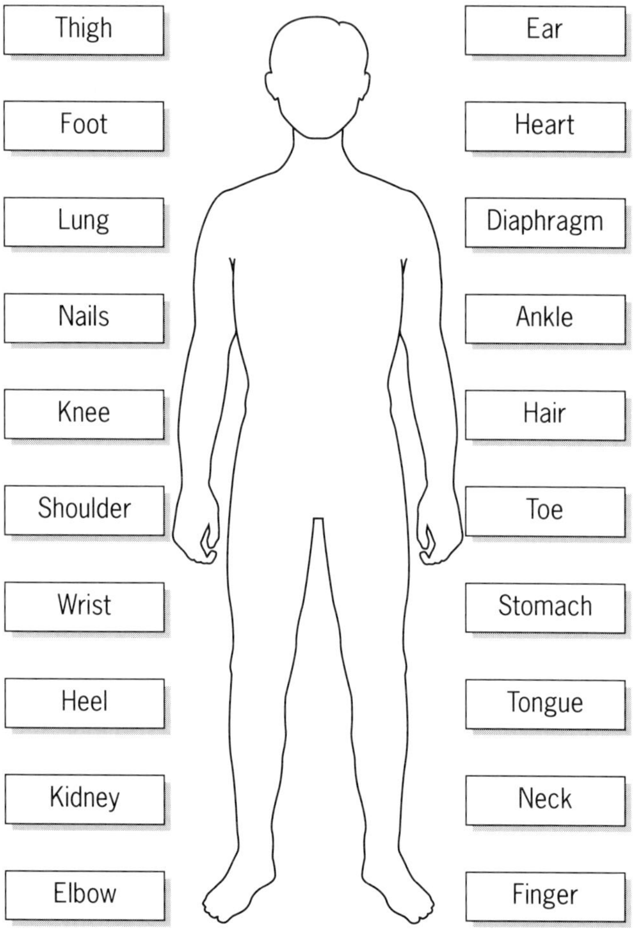

Thigh
Foot
Lung
Nails
Knee
Shoulder
Wrist
Heel
Kidney
Elbow
Ear
Heart
Diaphragm
Ankle
Hair
Toe
Stomach
Tongue
Neck
Finger

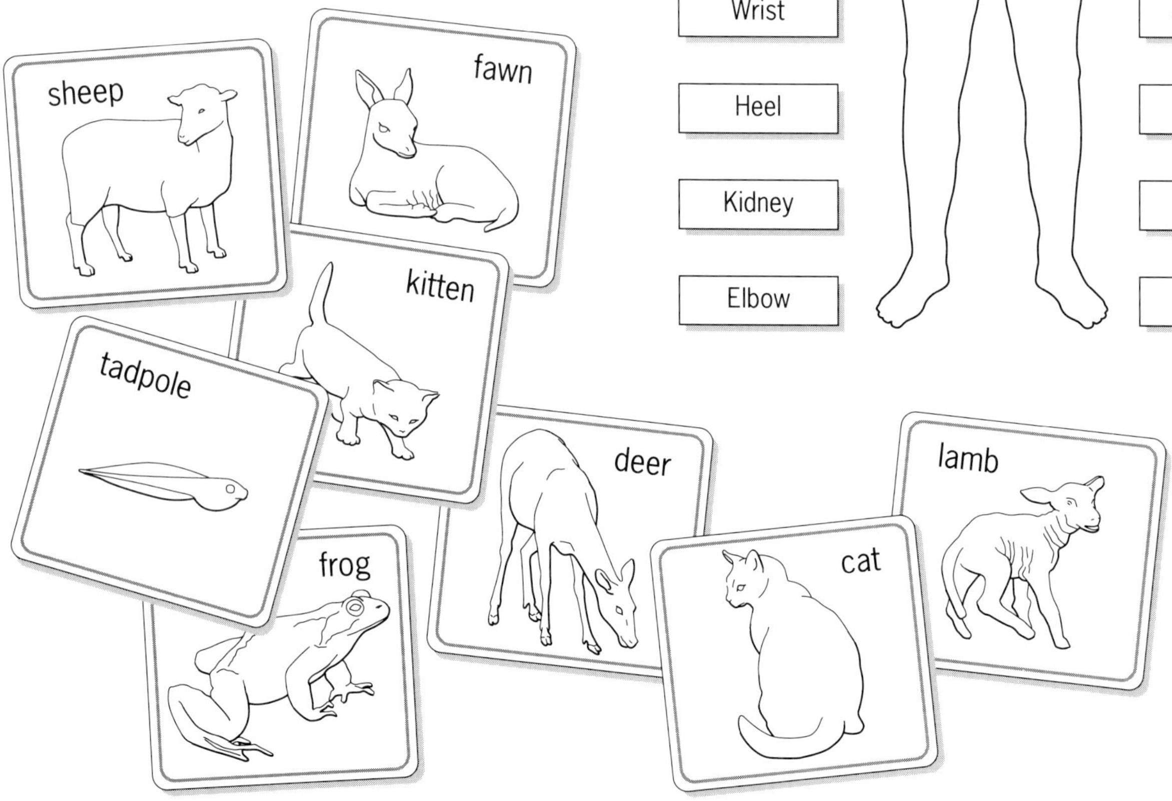

sheep
fawn
kitten
tadpole
deer
lamb
frog
cat

Minibeast search using a concept keyboard

Age range 5–8 years.

Ways of working Whole class for introduction of activity, then small groups.

Resources Concept keyboard and data collecting sheets.

Starting points Explain to the children that they are going to do a survey of minibeasts in the school grounds. They should make a record of which creatures they find, how many and note their special features.

Make a map of the grounds and use it as an overlay on a concept keyboard. When an area on the map is pressed the name and number of creatures found in that special place will be displayed on the screen.

Extensions and more ideas You can prepare a more sophisticated overlay with drawings on the concept keyboard and some words typed in to describe them. When you press a picture of a minibeast, it displays features about the creature.

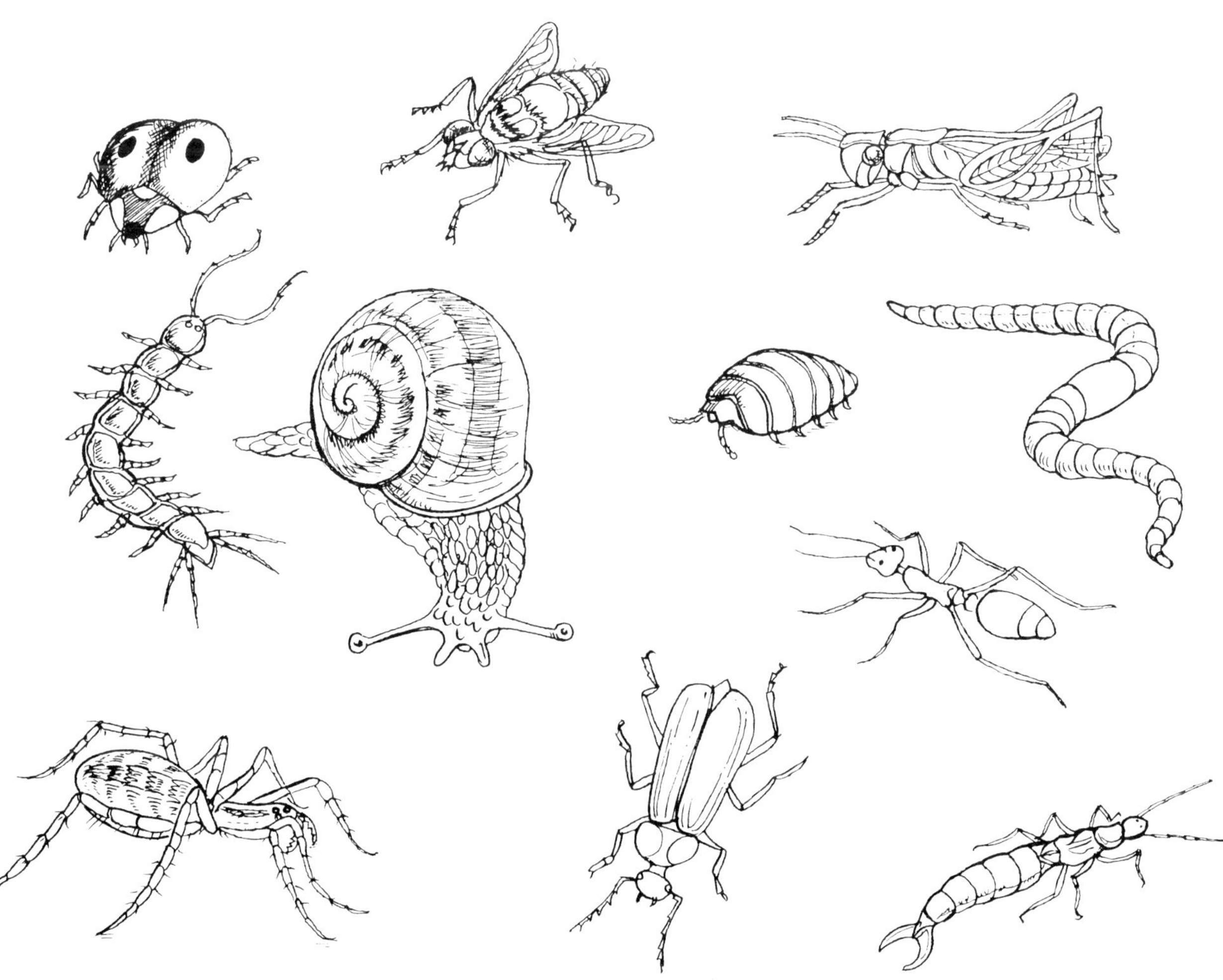

IT in cross-curricular themes

A cross-curricular theme incorporates some or all subjects of the primary curriculum. Using themes helps children to make connections effectively and offers opportunities for the reinforcement of ideas.

Working in this way involves carrying out research and helps to apply subject knowledge. Themes give plenty of scope for extending literacy and numeracy.

IT can enhance cross-curricular work in two ways:

- IT can be incorporated into subject-specific tasks planned as part of the theme
- it is possible for a software package to provide the focus and starting point for a range of activities which extend beyond the program.

In this section **four** themes are given as examples of using IT effectively to facilitate and enhance learning. Some ideas are presented as examples of structured lessons; other ideas are included for teachers to design their own structure to fit their style of teaching and the needs of the children.

1 Food

This is a very popular theme throughout the primary school. The suggestions show how IT can enhance some of the most frequently used activities.

2 Chinese dragons

This theme uses a software package ('Puff'), available for the BBC and Nimbus, as a starting point for this curriculum theme.

Adventure games, such as 'Puff', provide one of the most exciting applications of IT in the classroom. The programs are not, in fact, games but are simulated environments for children to experience and explore. This section is an example of what can be done. There are a wide range of adventure games for different age groups that can be incorporated into planning across the school.

3 Homes for gnomes

Creating a fantasy or fictional world motivates and opens up opportunities for creative and imaginative thinking.

The 'Homes for gnomes' theme is an enterprise project with many links with the real world. It offers children the challenges of problem-solving and an opportunity to use and develop their own initiative. IT can make a project like this come alive.

4 Europe

The 'European dimension' provides an example of how IT can enhance learning within History and Geography.

What did you have for breakfast?

Age range

5–7 years.

Ways of working

Whole class, groups, pairs, individuals.

Resources

Goldilocks story, packaging and pictures of a range of foods, a simple database program.

Starting points

With the whole class:

- read 'Goldilocks and the Three Bears'
- show children what you had for breakfast
- what did the children have?
- have a flip chart prepared with the children's names.

With the class divided into groups of 5 or 6, children cut out pictures of what they had for breakfast and stick them next to their names (either provide pictures or have the children draw them).

Children in pairs or individually input their personal data having had a demonstration by the teacher (peer group tutoring is useful here).

Repeat the activity for each group.

Back as a whole class, formulate some questions to explore, such as:

- what is the most popular breakfast food?
- what is the most popular cereal?
- do all the children have breakfast?

Let the children use the questions to produce graphs, charts, pictograms, etc.

Discuss the outcomes and interpretations.

Extensions and more ideas

The outcomes of this investigation can be displayed so that children will continue to think about the issues.

Investigating fruits

Age range 7–9 years.

Ways of working Whole class, groups, pairs.

Resources Collection of real fruits, pictures of and books on fruit, a suitable database program.

Starting points

- A visit to a local fruiterers or the fruit section of a big supermarket.
- A collection of fresh fruit in the classroom and a collection of other visual material.
- A discussion of the fruits, to formulate some questions the children want to investigate (use a flip chart as appropriate).

Some examples of questions:

What different fruits do we know about?
Are there fruits we haven't seen in the UK?
Where do each of the fruits grow?
Which fruits grow in the UK?
What do the different fruits cost?
Which is the most expensive?
Do all fruits have soft skin?
Which fruits are sweet?

The children can also think of questions and jot them down in their computer notebooks.

Discuss with the children how their questions can be turned into possible headings for collecting the data.

The list could look like this:

Name of fruit ....
Country of origin ....
Cost ....
Have stones ....
Have to peel ....
Juicy ....
and so on ....

Show an existing file from your chosen database to introduce technical terms and procedures such as:

HEADING FILE SAVE INTERROGATE

Fruit Words – by Amrit

Juicy
Fresh
Red and Green
Delicious
Rough
Bumpy
Sticky
Ripe
Stringy
Green
Lumpy
Spikey
Hard
Sour
Hairy
Squidgy
Soft
Delicate
Dry
Skin
Yellow
Slippery
Silky
Star shaped
Waxy
Stalk
Watery
Pink
Round
Papery

The children convert their headings to single word fields:

Fact sheet	
Name	....
Country	....
Cost	....
Seeds	....
Peel	....
Feel	....
Juicy	....
Skin	....

They can work in pairs or groups to input data from their fact sheets.

Interrogating the data base

How many fruits have seeds?

Which fruit is the most expensive?

If the computer gave the answer 'mango', this could lead to a further question and research.

Why is mango more expensive?

Extensions and more ideas

Other questions to investigate include:

- Why do some fruits have soft skin?
- Why do some fruits taste sweeter than others?
- Why do some skins peel more easily?
- Why don't some fruits grow in England?

The children can word-process their findings and display them.

Looking At Fruits.

We have been looking at fruits. We asked lots of questions about them, and then made our own Database to show our answers.

Name of Fruit.
Country it comes from?
How much it costs?
Does it have seeds?
Do you have to peel it to eat it?
What does it feel like?
Is it juicy?
What colour is it?

The graphs show all our results, and answer some of our other questions.

Which crisp?

Age range 8–11 years.

Ways of working Whole class, then groups.

Resources Copies of a consumer magazine, at least 8 packets of crisps of different brands (with brand name hidden), a data-handling package which allows at least 12 fields and a scoring system.

Starting points Talk about the purpose and uses of consumer surveys, collecting ideas from the children.

Explain that they are going to be part of a survey about crisps.

Set out bowls of crisps (labelled A–G) with a different brand in each bowl (having noted which brand is in which bowl).

Negotiate with the children a set of criteria which can be used to judge quality.

The children work in pairs but fill in individual results sheets.

Example of a data sheet:

BOWL A	
Feel	....
Cost	....
Colour	....
Shape	....
Flavour	....
Texture	....
Taste	....
and so on	....

All the information from the data sheet is entered into the database.

Use the interrogation facility to decide which is the best crisp.

Disclose the brand names at the end for discussion.

Extensions and more ideas

- Develop and word-process a consumer report of the survey and send copies to the manufacturers.
- A narrower search could be carried out by restricting it to one flavour from eight different brands – to find the best salt and vinegar crisps for example.

Crisp Investigation

We found out the different brands of crisps after our investigation. Here they are.

Bowl A = Smiths Square Crisps.
Bowl B = Smiths Crisps.
Bowl C = Hula Hoops.
Bowl D = Walkers Crisps.
Bowl E = Brannigans.
Bowl F = Chipsticks.
Bowl G = Tescos.

If we were to carry out another investigation, we would like to investigate different flavours.

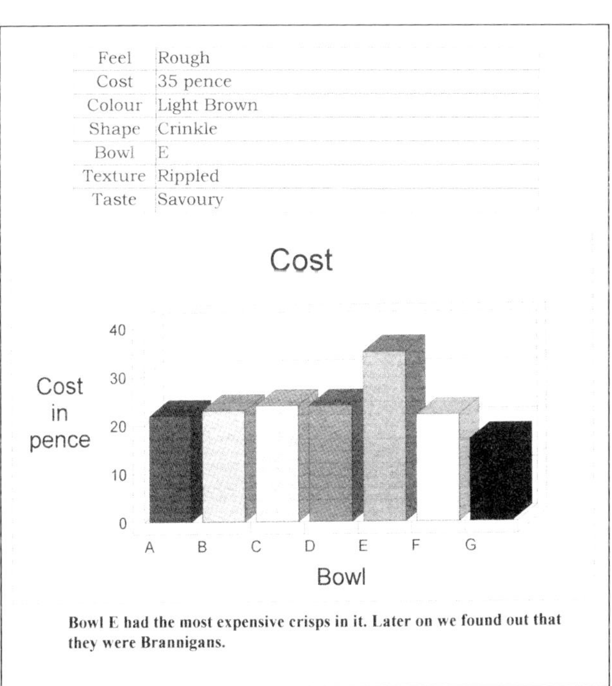

Feel	Rough
Cost	35 pence
Colour	Light Brown
Shape	Crinkle
Bowl	E
Texture	Rippled
Taste	Savoury

Bowl E had the most expensive crisps in it. Later on we found out that they were Brannigans.

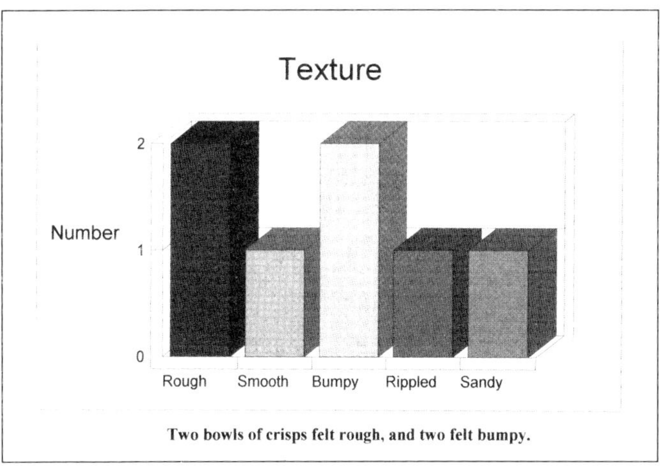

Two bowls of crisps felt rough, and two felt bumpy.

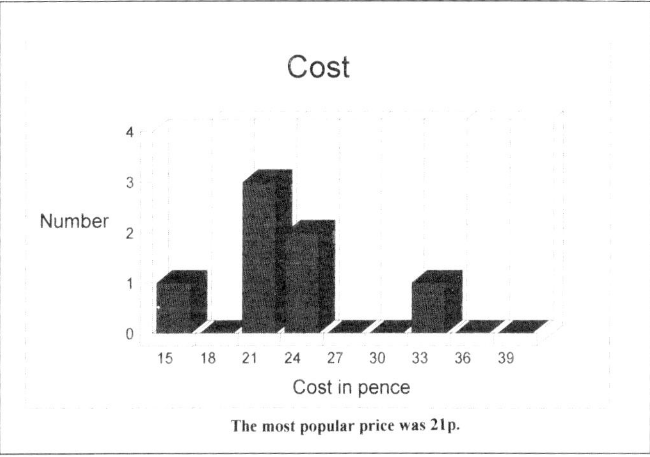

The most popular price was 21p.

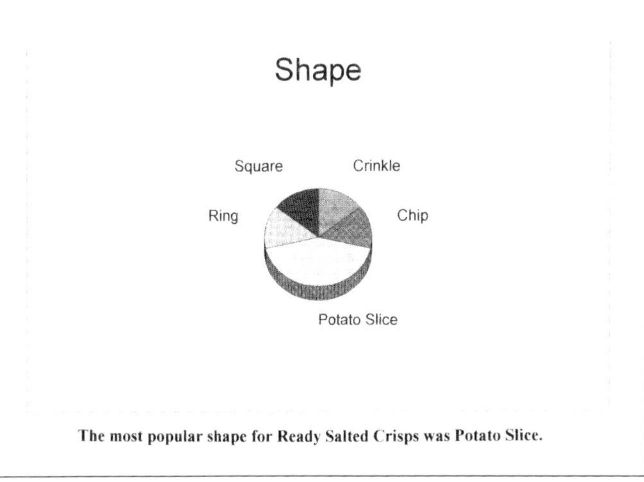

The most popular shape for Ready Salted Crisps was Potato Slice.

An incredible food story

Age range

5–11.

Ways of working

Groups or pairs.

Resources

A good collection of stories and poems about food, word-processing package to suit the age range, DTP package, concept keyboard, graphics package.

Starting points

Read a story or poems to the class.

Discuss possible fantasy food titles.

Some examples are:

The Story of the Incredible Sausages
The Biggest Hamburger in the World
The Mixed Fruit Tree
The Story of the Cute Cucumber
The Mouse-resistant Cheese
The Chimp's Banana

Having chosen a range of titles, decide the audience and ways of working.

Divide the class into groups or pairs to begin planning the outline of a story or poem, either on screen (for one group) or in a computer notebook and then move on to editing and publishing.

With very young children, the teacher may act as scribe or they could use pictures first - one group using a graphics package.

The teacher prepares basic vocabulary, phrases and pictures for one of the titles as a concept keyboard overlay for very young children.

Older children can write stories for a younger age range and word-process and illustrate them appropriately.

Older children could prepare a concept keyboard overlay for a simple version of the chosen title for younger emergent readers and writers.

Publish the stories and pictures as a story/poem collection for the class or school library.

Extensions and more ideas

As part of this topic work children can write letters:

- to manufacturers
- to supermarkets
- to local shops
- to organise an outing to a local hamburger restaurant.

Chinese dragons

A theme such as *Chinese dragons* can be an exciting starting point for curriculum planning. It also provides a motivating context for collaborative learning.

'Puff', an adventure game, can be used as a starting point for planning one curriculum area such as mathematics, as can be seen in the diagram below.

Alternatively, it can provide a stimulus for a programme of linked activities spanning all ten subjects, as shown overleaf.

Puff is a Chinese dragon who is trapped in a Chinese pagoda and waiting to be rescued. The adventure game involves following instructions, constructing maps and eventually finding Puff. Children are given many problem-solving challenges on their route to finding Puff.

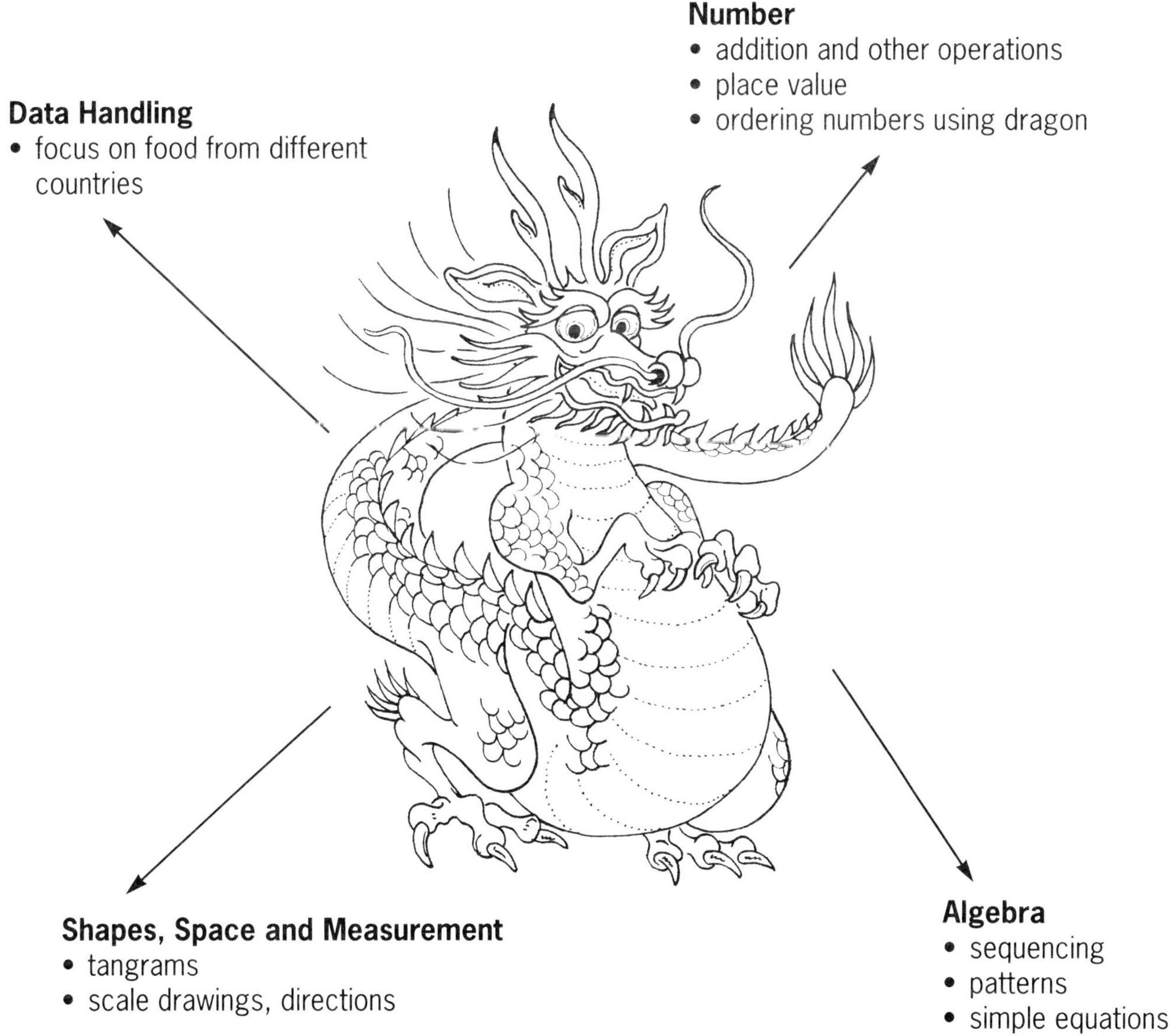

How 'Puff' can be used as a focus for Mathematics

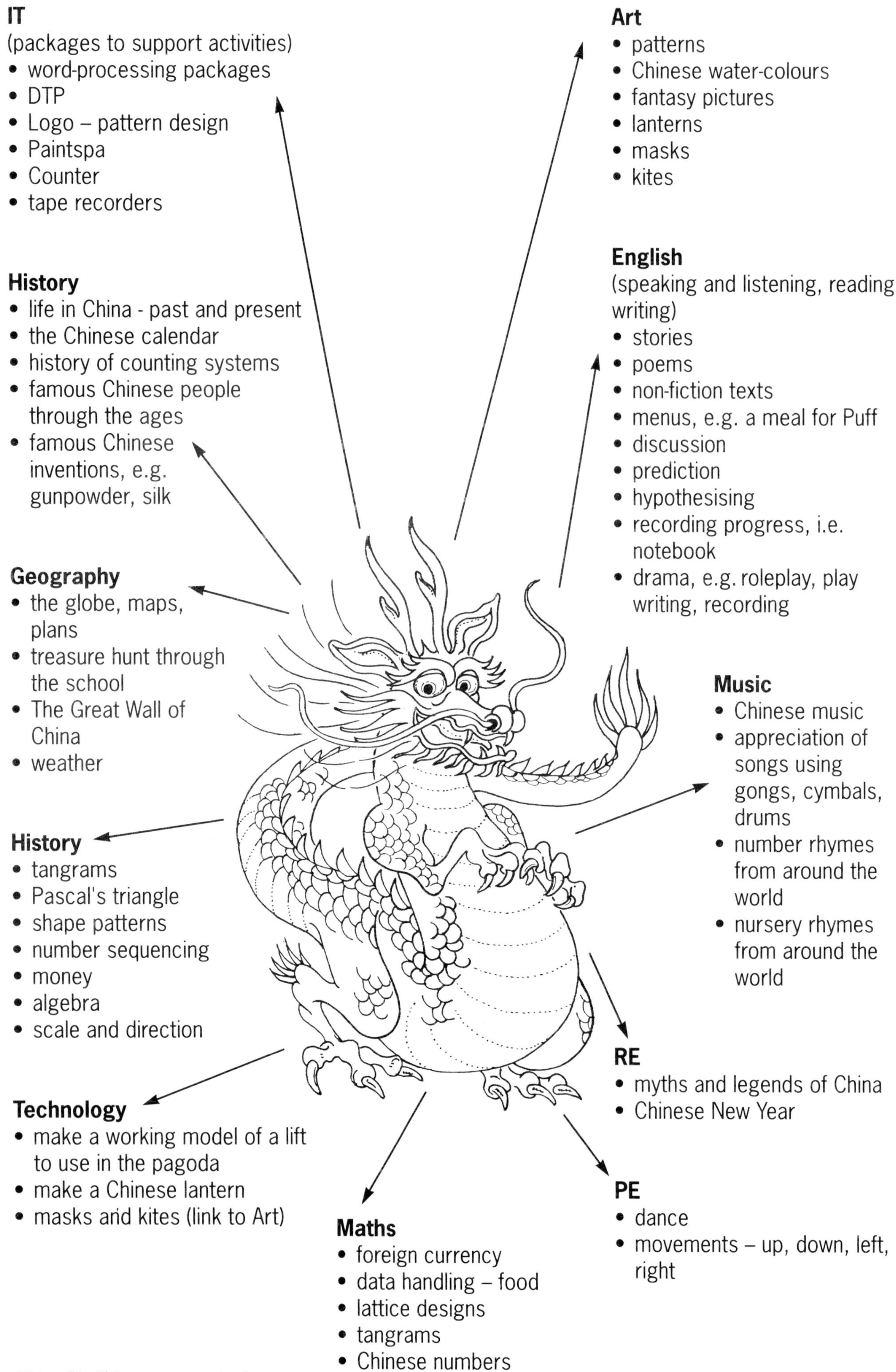

Using 'Puff' in a cross-curricular way

Rescue Puff

Age range 7–11 years.

Ways of working Class introduction, then small groups.

Resources Software package 'Puff' (Nimbus and BBC), computer notebook, resource material relating to China.

Starting points Read stories about China.

Introduce a world map and locate China in relation to your home setting.

Find out what your class already knows about China.

Then set the challenge (to rescue Puff from the pagoda) by reading the story from the teachers' notes ending with the letter:

Dragon's Rest,
Misty Wood,
China

Dear Friend,

In the year of the snake it was very hot and dry. It was far too hot for dragons' food to grow. All my friends died. Now there is only me left.

Please find me and help me to survive!

Puff

Discuss with the children the instructions for operating the program. Introduce them to a help chart that you have prepared to put alongside the computer. The teachers' notes with the software package will provide you with a list.

Provide each group (no more than four children per group; three is a good number) with a plan of the pagoda and instruct them to use their computer notebook for planning and recording their way through the challenge. By keeping a diary, logging their progress and saving their place in the adventure, groups can take turns to work at the computer for up to 45 minutes each.

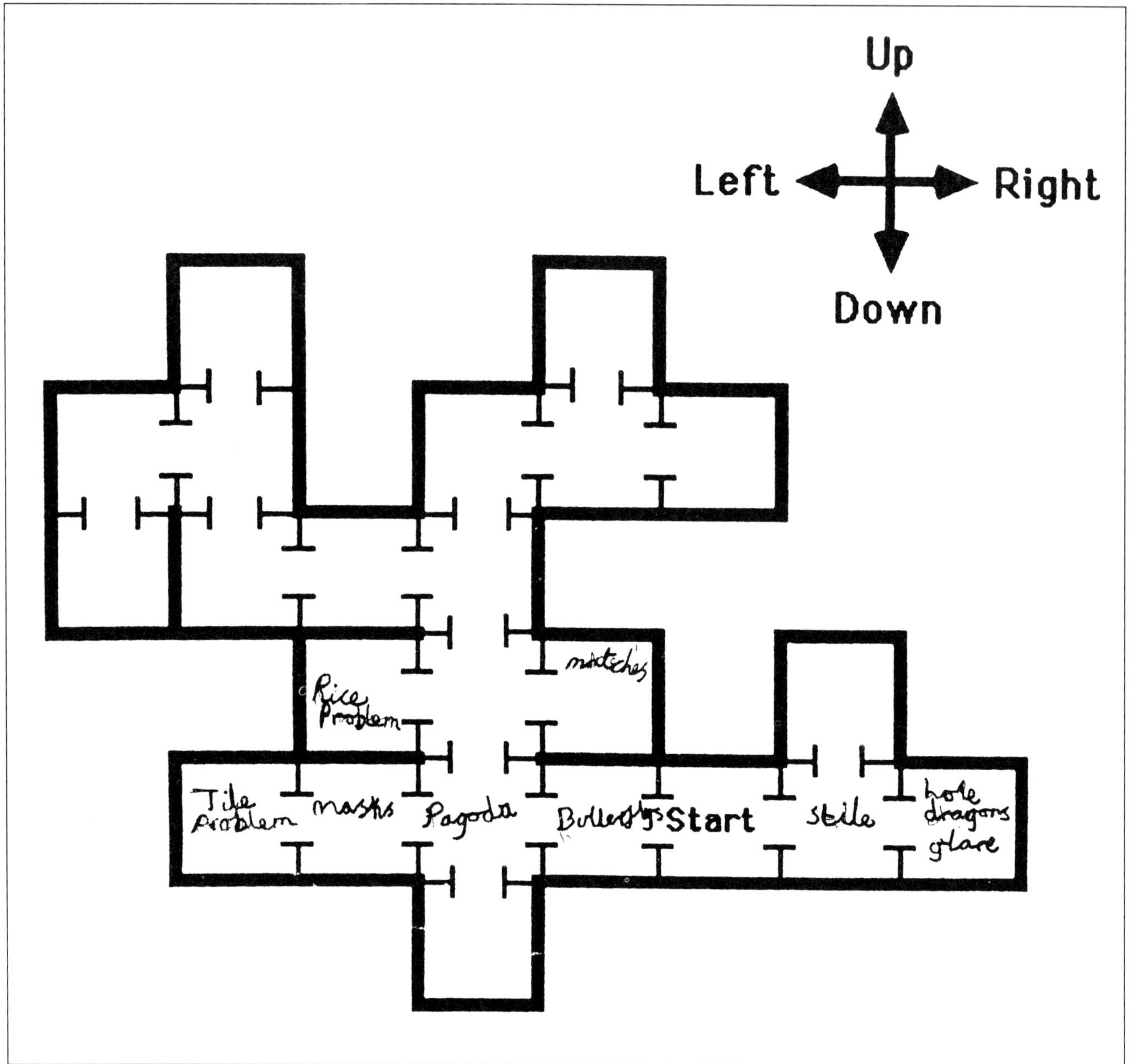

Extensions and more ideas

The following activities from the overall plan complement and extend those already built into the software package.

- Make Chinese lanterns and masks.
- Find out about Chinese writing and write a letter to Puff.
- Use a graphics package to create some kite designs.
- Word-process a collection of dragon poems for the class library.
- Use DTP to produce a newspaper article entitled 'Dragons – Friends or Foes?'.
- Design an alarm for Puff's room to make sure he is safe after his rescue.
- Research 10 facts about the Great Wall of China.

Homes for gnomes

This enterprise project is offered as an example of a meaningful and motivating context for young children, which provides scope for a range of curriculum activities. Using IT can enrich and enhance this and other similar projects.

Age range

5–8 years.

Ways of working

Whole class, then small groups.

Resources

A range of IT packages suitable for the age group and task and teacher-made resources for the task.

Starting points

Introduce the context that a letter (or fax) has arrived for the class. Ask the children if they know what a fax is. Read and show the letter below.

Gnomeland
Gnorwich
Date as postmark

Dear Blue Class,

We have heard about your kindness and great problem-solving abilities and wondered if you could help us.

In Gnomeland it is very cold, too crowded and we don't have enough facilities to support us all. We would like to stay as a community but we need some help to develop a new place to live.

Our requirements are:

- *12 homes, all with 4 rooms of identical size;*
- *we have old retired gnomes and families with children;*
- *each home should have a square garden;*
- *use your imagination to decide what other facilities we need;*
- *we would like a well-planned development.*

Perhaps you could work in groups and send us a number of plans. Also send a letter describing and explaining your decisions.

We trust that you will use your usual kindness and sensitivity to make thoughtful decisions.

Yours gnomely,

Gneville (Senior Gnome)

Discuss with the class the time plan and what the gnomes will need.

Ideas might include:

- 'a hospital'
- 'a house'
- 'a school'
- 'Gnomes like fishing, my next door neighbour has two gnomes beside her pond'
- 'they like animals'.

Next organise groups of 4 children and give each group cubes (multilink) and a large sheet of paper to design the homes and to plan a development.

Discussion points:

- Who are these houses for?
  (Bungalows for older people, flats for younger people.)
- They need sign posts and travel directions.
- They need shops and a hospital.
- A leisure centre.

After designing the development, each group should write an accompanying letter explaining their development, using a word-processing package.

Camber School,
Esher,
Surrey
Date as postmark

Dear Gneville,

Thank you for your letter to our class. Miss explained that you need our help. Everyone is excited. We hope you like our design the best. Tell the other Gnomes it took a long time. Is it true that you like animals? Mark wanted to put a dog kennel in every garden. Write back soon.

From,

Mark, Jessica, Sonia, Mandip

Then produce another letter from Gneville announcing which plan the gnomes would like to work on.

Gnomeland
Gnorwich
Date as postmark

Dear Blue Class,

I see you are using Information Technology a lot in your class. All your plans are excellent and it was very hard to have to choose one. But, we chose the one which showed your concern for the needs of all the gnomes, the old and the young. We have chosen plan 3. Your teacher said the whole class would like to work together to prepare a display to give us some ideas.

When the display is ready, please write and let me know so that we can visit you.

Love,

Gneville

Suggest that the children organise a display of what they can offer, in the classroom, and invite the gnomes to an exhibition of their work.

Discuss what is needed:

- Design a logo for Gnomeville.
- Create name boards for shops, road signs and other facilities. (Use Logo and word processing.)
- Design the first edition of the *Gnomeville Times* newspaper.
- Produce some posters.
- Write party invitations.
- Think up a menu.
- Produce poems and stories for the gnomes' library.
- Design a wallpaper for the houses.
- Compose a piece of music for the opening.
- Draw a map showing the gnomes how to get to the class.

Ideas are shown overleaf.

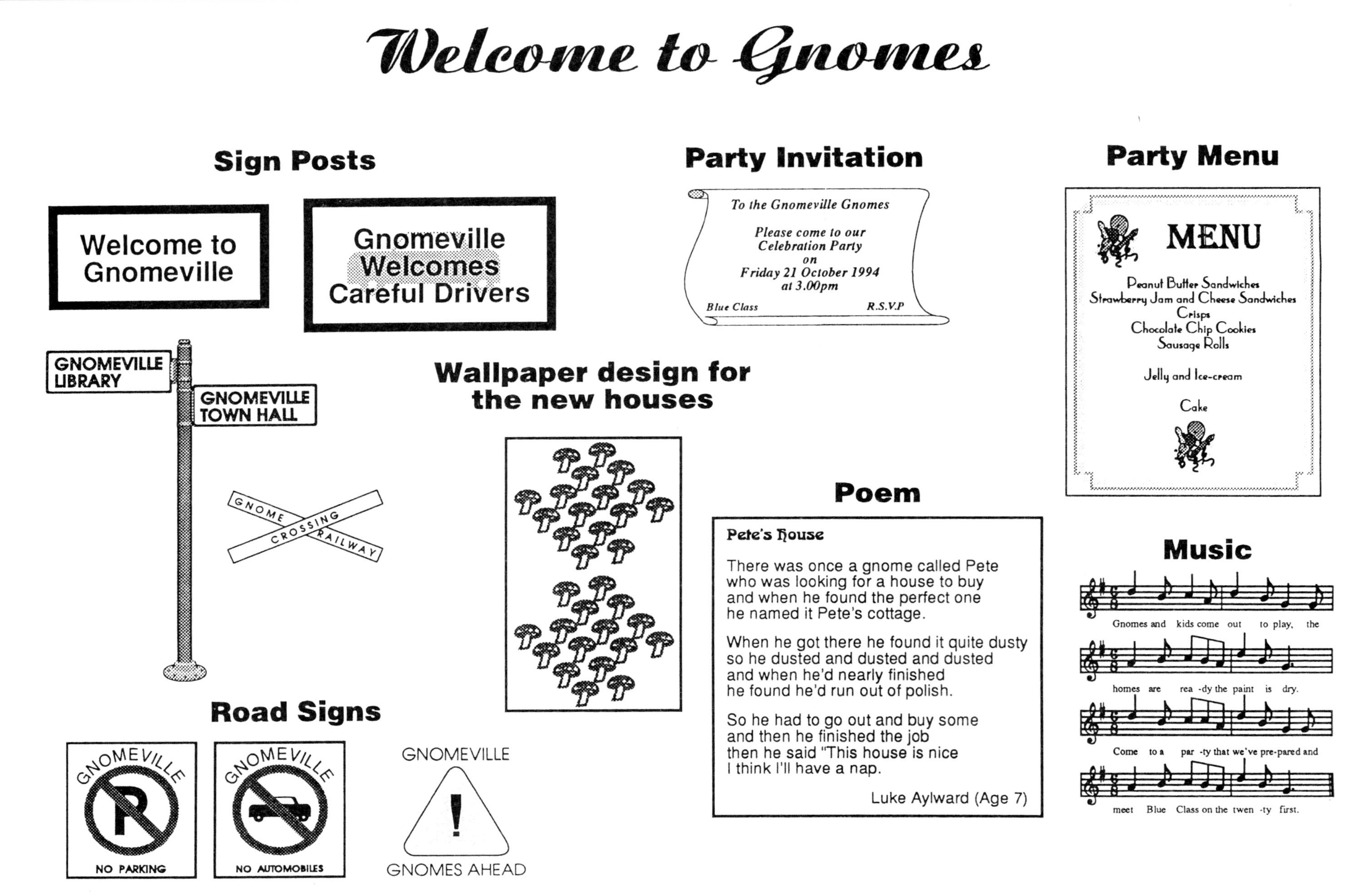
Welcome to Gnomes
Sign Posts
Welcome to Gnomeville
Gnomeville Welcomes Careful Drivers
GNOMEVILLE LIBRARY
GNOMEVILLE TOWN HALL
GNOME CROSSING RAILWAY
Road Signs
GNOMEVILLE
NO PARKING
GNOMEVILLE
NO AUTOMOBILES
GNOMEVILLE
!
GNOMES AHEAD
Wallpaper design for the new houses
Party Invitation
To the Gnomeville Gnomes
Please come to our Celebration Party on Friday 21 October 1994 at 3.00pm
Blue Class
R.S.V.P
Poem
Pete's House
There was once a gnome called Pete
who was looking for a house to buy
and when he found the perfect one
he named it Pete's cottage.
When he got there he found it quite dusty
so he dusted and dusted and dusted
and when he'd nearly finished
he found he'd run out of polish.
So he had to go out and buy some
and then he finished the job
then he said "This house is nice
I think I'll have a nap.
Luke Aylward (Age 7)
Party Menu
MENU
Peanut Butter Sandwiches
Strawberry Jam and Cheese Sandwiches
Crisps
Chocolate Chip Cookies
Sausage Rolls
Jelly and Ice-cream
Cake
Music
Gnomes and kids come out to play, the
homes are rea -dy the paint is dry.
Come to a par -ty that we've pre-pared and
meet Blue Class on the twen -ty first.

Europe

Listed below are examples of how you can plan your project on Europe to include IT.

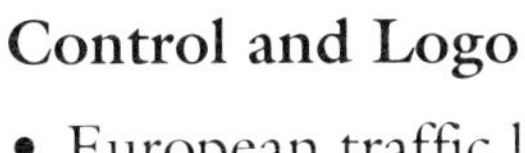

Control and Logo

- European traffic light sequence
- channel tunnel signal systems
- flags using Logo
- simulation of driving on the left/right
- turtle ferry
- flight plans/route plans

Communicating Information

- making continental number plates
- making continental road signs
- letters – to enthusiasts, tourist offices for information
- quiz book on Europe
- electronic mail
- DTP – a European newspaper
- holiday bookings
- languages – needs of different keyboards
- food, menus
- composing anthems
- designing stamps
- European cars

Handling Information

Databases:

- population
- capital cities
- rivers
- heights of mountains
- money
- people in positions of power
- weather patterns
- languages spoken

Spreadsheets:

- conversion of money

Your bumper quiz on Europe

Age range 9–11 years.

Ways of working Whole class and/or small groups.

Resources Reference books, brochures, word-processing package with graphics facility.

Starting points Explore the concept of a quiz.
Gather different designs.
Introduce and investigate the need for clarity, precision and ease of reference (e.g. Where would questions go? Where would the answers be?).
Choose a common format.
Each group chooses a European aspect.
Carry out research on the aspect chosen.
Draft six trial questions and answers per group.
Carry out a trial of the questions with another group.
Edit, plan lay-out and graphics.
Word-process.
Print and collate.
Produce final copy.

Extensions and more ideas

- Plan a quiz competition for your class or another class.
- Think about quiz formats to include crosswords or wordsearches as well on Europe.

Demystifying the IT Jargon

There are many terms used in IT which may be unfamiliar to you. In this section we try to provide a summary and brief explanation of these terms.

Adventure games

These are programs which involve using clues and moving about on the screen. You follow directions given on the computer screen, picking up and using objects offered as options.

CD-ROM (Compact Disc Read-Only Memory)

A CD-ROM is very similar to a music CD, but can be used on a computer. It has sound, pictures and moving images. A CD-ROM can store a large amount of information and can be very useful for project work.

Concept keyboard

This is an overlay keyboard used instead of the standard keyboard and plugs into the computer. Lights and buzzers can be made to operate from it. Its use encourages sequencing instructions and problem solving.

Database

This is a program which lets you store information by creating 'records' and 'files'. You can search, interrogate, retrieve and present the information using the database. Tables, charts and graphs can be printed.

Datalogging

This is a specially designed program which, with the use of sensors, can measure and record temperatures over a period of time. It can be used to monitor temperature.

Desk top publishing (DTP)

This is a computer package which enables the user to achieve different layouts and to combine graphics and text. Different fonts and type sizes are available. You can create borders and boxes to present work.

Electronic mail

This enables users to send and receive messages over long distances by using a modem which connects their computers using a telephone line.

Floor turtles

These are programmable robots which can be operated by connecting them to a computer. Roamers are similar in use and they can be operated without a computer, using batteries.

Logo

Logo is a programming language. By giving instructions to a computer, the user can create shapes and patterns. Turtle geometry is the most common use of Logo in a primary classroom, but Logo can also be used to generate number patterns and to control the movements of a floor turtle.

Modem

This is a device which converts computer information into a form which can be transmitted through a telephone.

Mouse

This is a peripheral which is used to move the pointer on the computer screen to give access to menus and for highlighting options.

Multimedia

CDs which can store images and sound, as well as data.

Peripherals

These are devices which can be plugged into a computer, e.g. mouse, concept keyboard overlays, printer.

Scanner

This is a peripheral which reads both text and pictures and feeds them into the computer which, in turn, interprets them and produces the images on the screen. These images can then be altered in size.

Sensor

This is used with datalogging programs to measure and record temperature, sound, light and movement.

Simulations

These are preprogrammed situations which enable the user to try different ideas and strategies.

Spreadsheet

This is a program which allows words and figures to be fed into the computer. The program has cells which are linked by formulas enabling data to be changed into alternative results.

Word-processor

This is a program which is used for writing, editing, formatting, saving and retrieving text when needed. The text can also be printed out.

Useful reading

Computers and the Primary Curriculum 3–13, Crompton, R., 1989.
The Falmer Press.

Information Technology 5–16 Curriculum Matters: 5,
HMSO, 1989.

Technology in the National Curriculum,
HMSO, 1990.

The Impact Report: An evaluation of the impact of Information Technology on Children's Achievements in Primary and Secondary Schools, D.M. Watson (Ed.), 1993.
Kings College, London.

Effective Teacher Assessment,
Mitchell, C. & Koshy, V., 1993.
Hodder and Stoughton.

I.T.'s English, Assessing English with Computers, NATE, 1988.

NCET (National Council for Educational Technology),
Sir William Lyons Rd,
Science Park,
Coventry
CV4 7EZ
(Publications available)

Children Using Computers, Straker, A., 1989.
Simon & Schuster.

Resources

A list of some of the more commonly used resources is given here. It is only a starting point and should be used as a personal record with comments entered as and when necessary. The addresses of the publishers, as they are at the time of writing this book, are given on page 108. A vast number of new programs and resources are being produced and there are constant changes to the publishers and their addresses. In a few cases it has not been possible to provide details of the publisher. The best way to keep up-to-date is to add resources to the lists as they appear or when you are more familiar with them. Space is provided for personalising and updating this list. The abbreviations used are:
Arc.= Archimedes, Nim. = Nimbus and AM = Apple Mac.

Resource	Publisher or write to for details:	Machine availability					Comments
		BBC	Arc.	Nim.	AM	PC	
Adventure Games and Simulations							
Treasure Hunt	NCET	✓					
Teddy Bears' Picnic	Sherston	✓					
Pond Life	Mercury (BBC) LETSS (Nimbus)	✓	✓	✓			
Puff	LETSS	✓		✓			
Martello Tower	LETSS			✓			
Granny's Garden	LETSS			✓			
L Game	ATM	✓		✓			
Moving In	SERMERC	✓		✓			
Logo – writing own adventure games	ATM	✓	✓	✓			

Resource	Publisher or write to for details:	Machine availability					Comments
		BBC	Arc.	Nim.	AM	PC	
Databases							
Clipboard	Black Cat			✓			
Datashow	NCET (BBC) LETSS (Nimbus)	✓		✓			
Datasweet		✓	✓	✓			
Our Facts	NCET (BBC)	✓		✓			
Branch	NCET	✓		✓			
IDelta	LETSS			✓			
Grass	Newman College	✓	✓	✓			
Junior Pinpoint	Longman		✓				
Key	LETSS (Nimbus)	✓		✓			
CD-ROMs							
Birds	RSPB		✓		✓	✓	
Dinosaurs	Media Design Interactive		✓		✓	✓	
Exploring Nature	Usborne				✓	✓	
The Times Newspaper	*The Times*				✓	✓	
CD-ROM Atlas	Heinemann					✓	
Living Books					✓	✓	

Resource	Publisher or write to for details:	Machine availability					Comments
		BBC	Arc.	Nim.	AM	PC	
Maths Specific							
Mathematical Investigations	NCET (BBC) LETSS (Nimbus)	✓		✓			
Smile	Smile Centre	✓		✓			
Number Games	LETSS			✓			
Spreadsheets							
Grasshopper	Newman college	✓	✓	✓			
Excel	Microsoft				✓	✓	
Eureka	Longman			✓			

Resource	Publisher or write to for details:	Machine availability					Comments
		BBC	Arc.	Nim.	AM	PC	
English							
Bookstore	ESM		✓		✓		
Fun with Text	ESM			✓			
Eye for Spelling	ESM	✓	✓	✓		✓	
Word-processing							
Caxton	LETSS				✓		
Folio	Tediman	✓					
Pendown	Longman	✓		✓			
Newspaper	SPA	✓					
First Word For Windows	Microsoft				✓		
Write On	SPA			✓			

Resource	Publisher or write to for details:	Machine availability					Comments
		BBC	Arc.	Nim.	AM	PC	
Tinyword	Northamptonshire			✓			
Allwrite	LETSS			✓			
Fairytales		✓					
Art							
Clip Art	Appian Way			✓		✓	
Kid Pix	See catalogues listed on p. 108				✓	✓	
Microsoft Fine Artist					✓	✓	
Paintspa				✓		✓	
Music							
Compose	LETSS			✓			

Resource	Publisher or write to for details:	Machine availability					Comments
		BBC	Arc.	Nim.	AM	PC	
DTP							
Aldus PageMaker	Aldus				✓	✓	
Microsoft Creative Writer	Microsoft			✓		✓	
Caxton Press	Newman College			✓			
Front Page Extra	Newman College	✓					
Microsoft Publisher	Microsoft			✓		✓	
Other programs							
Logo	Logotron RML (Research Machines Ltd (for Nimbus)	✓	✓	✓			
Electronic Mail	NCET		✓	✓		✓	
First Control	Philip Harris			✓			
First Sense	Philip Harris			✓			

Addresses of publishers

Advisory Unit for Microtechnology,
Endymion Road, Hatfield, Hertfordshire
AL10 8AU

Aldus Europe Ltd,
5 Mid New Cutlins,
Edinburgh E11 4DU

ATM (Association of Teachers of Mathematics),
7 Shaftesbury Street,
Derby DE3 8YB

Black Cat Associates,
3 Beacons View, Mount Street,
Breckon, Powys LD3 7LY

Cambridgeshire Software House,
The Town Hall, St Ives,
Huntingdon, Cambridgeshire PE17 4AL

ESM,
Duke Street, Wisbech, Cambridgeshire PE13 2AE

4 mation,
Linden Lee, Rock Park,
Barnstaple, Devon EX32 9AQ

LETSS
The Lodge, Crownwoods School, Riefield Road,
London SE9 0AQ

Logotron Ltd, Dales Brewery,
Gwydir Street,
Cambridge, CB1 2LJ

Longman Group UK Ltd,
5 Bentnick Street, London W1M 5RN

Mercury Educational Products,
8–10 Lower James Street,
London W1R 3PL

Microsoft, Microsoft Place, Winnesh,
Wokingham, Berks RG11 5TP

MUSE, Microcomputer Users in Education,
PO Box 43, Houghton on the Hill,
Leicestershire LE7 9GX

NCET (National Council for Educational
Technology),
Sir William Lyons Road, Science Park,
University of Warwick, Coventry CV4 7EZ

Newman College Computer Centre,
Genners Lane, Bartley Green,
Birmingham B3T 3NT

Northampton Computer Education Centre,
Teachers' Centre, Barry Road,
Northampton NN1 5JS

Philip Harris Education,
Lynn Lane, Shenton, Lichfield,
Staffordshire WS14 0EE

Research Machines Ltd,
1 Mill Street,
Oxford OX2 0BW

RESOURCE,
Exeter Road,
Doncaster DN2 4PY

Shell Centre for Mathematical Education,
University of Nottingham,
Nottingham NG7 2RD

Sherston Software,
Swan Barton, Malmesbury,
Wilts SN16 0LH

SERMERC,
University of Nottingham,
Nottingham NG7 2RD

The Smile Centre,
Isaac Newton PDC,
108 Lancaster Rd,
London W11 1QS

SPA,
PO Box 59, Leamington Spa,
Warks

Tediman Software,
PO Box 23,
Southampton SO9 7BD

The Times Network Systems Ltd,
Priory House, St John's Lane,
London EC1 4HD

Catalogues

A CD-ROM catalogue is available from:
Cambridge CD-ROM Ltd,
Combs Tannery, Stowmarket,
Suffolk IP14 2EN

An Apple Mac software catalogue is available from:
KRCS Group, Freepost NG 5132, Nottingham
NG1 1BR

	R/Yr 1	Yr 2	Yr 3	Yr 4	Yr 5	Yr 6
Communicating and handling information						
Controlling, monitoring and modelling						

Formative assessment record

Name: Date:

Activity:

Planned outcomes	What happened	Future action

Comments:

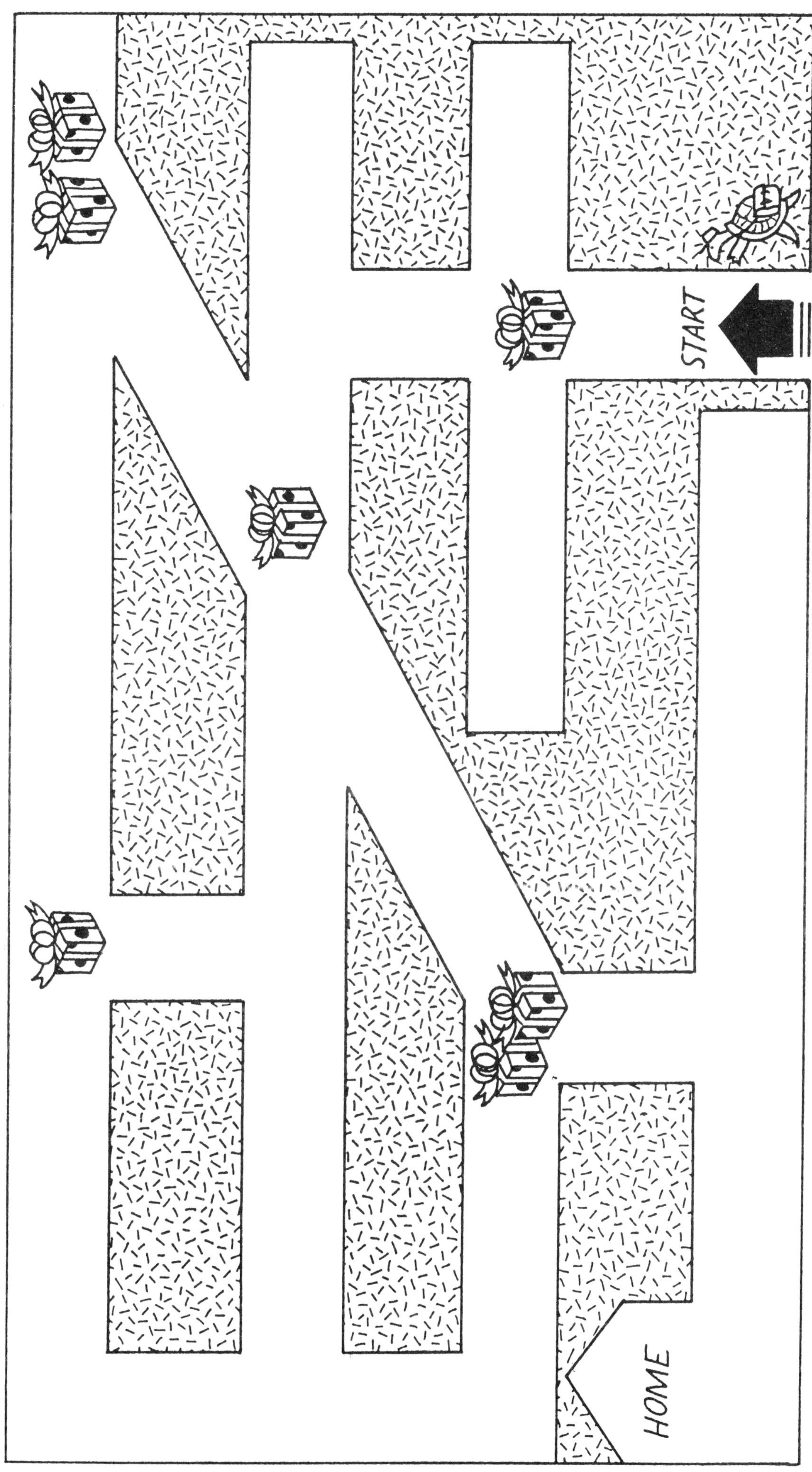
START
HOME

50
35
20
15
30
25
20
40
70
35
25
30

Mediaeval Pilgrims at a Shrine

Picture from 'THE SIGN' – JUNE 1934

DODDINGTON

A MILLENNIUM SOUVENIR

SPONSORSHIP

The compilation and publication of this book has been greatly assisted by sponsorship, which has also financed the growth of the Doddington Scrapbook to a second volume.

The sponsorship was by means of a Help The Aged Millennium Award Scheme Grant to the author and publisher, for which he expresses his sincere thanks.

BOOKS WRITTEN BY ERIC W. RUSSELL

"ERK'S EYE VIEW"
A story of RAF National Service in the 1950's.
Brewin Books ISBN 1 85858 054 4 (1994)

"WHEELS & THINGS".
A nostalgic collection of pictures of yesteryear.
Mostly 1930's/40's
Brewin Books ISBN 1 85858 093 5 (1996)

"DODDINGTON"
The story of a South Shropshire Hills Community.

Eric W. Russell ISBN 0 9530305 0 4 (1997)

DODDINGTON, CLEE HILL COMMON & RADAR STATION.

Cover picture together with all aerial views in this book taken on July 8th 1998

DEDICATION

This book is dedicated to the
residents of Doddington, including
their friends & relations

PAST

PRESENT

AND

FUTURE

First Published in 1999 by

Eric W. Russell,
"Oakwood Lodge"
Doddington,
Shropshire DY14 0NJ

Published to mark the Millennium, through the kind sponsorship of
The Help The Aged Millennium Awards Scheme.

ISBN 0 9530305 1 2

British Library Cataloguing in Publication Data
A Catalogue record for this book is available from
the British Library.

Typeset and printed by St Leonards Press, Ludlow, Shropshire SY8 1DL

Foreword

A visitor to Titterstone Clees will undoubtedly appreciate the most extensive views in Britain and be aware of industrial scars; but those of us who have lived here know that these Hills have experienced a rich tapestry of events ever since Jesus was born 2000 years ago. How pleased I am that the real reason for celebrating the Millennium has been stressed in this book.

My affection for the area and its people is beyond measure and I am never happier than when I am roaming Clee Hills.

Born at the Dhu Stone Inn, I experienced the hardship of quarrymen, miners and hill farmers. Accounts by members of well known local families reminds us of what everyone had to endure without mains water, electricity and other conveniences.

War time memories are vivid to me. Every night as darkness fell I could see search lights scanning the sky for enemy aircraft and hear the silence punctuated by explosions in cities. Local young men were killed, aircraft crashed into these hills and Italian and German prisoners of war worked in the quarries and on local farms.

I sat in my infant class with an evacuee from Leeds. I watched the Titterstone Clee forest being felled and with other small boys collected chips in a little cart to take home for firewood. When American soldiers brought their mobile crushers and other equipment to our quarries for making runways, I visited their camp with my father and for the first time in my life saw tinned peaches and pineapple. These were unknown luxuries during war time rationing days.

We are reminded that our Hills have a wealth of flora and fauna not apparent to the speeding motorist; and all budding poets are bound to be amused by Rusty of Clee.

We must thank Eric for filling in a few more pieces of our historical patchwork. I commend this book to young and old alike as a valuable Millennium memento.

ALF JENKINS
(Author of "Titterstone Clees").

PREFACE

People in our land and throughout the world will celebrate the coming of the new Millennium in a multitude of ways. In spite of these celebrations, we must not lose sight of the fact that the new Millennium marks the anniversary of the birth of Jesus Christ. I have sought to remind readers of this by the use of both words and pictures.

I have attempted to put together a collection of material of both local and national interest that will serve to make this book a souvenir of this unique occasion. I trust that the pages laid out for readers to enter details of their own family tree, will serve to make it a more personal possession.

Doddington can be traced back to the early days of the old Millennium, with a precise mention in the Domesday Book of 1086. That great work which was undertaken on the instructions of William the First (The Conqueror), mentions Earls Ditton as being in the parish of Doddington.

St George and St David are portrayed below as appropriate to representing the ethnic origins of the majority of the local population.

ST. GEORGE FOR ENGLAND
APRIL 23rd

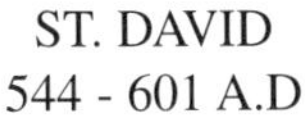
ST. DAVID
544 - 601 A.D

Be just, and fear not;
Let all the ends thou aim'st at be thy country's
Thy God's, and truth's.

King Henry VIII, Act 3

A CHRISTIAN MESSAGE FROM The Rt. Revd. Dr. John Saxbee. The Bishop & Archdeacon of LUDLOW.

THE HINGE OF HISTORY IS ON A STABLE DOOR IN BETHLEHEM.

FOR 2,000 YEARS WE HAVE BEEN CELEBRATING A BIRTH IN THAT LITTLE HILL TOP TOWN, AND SINGING ITS PRAISES:

"THE HOPES AND FEARS,
OF ALL THE YEARS,
ARE MET IN THEE TONIGHT".

WHATEVER YOU DO IN DODDINGTON TO MARK THE MILLENNIUM, BE SURE TO LOOK BACK WITH THANKSGIVING FOR JESUS CHRIST BORN AS ONE OF US AND STILL LIVING WITH US AND FOR US. BE GRATEFUL FOR THOSE WHO, BY FOLLOWING HIS EXAMPLE, HAVE BOUGHT LOVE, JOY AND PEACE TO YOUR LIVES OVER THE YEARS.

MARK THE MILLENNIUM AS A NEW START.

FOR YOU

YOUR FAMILY,

YOUR COMMUNITY

AND

YOUR FRIENDS.

ABOVE ALL, MAKE IT A NEW START WITH GOD.

BETHLEHEM - THE MANGER.

<u>THE HOLY LAND</u>

Stations of the Cross (not in sequence) left to right - top to bottom.
1. Calvary, Chapel of Nailing to the Cross. 2. Where Simon the Cyrenian took the Cross from Jesus.
3. Calvary, Chapel of the Raising of the Cross. .4 The Tomb.

1. Jericho - The Mount of Temptation. 2. The Tomb. 3. The Wailing Wall.
4. Bethlehem - Christmas Bells. 5. Bethlehem - Grotto of the Nativity.

AN ACCOUNT OF THE HISTORY OF METHODISM AT HOPTON BANK

There was a great religious revival in Britain from as early as the 1730's, bringing many new denominations of dissenters. It was not until towards the end of the 18th Century, however, that a Methodist Society was established at Hopton Bank. Initially the society held services in members' homes, but in 1837 a parcel of land was obtained from Mr John Dolphin and a Chapel-and-cottage was erected. (This is the cottage which lies in front of the present Chapel). During this time the Chapel was for some years the head of a circuit known as Hopton Bank Primitive Methodist Circuit. This later became the Ludlow Primitive Methodist Circuit and in 1932, when the different Methodist Churches amalgamated, the circuit became known as the Ludlow Methodist Circuit. Over the years the circuit has become the Shropshire South Circuit of the Methodist Church.

After the building of the Chapel, the congregation continued to grow and in 1860 the society decided to purchase an additional plot of land, adjacent to the existing Chapel to build a larger Chapel. This Chapel was eventually opened in 1880 and large congregations worshiped and attended other activities such as Concerts, Rallies and Services of Song. A large Sunday School was also maintained in the original Chapel at this time.

After the 1914 - 18 War, economic changes meant many families moved from the area and together with the death of older members, there was a decline in numbers attending the Chapel. When this decline continued after the 1939 - 45 War, the numbers gradually reached as low as 2 or 3 families that were left to maintain the Chapel. The society reluctantly decided to sell the old Chapel and use the proceeds to convert the larger Chapel into a Day Conference Centre, as well as a place of worship. This conversion was completed in time for the Centenary Celebrations in 1980 and the modernised premises have continued to be used for worship and community work.

The society at Hopton Bank remains small in number, but the work and witness for Christ continues with the provision of a monthly Luncheon Club, a Table Tennis Club, a fortnightly Activities Group for children, teas each Bank Holiday Monday and other organised activities such as "Songs of Praise". Special Services are held at Christmas and Easter, as well as every Sunday during the year.

The Chapel at Hopton Bank, within its Magnificent setting, continues to stand as a Christian presence within the communities on the east side of Titterstone Clee Hill.

ST. JOHN'S CHURCH DODDINGTON.

When I came to the Hill Group of Parishes in January 1993, and took my first Service at St. John's Church, Doddington, there were only six folk in the congregation and this was the norm. Over the next few years the numbers dwindled down to two.

Following the collapse of part of the ceiling over the gallery, quotations were called for the repairs, but this seemed an impossible task with so few Church members and a repair bill totalling over £10,000. A public meeting was called, with the Bishop of Ludlow presiding, to decide whether to go ahead and raise the necessary cash for the repairs or to close the Church. Some 60 people attended the Meeting and were unanimous in their decision that the Church should not be closed and that the repairs should be put in hand as soon as possible.

It was a forbidding task to have the repairs started and no money with which to pay the contractors. However two very generous parishioners offered interest free loans of £5,000 each which was an encouragement to others in the Parish to start fund raising.

The repairs were completed in February 1997 during particularly cold and wintry weather. Upon completion of the repairs, the redecoration of the Nave and Choir, and repairs to the electrical installation, a group of willing workers scrubbed the floors, varnished and oiled the pews, pulpit and lectern, as well as tidying and painting the Vestry.

The first Service after the improvements was held on Easter morning, and was followed on St. John's Day by a special Service of Thanksgiving to celebrate the 150th Anniversary of the Church's dedication and the completion of the repairs. The Bishop of Ludlow was the preacher on this occasion. Since then, the Lord Bishop of Hereford has paid three visits to Doddington Church - first in November 1997 and in July 1998 for Confirmations, and then in September 1998 for the Harvest Thanksgiving.

The Parish of Doddington has been held in high regard in the Diocesan circles as an example of what Parishioners can do when the "stakes are down". From having no Churchwardens, few Members on the PCC, no Secretary or Treasurer, it is good to know that all these posts have been filled and in addition two representatives elected on to Ludlow Deanery Synod.

It was a great privilege to have been associated with Doddington during this time of renewal, and to have been part of the resurgence in the life of the parish generally. It was of particular encouragement when, in 1997 we had five adult candidates presented to the Bishop of Hereford.

I wish both the Church and the Parish every blessing for the future.

MARK BURGESS

(Rev'd D. M. Burgess - Vicar 1993 - 1998)

KINGS AND QUEENS OF THE MILLENNIUM

978 - 1016 Ethelred (The Unready).
1016 - Edmund II (Ironside) Died aged 23 - Reigned 7 Months.
1016 - 1035 Cnut (Canute) Son of Swegn Forkbeard, King of Denmark.
1035 - 1040 Harold I (Harefoot).
1040 - 1042 Harthacanut.
1042 - 1066 Edward II (The Confessor).
1066 - Harold II (Godwinesson) Killed in battle aged 46.

THE HOUSE OF NORMANDY

1066 - 1087 William I (The Conqueror) Obtained the crown by conquest.
1087 - 1100 William II (Rufus) Killed aged 40.
1100 - 1135 Henry I (Beauclerk).
1135 - 1154 Stephen.

THE HOUSE OF ANJOU (PLANTAGENETS)

1154 - 1189 Henry II (Curtmantle).
1189 - 1199 Richard I (Coeur de Lion).
1199 - 1216 John (Lackland).
1216 - 1272 Henry III.
1272 - 1307 Edward I (Longshanks).
1307 - 1327 Edward II Deposed January 1327 - Killed September 1327 aged 43.
1327 - 1377 Edward III.
1377 - 1399 Richard II Deposed September 1399 - killed February 1400 aged 33.

THE HOUSE OF LANCASTER

1399 - 1413 Henry IV.
1413 - 1422 Henry V.
1422 - 1471 Henry VI Deposed March 1461, restored October 1470.
Deposed April 1471, killed May 1471 aged 49.

THE HOUSE OF YORK

1461 - 1483 Edward IV Acceded March 1461, deposed October 1470, restored April 1471.
1483 - Edward V Deposed June 1483, died July - September 1483 aged 12.
Reigned 2 months.
1483 - 1485 Richard III Killed in battle.

THE HOUSE OF TUDOR

1485 - 1509 Henry VII.
1509 - 1547 Henry VIII
Prince Arthur the elder brother of Henry died at Ludlow Castle in April 1502. Had Arthur lived, he would have been before Henry in the line of succession to the throne.
1547 - 1553 Edward VI.
1553 - Jane Deposed July 1553, executed February 1554 aged 16, reigned 14 days.
1553 - 1558 Mary I.
1558 - 1603 Elizabeth I.

THE HOUSE OF STUART

1603 - 1625 James I (VI of Scotland).
1625 - 1649 Charles I Executed 1649 aged 48.
COMMONWEALTH DECLARED 19th May 1649.
1649 - 1653 Government by a Council of State.
1653 - 1658 Oliver Cromwell - Lord Protector.
1658 - 1659 Richard Cromwell - Lord Protector.
1660 1685 Charles II.
1685 - 1688 James II (VII of Scotland) Reign ended with flight from Kingdom December 1688.
Interregnum 11th December 1688 to 12th February 1689.
1689 - 1702 William III (William of Orange). Son of William II Prince of Orange and Mary Stuart daughter of James II.
AND
1689 - 1694 Mary II.
1702 - 1714 Anne

THE HOUSE OF HANOVER

1714 - 1727 George I.
1727 - 1760 George II.
1760 - 1820 George III (Mad George) Regency 1811 - 1820, Prince of Wales Regent, owing to insanity of the King.
1820 - 1830 George IV.
1830 - 1837 William IV
1837 - 1901 Victoria.

THE HOUSE OF SAXE-COBURG AND GOTHA

1901 - 1910 Edward VII.

THE HOUSE OF WINDSOR

1910 - 1936 George V.
1936 - Edward VIII Abdicated, Reigned 10 months.
20th January to December 1936.
1936 - 1952 George VI.
1952 - Elizabeth II.

WHOM GOD PRESERVE

Happy is England! I could be content
To see no other verdure than it's own.

John Keats.

CLEE HILL COMMONERS ASSOCIATION

In response to my request, Mrs `Dot' Shorthouse, Secretary of the association, wrote a brief article about the organisation in January of 1999. The following is an edited compilation of her article.

"The Commoners Association is now over on hundred years old, having been founded in 1897. The minute books from the original meeting to the present day are still held by the association. On reading through the books of yesteryear one comes across the names of many families who are still active in the association. The organisation is run by a committee elected from the membership, the current executives being - Mr John Whiteman: Chairman, Mr Roddy Yapp: Vice Chairman, Mr Phillip Edwards: Treasurer, Mr Ernie Edwards: President, Mr John wheeler: Vice President, with myself as Secretary.

I'm proud to have been connected with the association for over twenty years and take much pleasure in listing a few of the associations achievements of recent years. The construction of cattle grids, fences etc., which have served to stop livestock straying off the common. There is evidence that on occasions livestock strayed as far as Hopton Wafers and Tenbury Wells. This particular enterprise was carried through by commoners of the day, with tremendous assistance from the small local population (see picture facing) who assisted with both fund raising and manual labour. It is unfortunate that we still get casualties to livestock, largely due to the speed at which some vehicles travel on the A4117 where it crosses the common from Clee Hill to Doddington. During the 1970's they had to face up to the threat of opencast coal mining, the plans for this enterprise were vigorously opposed. The same decade also saw major revisions to the regulations regarding commoners rights. The executive of the day spent considerable time in discussions and negotiations on the matter. Much of the discussion was with legal advisers, District & County Council and many other interested parties. The association still insist that all sheep are removed from the hill/common twice per year for dipping against scab. All committee members give their time and energy in the best interests of all members, for no personal financial gain.

An annual subscription is paid by members who are entitled to turn their stock onto the common for grazing. The association welcomes financial support by way of donations from clubs and other interested organisations. For a modest annual subscription of £5 - 00, membership is open to local people. Those who care about the unique environment in which we are privileged to live are particularly welcome.

I sincerely hope that the local communities will continue to support the association, both now and in the years of the next millennium. Old friends and supporters are always welcome at the associations general annual meeting which is held in May".

The 1979 sponsored walk, was an important part of the fund raising for the installation of cattle grids on the various roads leading on and off the common. During ensuing years the grids have served to prevent livestock straying off the common.

<u>GENEALOGY</u>

The study of genealogy is fascinating, absorbing and time consuming. I have studied the subject for well over thirty years, years during which I have accumulated a vast collection of material relating to the roots of many branches of my family. As the new Millennium draws closer it is surely a fitting time for each and every-one of us to give some thought to our ancestors. I have allowed space on this page and the two following for treasured family pictures with the intention of making this book a special personal possession. These pages are followed with three pages of charts for the creation of a personal family tree.

Page 19 (chart 1) shows your Paternal line to your Father.
Page 21 (chart 3) shows your Maternal line to your Mother.
Page 20 (chart 2) has your parents named at the top. Your name should be entered in the left upper panel marked ME.

There is provision in this chart for you, your brothers & sisters, your spouse, your children and grandchildren. It is appreciated that in the case of this book belonging to a child, it will be a considerable number of years before chart 2 is finally completed.

CHART ONE
PATERNAL LINE

SEE CHART 2

Father

Name:
Date Born:
Place Born:

Grandfather

Name:
Date Born:
Place Born:

Date Married:

Place Married:

Grandmother

Name:
Date Born:
Place Born:

Great Grandfather

Name:
Date Born:
Place Born:

Great Grandmother

Name:
Date Born:
Place Born:

Date Married:

Place Married:

Great Grandfather

Name:
Date Born:
Place Born:

Great Grandmother

Name:
Date Born:
Place Born:

Date Married:

Place Married:

CHART TWO

MY FAMILY TREE

FROM CHART 1

Father

Name:

Mother

Name:

FROM CHART 3

Date Married:

Place Married:

Me

Name:
Date Born:
Place Born:

My Brothers and Sisters

Date Married:

Place Married:

My Spouse

Name:
Date Born:
Place Born:

Our Children

Our Grandchildren

Chart Three

Maternal Line

See Chart 2

Mother

Name:
Date Born:
Place Born:

Grandfather

Name:
Date Born:
Place Born:

Date Married:

Place Married:

Grandmother

Name:
Date Born:
Place Born:

Great Grandfather

Namc:
Date Born:
Place Born:

Great Grandmother

Name:
Date Born:
Place Born:

Date Married:

Place Married:

Great Grandfather

Namc:
Date Born:
Place Born:

Great Grandmother

Name:
Date Born:
Place Born:

Date Married:

Place Married:

LEST WE FORGET

The poster that induced many thousands of our countrymen to join Kitchener's army in 1914.

Many men from Doddington answered the call to serve King and Country. Sadly - some made the ultimate sacrifice and did not return to their county of Shropshire. They are named on the war memorial in the church yard of St. John the Baptist Church, Doddington. In the case of three of them (C. Key, C. H. Woodhouse & J. Steadman) their names appear also on the war memorial at Cleobury Mortimer and on the Roll of Honour in St. Mary's church Cleobury Mortimer.

WE WILL REMEMBER THEM

The men named below were son's of the 19th Century they gave their lives for their fellow men in the 20th Century. Let us not forget their sacrifice as we go forward into the 21st Century and a new Millennium.

'THEIR MEMORY LIVES ON'

John Tennant Died 11th January 1917	age 36	Royal Warwickshire Regiment Buried at Doddington.
Frederick Weaver Died 23rd February 1919	age 20	Welch Regiment. Buried at Doddington.
William Ernest Corfield Died 6th December 1920		Worcestershire Regiment Buried at Doddington.
Cyril Key 2nd July 1916	age 19	Machine Gun Corps Thiepval Memorial, Somme, France.
James Steadman 22nd October 1917	age 22	Gloucestershire Regiment Tyne Cot Memorial, Flanders, Belgium
William Wiltshire 3rd November 1918		Kings Shropshire Light Infantry St. Sever Cemetery, Seine-Maritime, France.
Arnold Pugh 31st July 1917		Welch Regiment (formerly of KSLI) New Irish Farm Cemetery, Ypers, Belgium.
Samuel Richard Williams 22nd September 1918		Argyll and Sutherland Highlanders Mikra British Cemetery, Kalamaria, Greece
Walter Williams 16th February 1917		Cheshire Regiment Gezaincourt Cemetery, Somme, France.
Charles Henry Woodhouse 1st June 1918	age 31	Cheshire Regiment Soissons Memorial, Aisne, France.

FAITHFUL UNTO DEATH

1914 - 1918

LIVE THOU FOR ENGLAND
WE FOR ENGLAND DIED

A TRIBUTE

Thomas Botfield became owner of Hopton Court in 1798, and remained in residence with his wife Lucy (nee Skelhorne) until his death in 1843. Thomas was a direct descendant of Sir Geoffrey Boteville, one of a group of Knights brought from France by King John in 1210 to assist with quelling the rebellious actions of the Barons. During his years at Hopton Court, Thomas Botfield was not only an employer of considerable local labour, but also a major community benefactor. He financed the rebuilding of the church of St. Michael and All Angels at Hopton Wafers, but also the construction of the church of St. John the Baptist at Doddington, together with a fine Parsonage house now known as Doddington Lodge. In 1847 during the early stages of the construction of St. John's, Lucy Botfield, using her maiden name of Skelhorne, presented the church with some fine inscribed communion silver. For reasons of security this silver, still in the ownership of St. John's, is deposited at The Mappa Mundi Centre, Hereford, where it is on secure public display. Thomas Botfield also set up a trust on behalf of St. John's. The trust is still in existence and has for about 150 years provided a modest annual income, in the early years of the churches life it financed much of the cost of general maintenance and in more recent times has assisted with the annual running costs. Following the death of Thomas, Lucy carried on as Patroness until her death in 1856.

Thomas and Lucy Botfield are buried at Hopton Wafers and are remembered on a fine stone memorial in the church.

They had no children and the Hopton Court Estate passed to Beriah Botfield, a nephew, who with his wife, Isabella (nee Leighton), resided at the Court until his death in 1863. Beriah left no children.

The property of Hopton Court was by an old document entailed to Thomas Woodward, Rector of Hopton Wafers, although by that time (1863) this Thomas was deceased, he had been the son of another Thomas Woodward and his wife, Sarah (nee Skelhorne), a sister of Lucy Botfield. The Rev'd. Thomas Woodward and his wife had three sons, each of whom succeeded to the Hopton Court property. The eldest son, Thomas first had the Court. Following his death in 1887, the second son, Samuel inherited. In 1889 on the death of Samuel, the third son, Vice Admiral Robert Woodward CB together with his wife and family took up residence at Hopton Court. The Admiral and several subsequent members of his family carried on the Botfield tradition as Patrons of Doddington church and as active trustees of the original trust fund. In recent years the officials of the Diocese of Hereford have undertaken to act as trustees in consultation with the Minister and PCC as necessary.

`The Admiral' as he is now referred to by present members of the Woodward family is held in great affection by them. There is little doubt that he was the most flamboyant member of the family to have resided at Hopton Court. He was indeed a `character' in the nicest and fullest meaning of the word.

Admiral Woodward is buried at Hopton Wafers and a fine headstone marking his grave, reflects his status, loyal service and the commission he held.

I was privileged to be given access to personal Woodward family archives, which greatly assisted me in the writing of this brief tribute to the early Patrons of St. John's Church.

Lucy Botfield (from a portrait in Hopton Court).

The Botfield Memorial.

The 'Admiral's' grave.

Vice Admiral Robert Woodward.

AGRICULTURE

Over the past Millennium many industries have come to the Doddington area, with the exception of limited stone quarrying operations, they have disappeared. Whilst all of them left scars on the landscape, mother nature and time has healed most of the scars associated with these now defunct operations.

Long before man exploited the mineral riches of the area, agriculture flourished. Whilst agriculture is mostly controlled by mother nature in the shape of weather pattern, climate, land terrain and mankind's survival instinct , the way that the business of farming and animal husbandry is practised has constantly adapted over the past Millennium. The changes have been dramatic from about 1930 with not only the growth of mechanised aids to the farmer, but the introduction of the pneumatic tyre to the agricultural industry which has led to a rapid development of sophisticated machinery which has caused a decline in the need for agricultural workers. Our area of South Shropshire is one of the few remaining areas in England and Wales that has a landscape that allows the old methods to continue in parallel with the new technology.

A few years ago M. A. `Mac' Harrington wrote a Thesis entitled `Agriculture and the Tyre Man'. It is a comprehensive work which not only deals with technical aspects of tractors and Tyres, but contains a history of agriculture from 3,300 BC to the present day. The following is an extract from that Thesis in relation to the past Millennium.

The coming of the Norman's in AD 1066 did not result in much change on the farm. The Saxon system is known as the manorial system and it was the Norman's who extended this to cover the whole country. This is shown in detail in the Doomsday Book - the result of a survey of 1086. In it every estate is noted down with all particulars of agricultural importance.

Livestock of all kinds played an increasingly important part in the lives of the people, who needed ever-greater supplies of all animal products. Horses became more numerous on the farms. Wild rabbits became an important article of food and a nuisance to crops during the 13th Century onwards.

The beginning of the 14th Century saw a decline in the manorial system of agriculture and much unrest among the people. Markets were being developed and money was more plentiful, but the land was becoming impoverished by over-cropping to feed the people and livestock. Also a period of bad seasons from 1312-21 caused famine and disease. Changes had to come and the disaster of the Black Death precipitated them in 1348 and succeeding years. Almost half the population died from this and similar disease before the end of the century.`

The consequent shortage of workers and farmers led to the break-up of the manorial system, and much land became derelict. Village communities disintegrated and individuals scattered to seek a living as best they could. To protect agricultural interests the Government intervened. A Royal proclamation of 1349 ordered all men and women, with certain exceptions, to work on the land where they lived at the wage rate current in 1346.

Much land reverted to pasture on which sheep were grazed as they needed little labour, especially as some of the land was now being enclosed. Wool was also very valuable.

Agriculture deteriorated from the time of the Black Death up to the end of the 15th Century, mostly because of the lack of any system such as the manors, where everyone and everything fitted into a progressive programme. The Wars of the Roses further aggravated the situation. There was no real change for the better either of livestock, crops, implements or general farming conditions.

The 16th Century saw a speeding up of two processes, first the amalgamation of scattered strips into single farms, and later the enclosure of more land for sheep. The more settled conditions also encouraged better farming, while the growth of towns and overseas trade brought markets for farm produce and more money, and ushered in the yeomen of England - real men of the land and proud of their status. Livestock was improved by better crops and better breeding.

Implements were being improved to meet the demands for better farming. Hay was made and stored for winter fodder. Turkeys were introduced about 1537 and the farmyard poultry included guinea-fowl, peacocks, pigeons, ducks, geese and wild birds fattened in cages.

It was not until the 17th Century that farm animals were recorded according to district, the starting point for the various breeds known today. During this century experiments were made to find the best types of farm crops for each district. Implements were more plentiful and of improved design and capacity. Corn was being dibbled-in instead of being sown broadcast. Dressings of manure were more plentiful and various distinctions were made between different types of soil, both arable and pasture. Lucerne, sainforn, artificial grasses and turnips were gaining in favour, but not until the 18th Century did they become widely known. This period saw great improvements in agriculture, brought about by such men as Coke of Norfolk, Townsend of Raynham, Bakewell of Dishley, Webster of Canley, the brothers of Ketton, Jethro Tull and many others. All livestock was greatly improved, soil fertility was built up to produce better crops, which were also becoming more varied. Improved crops provided more for livestock and for market. The manure from one and the money from the other led to greater prosperity. Land was continually being enclosed and reclaimed to bring further agricultural benefits to nearly all districts, and this laid the firm foundations on which to build the present system of farming.

The 19th Century is noted for scientific progress in relation to agriculture. The fertiliser industry was started by Sir J. B. Lawes, who with Sir H. Gilbert founded the experimental farm and laboratories at Rothansted, where much important work on crops and soils was conducted.

The area of the United Kingdom under cultivation peaked at about 33 million acres in the 1880's. By the 1970's the total stood at about 29 1/2 million acres, much of the decrease was directly associated with the need for land for such things as roads, housing and industrial development. There was also a remarkable increase in crop yields over this period.

The 20th Century has not only seen an improvement in land and livestock management, but the most notable advance has been in plant breeding and the development of mechanical aids to farming.

Figures for the early 1970's show that England had a total of 324,390 tractors, Shropshire had 10,290, whilst the neighbouring counties of Hereford (6,320), Worcestershire (5,430) and Staffordshire (8,160) were far less mechanised at that time.

LISTER SEED DRILL OF THE 1880's

The Clee Hill area has long been popular with vehicle manufactures for the testing and proving of their products, both on and off the road.

Shown immediately below is an experimental BMC vehicle passing Doddington Church, circa 1964. The bottom picture is of a Ford model 'N'. The tipper version of this vehicle would have at one time been a familiar sight in the quarries.

ALFRED EDWARD HOUSMAN 1859 - 1936 A TRIBUTE

A SON OF WORCESTERSHIRE - A LOVER OF SHROPSHIRE

During my early childhood, my grandfather, a Salopian by birth, talked of many things associated with his youth in Shrewsbury. He often spoke of A Shropshire Lad. Whilst I was far too young to understand much of what he talked of, a great deal of what he said remained in my memory, no doubt as a result of the sincerity with which he spoke. As I've got older I have come to realise what great love he had for his native county. I have also come to appreciate the works of Housman in his book 'A Shropshire Lad', in which with his poetry and fine use of our language, demonstrates his deep love of Shropshire. Housman looked towards Shropshire from his Worcestershire home. He journeyed to and wrote about the county over Abberley Hills. I consider myself more fortunate than Housman, as I travelled over the Abberley's and settled in Shropshire. This has a certain logic as many of my ancestors came from the county, including five great grandparents from South Shropshire.

A SHROPSHIRE LAD - A E HOUSMAN

1887
From Clee to heaven the beacon burns,
The Shires have seen it plain,
From north to south the sign returns
And beacons burn again.

Look left, look right, the hills are bright,
The dales are light between
Because 'tis fifty years tonight
That God has saved the Queen.

Now, when the flame they watch not towers
About the soil they trod,
Lads, we'll remember friends of ours
Who shared the work with God.

The skies that knit their heartstrings right,
To fields that bred them brave,
The saviours come not home to-night:
Themselves they could not save.

It dawns in Asia, tombstones show
And Shropshire names are read;
And the Nile spills his overflow
Beside the Severn's dead.

THE RECRUIT
Leave your home behind you lad,
And reach your friend your hand,
And go, and luck go with you
While Ludlow tower shall stand.

Oh, come home of Sunday
When Ludlow streets are still
And Ludlow bells are calling
To farm and lane and mill.

Or come you home of Monday
When Ludlow market hums
And Ludlow chimes are playing
'The conquering hero comes'.

Come you home a hero,
Or come not home at all,
The lads you leave will mind you
Till Ludlow tower shall fall.

And you will list the bugle
That blows in lands of morn,
And makes the foes of England
Be sorry you were born.

When I came at last to Ludlow
Amidst the moonlight pale,
Two friends kept step beside me,
Two honest lads and hale.
Now Dick lies in the churchyard,
And Ned lies in the jail,
And I come home to Ludlow
Amidst the moonlight pale.

When I was one-and-twenty
I heard a wise man say,
'Give crowns and pounds and guineas
But not your heart away;
Give pearls away and rubies
But keep your fancy free'.
But I was one-and-twenty,
No use to talk to me.

THE INDUSTRIAL PAST.

In the late 17th and early 18th centuries the coal mining communities on the slopes of Titterstone Clee grew substantially . Coal was sent to local towns, iron ore was produced for nearby blast furnaces and coal was employed in the making of tobacco pipes, bricks, tiles, pottery called Clee Hill ware, and possibly for glass making. Most of the miners occupied squatters cottages, of which there were 49 on the wastes of Snitton township alone in 1745, a total which had grown to 68 in 1778. In the late 18th century two coke-fired ironworks were built on Clee Hill. The Cornbrook Furnace was constructed by 1794, although it was only making 292 tons of iron a year in 1805, and was out of blast by the 1820's. The Knowbury works was built in 1804-05. When it was offered for sale in 1851 it included a forge, a rolling mill and a slitting mill, as well as a blast furnace. The mining of coal on the Clee Hills continued into the 20th century, but declined in importance as the quarrying of the local dhustone for road metal expanded.

(Ref. A History of Shropshire by Barrie Trinder).

The once thriving coal mining industry of the Shropshire/Worcestershire border area is long gone. In the heyday of the industry, pits both large and small abounded in the area. It is difficult to imagine the conditions that the industries workers laboured and lived under, often near the poverty line. Survival must have been very difficult in the 1800's.

In the 1870's miners worked 64 hours a week, 6.00a.m to 4.00p.m on Mondays & Saturdays, and 6.00a.m to 5.00p.m on the other four weekdays.

By 1920 the men worked 8 hour shifts on weekdays & 6 hours on Saturdays. In the early part of this century the pit head price of best coal was 16/= per ton. A miners wage was £3-10-0 a week, loading and haulage workers were paid £1-10-0 and 14 year old boys working as pony drivers 15/= a week. House rents were 3/6 per week, cider was 2d a pint and tobacco cost 4d an ounce.

(The Ref. To hours and wages is from 'Rock' by Robert D Thompson).

A short distance from the slopes of Clee Hill on the banks of the river Severn at Dowles (Shropshire), there was once a gasworks which was owned by the Bewdley Gas, Light & Coke Company. In the mid 1800's my Gt. Gt. Grandfather was the manager of this establishment and lived in a cottage on the premises with his family, indeed in 1854 my Gt. Grandfather was born at the cottage, which is now known as Severnside. In the 1850's' Thomas Russell worked 7 days a week and virtually ran the works single handed, he was paid 18/= a week, had a free cottage, allotment garden and coke for his domestic use. Apart from making the gas he had to collect the dues from the customers, walk to and from Bewdley, twice a day, to turn the public lighting on and off. His reward for performing this extra task was £11- per year. His one 'perk' was that he was permitted to buy coke from the company and 'hawk' it round the town for the residents to purchase. Not much of a perk by modern standards. In the 1850's coal was brought to Bewdley railway sidings by train, transferred to horse drawn wagons and delivered to the gas works at 21/= per ton.

(Information from Russell Family archives).

Some may consider it strange that I have chosen to write briefly of the Clee Hill quarrying industry in a chapter that is headed 'The Industrial Past'. The quarrying industry is thriving and hopefully has a future, but more importantly it also has a past which has played a major role in the shaping of the area (both commercially and physically) as we now know it. It is indeed the correct chapter.

Man has for the past eight hundred years (or there abouts) extracted minerals such as coal, iron-ore and dolerite from Titterstone Clee. To those unfamiliar with the area, dolerite is the hard dark blue/grey rock which abounds in the area and is locally known as 'dhustone'. Of the once thriving industries of the area (other that the oldest - agriculture) only stone quarrying now remains.

Back in the early part of the century three quarries operated on Titterstone Clee. The total annual stone extraction at that time was in the region of 410,000 tonnes with a labour force of several hundred men. There is no doubt at that time the work was highly labour intensive, with the labour force enduring harsh conditions to earn a modest wage.

By 1998 only one quarry operates on the hill. This being ARC's Clee Hill quarry which is located just off the A4117 Cleobury Mortimer to Ludlow road at a height of approximately 1,500 feet above sea level and a short distance from Clee Hill village. There is little doubt that this quarry has survived and indeed prospered due to the introduction and effective use of modern production and processing technology. Technology and methods which allow the company to annually produce in the region of 320,000 tonnes with a labour force of just 19 men.

In recent years ARC has co-operated and consulted with villagers, local authority and other interested agencies to ensure that not only their present operation, but also those in the foreseeable future take full account of the local unique environmental issues of Titterstone Clee.

At the time of the open day at Clee Hill quarry in 1998, the company issued a well documented information sheet. I acknowledge the assistance of that information sheet in compiling this short article

This picture clearly shows the marquee erected in Clayton's field in readiness for the church fete of 11th July 1998. It was at this event that sufficient money was raised to finally pay off the debt for the restoration of the church roof.

TITTERSTONE CLEE

If any consciousness at all remains
You surely must remember Titterstone Clee
Where we escaped from the lanes
Heavy with heat and the hedges trapping
The stink of petrol. In a small dark church
We'd found some coolness, but the air was musty
Tarnishing the oil lamp's brass.
Then as we climbed a breeze began to stir
And eddied and swirled around us
Growing ever fresher till we stood
Upon the summit alone with the earth and sky.
Below the Midlands stretched, shire upon patchwork shire
Without a hill between us and the Urals,
But there was no sound but the bleat of tolerant sheep
And muffled rumblings from a distant quarry,
No motion but a tractor's beetle progress
A thousand feet below us.

Alone as pioneers we rediscovered
Our mutual love, that strange discovery
So often made, each time with an amazement
No Columbus had experienced.
Shropshire that day was a rediscovered Eden
And we it's sole possessors. Earth was happy
To share your qualities, the strength of rock,
The gentleness of turf, The sun
Kissed with our passion and the winds caressed us
For we were earth and sky, our love the power
That moved them in their courses.

That is a spot where I shall not return.
Though you remain it's guardian spirit
To bless all lovers coming there
Death's fiery sword debars me from that Eden.
Elsewhere the sun may kiss me with your strength,
The winds caress me with your gentleness,
But there your body's absence would torment me
And I should walk an excommunicate
Excluded from the sacraments of love.

Charles Hobday.
(Printed with permission of Peter & Ginny Barnfield of XENIA PRESS).

Could the small dark church with tarnished oil lamp's be our church of St. John's, Doddington?

SNIPPETS

TITHES.

I personally believe the tithe to have been one of the most unjust taxes in our nations long history of taxation. This particular tax discriminated against rural/country dwellers, many of whom produced barely enough to maintain themselves and their families.

The essence of the tithe was that one tenth of the main produce of the land and relating to both stock and labour such as wool, pigs, milk etc., was paid to the church. The Tithe Commutation Act of 1836 allowed tithes to be commuted to a rent-charge based on the price of corn. Tithes were abolished in 1936.

An example of the tithe for 1840 shows that Ann Palmer (nee Crump) a widow of fifty years of age, farmed the Court Farm at Neen Sollars which at the time totalled 127 acres. The rent chargeable to the Rector was assessed at £27-. This seemed an unrealistic sum as the tithe map of the time shows that most of the land was used for grazing with very little cultivated. Indeed!! a very unjust tax.

Ann Palmer was my gt. gt. gt. grandmother.

MRS GERTRUDE BYTHEWAY.

On Easter Sunday (12th April 1998) a plaque was dedicated at St. John's church Doddington in memory of the late Mrs Gertrude Bytheway. She had devoted many years of her life to the service of the church in the capacity of Church Warden. She had also been a kingpin of many of the organisations associated with her village community.

THE DODDINGTON CHURCHYARD GHOST.

This story has been related to me by many people, I doubt if any of them witnessed the original incident. There is little doubt that the tale has been told on many occasions, most of these occasions have been at times when alcohol was being consumed. On some (or all) of these occasions the story teller has perhaps been guilty of a modicum of exaggeration (artists licence). In spite of this, the story has merit and a ring of truth about it.

The story goes that some years ago, a group of local men were walking home after spending a congenial evening drinking in a local hostelry. As they passed Doddington churchyard they heard clumping footsteps and rattling chains on the other side of the wall. One member of the party who had consumed a little more than the others volunteered to investigate. He entered the churchyard alone, verbally encouraged by his companions, non of whom made any move to accompany him in his quest. Once in the churchyard he walked furtively in the direction of the ghostly noises. He then came upon a donkey who was walking around dragging a piece of chain of which one end was attached to the unhappy beasts bridle.

So the Doddington ghost turned out to be nothing more than a local man's donkey which had broken free from it's tether.

THE DODDINGTON WAR MEMORIAL

In June of 1998 the drawing of the war memorial, plus all the references to it contained in the 'DODDINGTON' book were included in the National War Memorials data base which is held by the Imperial War Museum, London.

CHARACTERS

There are several definitions of this word in the dictionary, the one closest to that I write of, is 'An odd or eccentric person'. During my sixty plus years on this earth I have been privileged to have known several characters, I have indeed been lucky as in our modern age there is little room for genuine characters. I personally define a character as being individual in style of dress, physical features, behaviour pattern or other personal attributes that cause no offence to their fellow beings. Many of the older residents of the area have spoken of one, Reuben Turner, who by all accounts was a character of the first order.

His mode of transport was a donkey cart with which he used to go about his daily work. When the working day was over it became his form of conveyance to one of the many local hostelries. There is no doubt that from the many who remember Rueben he was a man who enjoyed his ale. The story is told that on one occasion when he was drinking with friends, some of the local lads removed his donkey from the shafts of his cart, put the shafts through a five bar gate and then re-harnessed his donkey in the shafts. As well as his ability to drink ale, people have also spoken with great respect of his ability to do a days work. I have been told that there was non finer at handling a scythe at harvest time.

There is little doubt that this character was a much loved member of the community.

OF HOME MADE WINE - MRS GUMBLEY'S BEVERAGE

It is always a pleasure to sit and chat with Sam Gumbley. We talk of many things, including many of the wrongs of this world, which we put right, as men do. I most value the stories Sam relates of his youth, including bits about the characters and events of that time. Sam's mother like most country ladies of her era produced annually vast quantities of wine from the various local fruits. To those of us who have tasted and come to love these traditional beverages, we have learned to treat them with respect and to consume them in moderation. Old Chris Cole would often stop by the Gumbley home with his snap box at dinner time. One particularly hot day, Sam's mother gave Chris some of her wine instead of the customary glass of cold water. The result was that Sam had to find the road man that looked after Earls Ditton Lane and with his help get Chris back to his lodgings at Hopton Wafers.

At sheep dipping time it was customary in years gone by for the local constable to stand and observe that the operation was carried out. On one particularly hot day those taking part in the operation kept cool by consuming large quantities of wine. Sam's mother remarked to the constable, 'Pity you can't have a drink while your in uniform'. To which he was alleged to have replied, 'If it means getting a glass of wine missus, I'll take my ruddy clothes off'!!!

True or false?. It doesn't matter; it's a good tale and worthy of mention.

PEEPING TOMS (BOY'S WILL BE BOY'S)

The Second World War saw the greatest influx of people to Clee Hill area since the growth of the mining and quarrying industries several decades earlier. By far the greatest group to arrive at Doddington were the RAF & WAAF personnel charged with establishing and operating the radar station known as Royal Air Force Clee Hill. The Air Ministry took over the Lodge, initially to accommodate airmen. The airmen later moved to hutted accommodation high on the hill. This move allowed the WAAF personnel who had been billeted with civilian families over a wide area to move into the Lodge. It became necessary to construct an additional ablution block for the WAAF's, this was sited in the Lodge grounds on a plot directly across the road from the old post office (a house now occupies the plot). When the building was put into use, I'm told the local male population of varying ages knew every crack and fault in the buildings fabric that would allow them to peep into that magical, forbidden female domain. The peeper's no doubt grew up to have a far greater knowledge of the female anatomy than did their more timid contemporaries.

MEDIEVAL VERSE

Wretched is the hall...each day in the week
There the lord and lady liketh not to sit;
Now have the rich a rule to eat by themselves
In the privy parlour...for poor mans sake,
Or in a chamber with a fireplace, and leave the chief hall
That was made for meals, for men to eat in...

A cleric's duty is to serve Christ and leave
carting and labouring to ignorant serfs. And no
one should take Holy Orders unless he comes
from a family of freemen...Serfs and beggars'
children should toil with their hands, while men
of noble birth should serve God and their fellow
men as befits their rank....

From 'The Vision of Piers Plowman' circa 1362 by Langland.
It is possible that Langland was born in the parish of Cleobury Mortimer in 1322.

GORSE BURNING

Many years ago it was the custom to burn the gorse (goss) off the surface of the local common land. I have been told that on one occasion as this operation was in progress, a local man of good repute and of some importance, suffered great embarrassment during the burning operations. As the fire neared a large patch of gorse, he was observed to stand up from behind it. He was closely followed by a young woman who appeared flustered and dishevelled. This story was related to me in hushed tones from behind the narrators hand. Is it true?, or just a good tale? Will we ever know the truth?, maybe!!!

FIRST PAY PACKET

In January 1950 I started work as an apprentice at the former Morris Commercial Cars factory. After two weeks I received my first pay packet, we were paid on a week in hand basis. I proudly carried it home and handed it, unopened to my mother. She took it, looked at it and handed it back with the words 'This is the only pay packet that you will ever truly call your own'. How true were her words!! That magical first packet contained the sum of 25/= (£1-25p), oh how times have changed.

SCIENCE - GOOD AND BAD

There is little doubt that during the last few decades of the old Millennium mankind has made far more scientific advancement than during the previous one thousand years.

One must particularly applaud advances in medical sciences of which the benefits are obvious.

Other sciences of a more destructive and sinister nature have also made great advances. The unfortunate thing is that the application of the latter is often seen to become perverted by mankind's constant thirst for power, domination of others and wealth. I hope and pray that in the new Millennium the humane applications of science will prosper, whilst the perverted applications decline.

ROPE (A GIFT - COURTESY OF THE ROYAL AIR FORCE !!!)

When the RAF radar station was established on the hill above Doddington, a person in authority decided that the path from the village to the station should be well defined and marked. At regular intervals along the entire length of the path he had wooden stakes driven into the ground. He then had Air Ministry specification rope suspended from stake to stake at about waist height. The purpose of this exercise was to provide a guide for RAF personnel to move to and from the station in all weather conditions. To a civilian population that had by this stage of the war got thoroughly brassed off with shortages, the temptation of this unguarded rope was too great a temptation to resist. I'm told the entire length of rope disappeared during the first night. It was split up into useful lengths and did good service for many years in numerous local homes.

A TRAGIC OCCURRENCE

Edited account of a Coroners inquest held at Ludlow Guildhall and reported in the Shrewsbury Chronicle on May 9th 1845.

Fatal Accidents - An inquest was held at Guildhall, on 29th ult., before W. Downes, Esq., Coroner, on view of the body of Edward Lewis. It appeared from the evidence, that the deceased was in the habit of attending at the George Inn on market and fair days for the purpose of assisting the ostler, and on Monday 28th ult., was thus employed when cries were heard by the ostler for help, and on his repairing to the stable, the poor fellow said that Mr. Oven's horse had kicked him and caused a terrible rupture. He was immediately assisted home and medical aid called in, but he gradually sunk and died next morning. He has left a wife and six children.

Verdict, "Accidental Death".

Edward Lewis was my Gt. Gt. Grandfather.

In it's heyday The George Hotel provided livery for up to forty horses.

TOMMY OAKLEY'S SALVE

There is no doubt that in the past life on Clee Hill was harsh, harsher than those of us living in modern society can imagine. In the severe weather of winter it was particularly tough on the men who carried out various tasks in the quarries. The skin on their hands cracked and got cut. To ease their discomfort a little they didn't turn to the Doctor, but to the local cobbler, Tommy Oakley. From the various waxes and sealants used in his trade he produced a preparation which became known locally as 'Tommy Oakley's Salve'. Many of the quarry workers used this preparation on their cut and cracked hands and swore that it provided a degree of insulation that eased the pain as they went about their work.

The men of Clee Hill village and the Tenbury Road area used a similar preparation which was made from a secret formula and known as Howell's Salve. This was made and supplied by Mr. Howell. It is said that when the salve was applied warm it gave great relief to the sore and cut hands of quarry workers.

FOURTEENTH OLYMPIAD

In 1948 England hosted the Olympic Games. These were not only the first post war Games, but the first to be held since the Nazi propaganda dominated Munich Games of 1936. On the conclusion of the 1948 Games, several Eastern European athletes decided against returning to the their homelands.

TRAP ONE

Over a period of many years an essential everyday 'office' has been given a vast assortment of names. Some of these being acceptable, some acceptable yet risque, others totally unacceptable in print. Familiar names being privvy, girls/boys room, lavvy, bog, loo etc.

When I started work in 1950 it was a familiar sight to see men sloping off from their workplace at about 8.30a.m. (we started work at 7.30). Many of them would have a bulge in their overall pocket which would be caused by The Daily Mirror or The Herald, both considered working men's papers. The destination of those errant workers would be a place in the factories basement that many considered to be a reading room. When the foreman missed a worker and asked 'where's So & So' he would get the answer 'in trap one'.

BATH NIGHT

Friday was the weekly bath night, a well established ritual that even had a pecking order for the weekly dunk and back scrub. First in would be the wage earners, then older family members, followed by children with the youngest at the back of the queue. In the case of very large families the bath water may well have made some children dirtier than before they were dunked. I'm ahead of myself, for before the ritual could begin the bath had to be prepared.

The bath was made of galvanized metal, was about five feet long and when not in use hung from a six inch nail on the outside wall of the kitchen. The start of the ritual was heralded by the boiler being filled with water and the fire being lit, making sure that a bucket of slack was at hand for keeping the fire built up. When the water was hot, the bath was brought into the kitchen and hot water was ladled from the boiler, but not too much as some hot water needed to be saved for the later bathers. As the pecking order progressed each bather poured one ladle of bath water down the sink and replaced it with a ladle of fresh hot water from the boiler.

When all the family had bathed the ritual concluded with what to the elected person was the most unpleasant part of the ritual, emptying the ruddy bath. Water was ladled from the bath until the bath was light enough to be slid along the floor. At this stage the back door was opened, the bath was slid to the doorstep and tipped up so that the remaining water would run down the outside drain. As the bath was slid, the water was guaranteed to slop from end to end of the bath with a fair amount splashing over the feet of the hapless emptier.

How nice it is to now be able to turn on a hot tap, run a bath of water and remove the plug when finished. These modern innovations which are now the accepted way of life are much appreciated by those of us who remember the old days.

AGRICULTURAL WAGES

In February of 1949 it was announced that from 13th March agricultural workers would receive an increase in their weekly minimum pay, this increase coupled to a reduction in working hours. Minimum male rate to rise from £4-10-0 to £4-14-0. In the case of women and juveniles the minimum rate would go from £3-8-0 to £3-11-0. At the same time the working week was to be reduced by one hour, from 48 to 47 hours.

AVIATION

In 1949 an American Super Fortress bomber made the first non-stop circumnavigation of the Earth. The distance covered was approximately 23,000 miles, about 1,500 miles less than if the flight had followed the line of the equator. To achieve this feat the aircraft had to refuel in flight on four occasions. The journey was completed at an average speed of 239 miles per hour.

TRANSATLANTIC RESIDENTS

By 1944 many hundreds of American servicemen (GI's) arrived in the Clee Hill area. Their arrival heralded the build up of allied military might prior to the D Day invasion of the European mainland. At least one local girl, Jessie Teague, daughter of the licensee of The Gate Hangs Well married one of these American soldiers. During 1998 the now Jessie Davidson of Ontonagon USA wrote to me a delightful letter. An edited version of part of that letter is printed below.

'The 463rd Anti Aircraft battery sailed from the USA and during 1944 landed in Scotland. They then travelled by road to Shropshire. The first night in the area was spent on Catherton Common, the following day a tented town of considerable size mushroomed up on Cleeton St Mary's Common and extended to the banks of the Crumps Brook. The 463rd remained for about seven weeks and then moved rapidly overnight to their embarkation point in readiness for the D Day invasion. The men who had been local residents for that brief seven weeks landed on Omaha beach immediately after the initial invasion troops. They joined with the 79th Division and carried on through France to Germany'.

Jessie Teague and her American soldier, Chester Davidson married at Silvington church and now live in quiet retirement.

INFLATION

During the latter part of the present century we have experienced inflation, which at times during the period has grown at an alarming rate. It is only when we compare prices of specific items over a given period that we can appreciate just how great is the variation in prices. For example. A tractor operator purchasing standard 12 inch front and 23 inch rear tyres in 1970 would have paid in the region of £38- and £137- respectively. Some thirty years on, for comparable tyres (ply ratings have increased) he would have to pay in the region of £190- & £300- each. Makes you think!!.

TITANIC DISASTER - GREAT LOSS OF LIFE

The above headlines appeared in the press in April of 1912. The White Star liner Titanic left Southampton for her maiden voyage to New York on April 10th 1912. Some four days into the voyage, the liner struck an iceberg and sank within a few hours. Of the 2,201 souls on board, only 711 survived.

There were strong West Midland links with the ship, as many companies from the area had supplied equipment and fittings. The major of these being anchors and chains from the Black Country and berths from Messers Hoskins & Sewells of Bordesley, Birmingham.

AN OBSERVATION AND THOUGHT

As a genealogist and historian, I'm often accused of living in the past. This accusation is rubbish and totally unfounded, and will hopefully be proved so by the following thoughts which I commit to paper!!

My grandparents, whom I remember well, lived during two centuries and one Millennium.
My parents lived during one century and one Millennium.
My mother and father in law lived during two centuries and one Millennium.
My wife and me, together with our children and grandchildren have already lived in one century and one Millennium. By God's will we shall hopefully live into the next century and Millennium. This will number us among the small percentage of mankind to have this unique experience.

There is however a smaller group of beings who having been born in the latter years of the 19th century, lived throughout the 20th century and will be alive to see the dawn of the 21st century, they will perhaps be the only people in the history of our world to have lived during no less than three centuries and two Millenniums.

The above thoughts were committed to paper in February 1999

MOTORCYCLES

Back in the 1930's it is likely that many of the young men of Doddington, in common with today's young men, dreamed of owning a brand new gleaming motorcycle. Prices for that time appear now to be very `modest', but with the low pay of the 1930's the prospect of buying a motorcycle was little more than a daydream. To those who could afford to buy, there was a tremendous selection of Midlands produced machines available. A few examples of 1938 models and prices are shown below.

Velocette, Birmingham	249cc	Two stroke	£44 - 00
	348cc	OHC	£74 - 00
Rudge, Coventry	449cc	OHC	£69 - 10s
Raynal, Handsworth, Birmingham. Motorised bicycle	98cc		£18 - 18s
OK Supreme, Greet, Birmingham.	248cc	OHV	£42 - 00
Ariel, Selly Oak, Birmingham.	599cc	'AF Square Four'	£82 - 7- 6d
BSA, Small Heath, Birmingham.	348cc	Silver Star	£58 - 5s
	498cc	Gold Star	£80 - 00
Excelsior, Tyseley, Birmingham.	249cc	Norseman	£51 - 00
Levis, Stechford, Birmingham.	346cc		£52 - 00
New Imperial, Hall Green, Birmingham.	346cc	`Grand Prix'	£60 - 10s
Norton, Aston, Birmingham	490cc	Model `16H'	£63 - 16 - 6d
	400cc	`International'	£102 - 11 - 6d

Swallow Sidecar's, Coventry offered a wide range of sporty sidecars, with a two adult version for £22 - 10s.

Watsonian of Birmingham offered a fabric covered single hammock seat model for £12 - 5s.

During the 1930's BSA, in parallel with their motorcycle business produced a range of four seater 10HP cars which sold for under £300 - 00.

"Young" Alan Webb with his first Motor Cycle - 1942

IN LIVING MEMORY - "I REMEMBER"

The Tennant family have lived and prospered in the Clee Hill and Doddington area throughout the twentieth century. The following references to the family were written by Jim Tennant in 1998.

'My grandfather, John Tennant, arrived on Clee Hill at the start of the century in the year 1900. He was attracted to the area by the vast number of small coal mines and the promise of regular work. The family, particularly the younger members, were dismayed at the desolate and remote area to which they had been brought. Coming from Pargeter Street in Walsall to their new home at Top Whatsill was guaranteed to shock and alarm them. Grandfather had a horse and cart with which he took coal from the pit heads to the railway sidings at the granite quarry. The family eventually moved to number 2 Cornbrook, which they considered to be a little closer to civilisation. When the pits closed, the men of our family, including my father started to work in the quarry. In 1919 my father, Enoch Tennant, married and set up home at the cottage in Fairy Glen. I had one brother and four sisters, all of us being baptised at Doddington. My father was one of a considerable number of children of which several served in the Great War. One of his brothers, John, died of his wounds and is buried at Doddington. His grave is marked with a military headstone which bears the insignia of his regiment!'.

Pictured below - John Tennant (senior) and the Tennant family at Fairy Glen.

I have met and spoken with Kay Grainger on numerous occasions during her frequent visits to Doddington, visits that are made for the express purpose of tending family graves. It became obvious during those conversations that Kay had a deep love and affection for Doddington. In September of 1998 I invited her to write of her child-hood memories for inclusion in the Millennium Book. The following are edited extracts from those written memories.

"My mother (Margaret Morgan) was born in Doddington, the twin sister of George, whom I believe was a bit of a character. There was another brother John (Jack), plus sisters Doris, Florence (Flo) & Gertrude. In 1936 mother left Doddington to go into domestic service at Kings Norton. It was there that she met my father, Daniel Henry Claverley and they married at Doddington on 27th March 1937. Sadly my father died in India during the war, I was only five months old at the time.

My earliest memories of Doddington are of travelling from Birmingham on the bus, dressed in my Sunday best. I would scramble off the bus and happily skip down Earls Ditton Lane towards Gran's cottage. I normally ended up in the ditch or a cow pat and started my visit by being cleaned up in the brew house boiler.

Gran's cottage had no mains services and we went to bed by candlelight, I loved to lie in bed listening to the sheep. My mother, sister & me normally slept in Gran's big bed. One Easter auntie Flo & uncle Albert also visited and heavy snow meant that they also had to stay the night at gran's. Sleeping arrangements for the night resulted in mother & auntie Flo sleeping at the top of the bed, whilst my sister & me slept at the bottom. Sleep was impossible as I had a toe in my ear for most of the night.

In the mornings we would rush down to the garden wall and watch Teddy Webb ride by as he drove his cows out to graze after milking. We often saw the operation in reverse in the evening. As a child I could never understand how the cows knew which way to turn at the end of the lane.

Uncle George often got us to pick gooseberries (gooz gogs) from the garden, he then took them to Tenbury market. When he came from the market he would give us a penny each. Clutching our pennies we would happily run up the lane to spend them at Mabel Dolphins post office. She was so patient as we normally took ages to make our choice, which was usually pear drops, the nicest I can ever recall tasting. At times we would walk along the road to the little wooden hut at Foxwood to spend our coppers, but it was never as good as going into Dolphins to the happy sound of the tinkling door bell.

We sometimes walked over the common to get milk from a farm or bread from Goodman's at Coreley. On other occasions we would walk to Ditton Mill and play in the stream. It was usual in the season to pick blackberries on the way back from the mill, but there were never enough left for a pie when we arrived back at gran's. Our playmates at Doddington were Peggy & Rosie Day who lived in the cottage just across the lane. We had great fun playing in the hay loft which was over the pigsty. On one occasion when in the loft we heard thunder in the distance. Thunder always frightened me and in my panic I fell from the loft into the sty. This resulted in another trip to the brew house to be cleaned up.

Many happy hours were spent looking for hen and duck eggs on the area that is now Doddington Heights. We handed the collected eggs to Mrs Edwards who gave us pennies to spend. These pennies were of course spent at Dolphins shop. We also spent many happy hours roaming over the hills with Peggy, Rosie and Frances Breakwell. Much of the time was spent in childish daydreaming, we spent endless hours talking together of what we would be and do when we grew up, a bit like The Last Of The Summer Wine in reverse. I know the things I dreamt of never came to fruition, I wonder about the hopes of the others of our happy little band?

When gran had eggs to sell she took us with her to Cleobury market on Wednesdays. If we had a few coppers to spend we made a brief visit to the local toy shop. On occasions we would watch the cattle being sold in the area that is now the car park behind the Talbot Hotel (Talbot Square). Dinner was normally at auntie Ethel's and then back to Doddington by bus. A free ride if my cousin was driver, a free ride was always a bonus.

Uncle George was the local cobbler and had his workshop in the garden. The workshop is still there, but I imagine that the wonderful smell of leather and his collection of cigarette cards that adorned the walls have long gone. One can still dream of the sights and smells of a past childhood.

I clearly recall joining many other folk on the common to help with the rounding up of sheep for dipping and shearing. On at least one occasion I admit to trying to send them the wrong way as I believed any delay in completing the operation would in turn delay our return to Birmingham. I would much have preferred to have remained at Doddington'.

Pictured below - Mrs. Laura Morgan, Mr. John Morgan, The Morgan 'Girls' on the occasion of the marriage of Gertrude to Frank Iliffe in July 1937.
Left to right - Margaret, Florence, Gertrude & Doris.

The following edited extracts are from Bruce Astbury's excellent article on his childhood and informative years at the 'Finger'. His complete article is contained in the Doddington Scrapbook.

"My first recollection of the Finger was 9th October 1940. I was five at the time and stood at Gran Turner's gate watching the van as it went up the lane towards our new home. Although my dad's family had a long association with the licensed trade, the Finger was to be the first venture of my parents (Edith 'Ede' and Asher Astbury) in the business.

The official name of the house was The Miners Arms, but for many years had been referred to as The Finger. In later years my mother had it officially renamed. The new house was wondrous to me with it's Calor gas lighting, no more smelly oil lamps or candles. The house did however still have typical country toilets which were sited down the garden at a 'safe' distance.

Beer was kept in the cellar and tapped from the barrel directly into drinking vessels or large jugs. Wine and spirits were also kept in the cellar and measured out in pewter measures. There was no bar and drinks had to be delivered to the customers tables.

We were fortunate having my grandparents living near by, as with dad working all day on war work, the assistance that my grandfather (Reuben Turner) gave was invaluable. Grandfather never went to bed, he took odd naps as and when he could. He enjoyed working at night, he often sat by the fire making clogs and on occasions would work in the moonlight cutting the dew soaked grass with his scythe. On one occasion he cut Hall's seven acre field at Hopton Bank, without ever leaving it. He also did his grave digging at night and frightened many an unsuspecting passer by. I later realised that our house would always be full of people, particularly as we often stayed open all night. We counted our customers as not only friends, but also family members.

One dark, foggy night two men arrived and asked for accommodation. My mother and several regulars became alarmed as they thought the Germans had arrived. The callers managed to convince mother that all was well and they were permitted to stay. They had several large boxes which caused some alarm, but it transpired that they were carrying out tests to establish a suitable location for a radar station. Their tests resulted in Royal Air Force Clee Hill being established.

School days were very happy at Hopton Wafers and at the age of seven I got my first long trousers. Was I proud of them? No! I ripped them on purpose so that I could have them patched the same as the other boys.

My friends and I often played football in the road at Hopton Bank, there was so little traffic that it didn't spoil our play. One evening my friend Stuart Howells and I became bored and decided on a prank to pass our time. With the use of trimmings and small trees from a hedge that had recently been laid we built a barrier across the road. It was a fine structure, six feet high with the appearance of a perfect hedge. When completed we hid to see what would happen. The service bus approached, stopped, with both driver and conductor getting off. They viewed our magnificent barrier with looks of disbelief and amazement. Their next task was to remove the barrier to allow the bus to proceed on it's route. A task they carried out with a vocabulary of swear words that I have not heard bettered to this day. By the time the road was cleared we had retreated to our homes, contented with our evenings mischief".

"I have very vivid memories of standing outside the Finger at night-time during the war and watching with awe the bombing, search lights and anti-aircraft fire over the West Midland towns. I would go back inside to what seemed a normal world with little visible signs of war, other than the blacked out windows.

When I was about eight the 'Yanks' arrived, hundreds of them were in a camp on the common at the end of Cleeton Road. At night there would be at least 200 thirsty soldiers waiting to be served. During the day a jeep loaded with 'Jerry Cans' would arrive at Hall's to collect water from the spout. It was no doubt the same cans that were filled at the Finger later in the day, to provide beer for the men who had to remain in camp at night. At that time beer was 8d per pint. I accumulated large quantities of gum and candy by continually asking 'Got any gum chum?' (this is pure nostalgia as most of our generation asked the same when we say G.I's). I came out in boils and Mum said 'That's what chewing gum does for you', so I was reluctantly compelled to put my hoard into a wheel barrow and tip it into a pit head. Unfortunately, this did not cure my boils.

Our cider was supplied by Charlie Robinson (he later founded Well's drink company), it sold at 4d per pint and was strong, especially the Christmas brew. This special brew was matured in rum casks and the smell lingered. Our regulars who normally managed eight or nine pints a night could only manage one of the special brew. Dad used to tell the RAF boys that he could get them drunk for two shillings, and he frequently did.

In 1944 my brother Howard was born. I had to spend some time looking after him as Mum was so busy. He spent much of his time in an improvised play pen (a beer barrel with one end knocked out), this allowed Mum to get on with her work. At the age of five he found the cider that was behind the rick for the hay makers. He consumed enough to get drunk and spent the rest of the day in bed. He was a very subdued little brother for the next few days.

Harvest time was always very special, neighbours helped each other and took their refreshments in the field. On one occasion we didn't finish until eleven at night, it was still light as in wartime we had 'double summertime' with the clocks being altered by two hours. We sat in the field taking our refreshment at midnight; never has pork pie, apple pie, sandwiches and 'home brew' tasted as good as that night.

Revd. Peers was in charge at Doddingrton Church. He formed the Church Lad's Brigade. We played snooker at Hopton Rectory, many of us were provided with instruments. In my case a cornet, bugle and kettle drum. I never learned to play, but was happily able to 'blow and bang'. On reflection he was such a generous man with an understanding of youth. When he moved to London he invited three of us to visit and stay at his home for a weekend. The highlight of the weekend was as a result of him giving us tickets for the Folies Bergeres. He transported us to the theatre and collected us after the show, he didn't share the experience of the show with us. It was a weekend that was savoured by three naïve country boys. We later related our story to our contemporaries with appropriate nudges and winks.

Georgie Morgan had his favourite seat by the fire in the bar. He often sat there sorting the rubbish from his pocket and throwing it on the fire. One night as he did this he suddenly realised he had also thrown his money on the fire. In spite of his frantic efforts to retrieve it, the fire was too hot and he spent the rest of the night jumping up and down with rage at the loss of his hard earned cash.

Another customer I remember well was Jackie Webb. He was a marvellous story teller and had a habit of telling me ghost stories before I went to bed. I often went to bed terrified especially as there was definitely something strange and ghostly about the Finger. Several people remarked about it and gran only ever stayed over night on one occasion".

“I can say in all honesty that many of our regulars treated the pub like home. At times it was possible when venturing out on a cold morning to see the outline of a human body etched in the frost, next to a sleeping cow. No doubt caused by one of our customers who needed a warm place to sleep for a few hours.

Dad eventually bought an ex WD V8 truck. It was mainly used to collect the pig ‘swill’ from the RAF camp. This became my job and at the age of fourteen I became an experienced driver. On one occasion dad drove to market to buy pigs; he returned home with ten human passengers in addition to several pigs.

During the war years we kept two pigs which provided us annually with ham and bacon. In later years we kept 100 pigs, they were largely fed on swill from the RAF camp. One evening dad returned from checking the pigs with a rat up his trousers. He asked Flaxer to get it out, but he would have nothing to do with it. Ben Key came to the rescue and stabbed it with a knife.

At the age of eleven I went to Cleobury School, at about the same time a local cricket club was formed, it was great fun and kept us occupied. Derek Bytheway was the organiser and we practised in Cuckoo Quarry. We became quite successful, thanks to Derek. Many of my companions of those carefree days have remained friends. Ron Hall was best man when I married and is now my brother-in-law.

These are but a few stories of my days at the Finger. Memories flood back, such things as the smell of wax polish and flowers. The huge fire and it’s heat which extended a welcome to our customers and friends, especially on cold nights. I now look back in amazement on the occasions I came down after a nights sleep to find the public rooms completely redecorated. Mum would have worked all night, papering and painting in order to maintain the high standards she demanded for our customers.

I also remember lying in bed listening to the sounds of country people in the rooms below, enjoying themselves on a night out with friends. I recall those voices well, Dennis Crowther singing and telling tales of the Clee Hills. Bill Briscoe with his accordion and Billy Hall crooning into his glass. I could also distinguish the voices of Tom & Ben Key, Ted Bradley (Flaxer), George Morgan (Stripes), Stan Price (a brilliant darts player), Jumbo Price the ‘thrower out’, Sam Wiltshire, Benny Jones, Benny & Joe Bishop, Ted Broome, Mike Mantle, Ken Butcher, Sammo Warrington, Jim Price (Sailor), Jim Warrington, Jack, Fred & Alan Webb, Charlie Woodhouse, Tom (Sire) and Jack Martin. These and many more were our ‘regulars’ and were often accompanied by their wives and girlfriends. They were in fact customers, friends and the most friendly and delightful people to be associated with. I am proud to have known them.

I left the Finger at the age of twenty one to do my National Service in the RAF and to marry my wife Margaret.

Dad died a few years after I left the Finger. Howard married and moved away. Mum carried on for a while, finally selling up and retiring in 1972. Sadly she died a mere three months later.

I consider myself lucky to have grown up in that wonderful, friendly, happy and often funny environment, surrounded by friends and the beautiful Clee Hills. My one daughter has produced a delightful pen and ink drawing of the ‘Lady’s Finger’ - Ede’s Pub. The picture gives life to the stories I relate to my daughters and grandchildren of my young days at the ‘FINGER’.

They were good years and I treasure my golden memories of them”.

DENNIS CROWTHER - A CHARACTER & GENTLEMAN

Dennis is a Clee Hill man both in his heart and by birth, with a deep love and regard for his lifelong environment. He is well known for his stories, anecdotes, folk songs, but mainly for his poetry. His use of words enables the reader or listener to conjure up a mental picture of what the poetry seeks to portray. Much of it paints a vivid picture of Clee Hill life, past and present.

The following are a couple of examples of his work (one humorous, one serious), from his book `Reminiscences of Titterstone Clee'

RUSTY OF CLEE

Below the castle walls of Clun the dog show there took place
the highlight of the week it was - full of elegance and grace
Where dogs from all the Midlands were paraded on the ground
and I entered Rusty Crowther there for the price of a half crown.

O! I lined up with the pedigrees to pay my entrance fee
and she entered him down in her ledger by the name of Rusty of Clee
and as I gave her my money Rusty gave her a winning look
and lifted his foot from off the ground
and piddled all over her book.

O! I took my dog out in the ring beneath the blazing sun
the field was full of daisies - he piddled on every one
he lay on his back in a cow-pat and there he did remain
then he imitated a fountain, he piddled straight over a Dane.

I lined up with the pedigrees all groomed and looking alert
Rusty stood next to a Greyhound and gave him a crafty squirt
the judge came forward friendly like to have a closer view
and Rusty sat back on his haunches and piddled all over his shoe.

The judge said walk the dog about the test it had begun
I pulled upon the bindertwine till his neck was three foot long
O! he showed a lovely set of teeth, O! what a lovely grin
then he got his own back - he piddled against the wind.

The best dogs they were singled out beneath the castle wall
and Rusty stood so proudly there that he come last of all
he rolled among the cow-muck he howled with sheer delight
and a lady patted him on the head and he piddled on her for spite.

O! I tried to get him on the bus to make our way for wum
his eyes stood out like organ stops coz he didn't want to come
for he'd thoroughly enjoyed himself and stood me in disgrace
and I bet if I take him to Clun again he'll piddle all over the place.

Clunton and Clunbury
Clungunford and Clun,
Are the quietest places
Under the sun.

TITTERSTONE CLEE

The air is still on Titterstone the highest point of Clee
I sat there reminiscing, of the days that used to be -
of horses and of Quarrymen, that trod the Quarry floor
but now it is deserted, they've gone for evermore.

I gazed down to the valley, with the mist a lying there -
with trees and steeple poking through, most wondrous I declare
and sounds upon the still air for miles around there be -
as I sat reminiscing upon Titterstone Clee.

The ghostly sound of hammers, up underneath the face
the sound of trucks and horses, made my imagination race
I could hear the Blacksmith cussin', as a shoe he tried to free
as I sat reminiscing upon Titterstone Clee.

I heard the bull go for their break, I saw them all sit down
with dinners tied in handkerchiefs, and cider from the Dhustone
with pitch and toss, and games of cards, let's have the best of three
it gives me time to reminisce up on Titterstone Clee.

Now Quarrymen are moving I hear no sound at all
they move like in slow motion up to the granite wall
the horses move without a sound, twas indeed a ghostly sight -
as I sat reminiscing beneath the sky so bright.

Silent hammers, strike the stone, a silent train passed through
and this dream of mine of bygone days, faded from my view -
I sat in utter silence back to reality
now I finished reminiscing up on Titterstone Clee.

"The reader will not credit that such things could be,
But I was there and saw it"!!!
Izaak Walton.

VISUAL NOSTALGIA

On 7th March 1947 the Ludlow newspaper reported that the worst blizzards for fifty years had resulted in Ludlow being totally cut off by road. The report went on to say that due to the depth and quantity of snow it had not been possible to use snow-ploughs on Clee Hill.

The picture immediately below shows RAF Clee Hill (which was sited above Doddington) receiving essential supplies by parachute during that now long gone infamous winter. The Airman nearest the parachute is 'Jock' MacPherson who now lives in Ludlow.

The bottom picture shows the RAF Radar Masts and gives an indication of the stations location.

Horizontal icicles February 1976 and February 1986.
Earls Ditton Lane February 1996 and The Common February 1998.

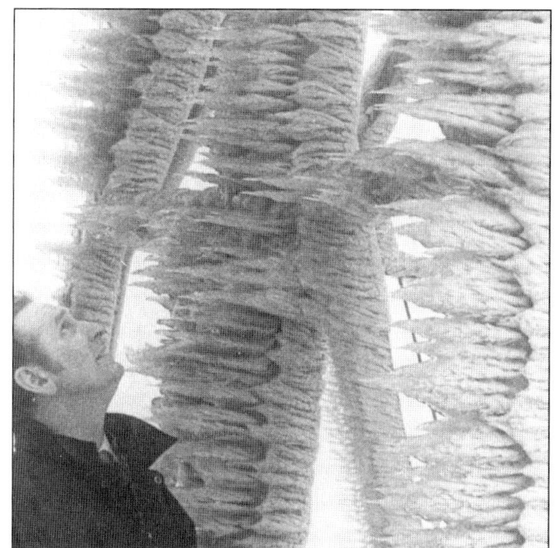

As Birmingham Distributors we always have a fine selection of Used Morris Cars. All are offered for sale in good road-worthy condition. With those purchased at £50 and over we give our "Money-Back" Guarantee. Ask for copy and full list. Attractive and confidential terms offered to all Morris and Wolseley employees.

Here are one or two:—

MORRIS 8 COACHBUILT SALOON. Sliding roof. Latest Series. Very good condition and appearance throughout	£75
MORRIS 10 SALOON DE LUXE, Series Model. Very good appearance and condition throughout	£100
MORRIS 12/4 SALOON, 1935 DE LUXE Model, complete with full equipment and sliding roof	£85
MORRIS SERIES II SALOON DE LUXE, 25 h.p. Complete with full equipment and in first class order	£125
MORRIS OXFORD 16 h.p. 1935 DE LUXE Model, in good mechanical order and clean condition. A very roomy five-seater with large luggage grid	£100

Showrooms :
49 JOHN BRIGHT STREET, BIRMINGHAM
opposite Alexandra Theatre. *Telephone : Mid. 4001-5*

Above right -
Authors first car (BNA 380)
Bought for £45 - in 1954
and same as the Morris Oxford
in the Advert of 1937.

Player's Please

MEDIUM or MILD

BOTH BLENDS ARE
CORK-TIPPED or PLAIN
10 for 6D 20 for 11½D

BSA Deluxe Saloon
£255 ex works (1934)

Advertisements from
'The Sign'
August 1930 Edition.

CHURCH TRAVELLERS' CLUB.

Chairman: LORD SAYE AND SELE.

OBER-AMMERGAU PASSION PLAY.

9 Days' Tour. OBER-AMMERGAU AND BRUGES OR HEYST, from **£10. 19s. 6d.** upwards.

Tours at varying rates including
COLOGNE, MUNICH, NUREMBERG, ROTHENBURG,
THE TYROL, THE BAVARIAN ALPS.

Special Illustrated Booklet.

Some specimen Tours.

Tour	£	s.	d.
INTERLAKEN (10 Days' Tour)	£8	5	6
MONTREUX—CLARENS (10 Days' Tour) ..	£7	16	0
LUCERNE (10 Days' Tour)	£7	15	0
NICE (10 Days' Tour)	£11	10	0
ROME (1 night Milan or Turin)	£15	15	0

GRAND CRUISE ROUND ITALY.

August 26th, September 9th and 23rd, October 7th, visiting Naples, Palermo, Taormina, Malta, Venice, etc. Inclusive costs, 19 days, 28 guineas and 35 guineas.

SUMMER HANDBOOK, 112 pages, Illustrated,
from SECRETARY,
(Dept. Y.), 3 ALBANY COURTYARD, PICCADILLY, LONDON, W.1.

SELFRIDGES

For All Postal Shopping

You may order any of these Bargains by post or telephone with perfect confidence. Satisfaction is assured or your money will be refunded without quibble. Post Orders are executed by specially trained assistants who are skilled in interpreting customers' requirements.

A REMARKABLE BOOK OFFER

HANDSOME BIBLES *in Coloured Bindings*

A very handsome BIBLE which is exclusive to Selfridge's Book Department. Bound in a very hard-wearing, new material that resembles the finest Morocco leather but will give almost better wear. In 8 colours, Violet, Purple, Maroon, Green, Blue, Scarlet, Brown or Black. Very light in weight, being printed on very thin paper, but the type is **clear and bold.** Full gilt edges, and bookmarker. 8 maps in Colour. A most remarkable offer at the price of **5/-** each

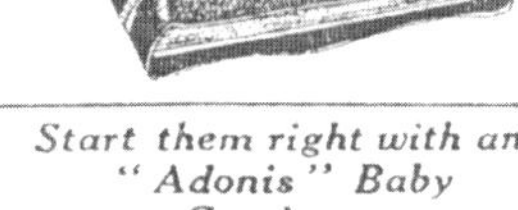

Postage 6d. extra.

Ground Floor, Aisle 8.

Orders 10/- and over, Post Free.

Start them right with an "Adonis" Baby Carriage.

A smart and roomy carriage measuring 33½" by 16" on bed level, generously upholstered with well padded seats, which are loose and easy to clean. The hood and storm aprons are of black leather duck having corner protectors, braid to front of hood and heavy quality black covered joints. Wheels are ball-bearing, tangent spoke, easy riding, well tempered springs, without straps. Body has lined safety strap and wheels fitted mudguards. Colours: Navy/Navy, Navy/Fawn. PRICE each **£8 8s.**

Or delivered after the first of 12 monthly payments of **14/8.** Carriage Paid in England and Wales.

Perambulator Dept.—Second Floor.

BEACH AND BATHING WEAR

TOWELLING BATHING CAPES

Wonderful offer for Women. These capes are absolutely indispensable for bathing. They comprise all colours and can be worn with any colour bathing costume. PRICE, each Post Free. **3/6**

Bargain Basement, Aisle 18B.

Wool Stockinette BATHING COSTUMES

Well cut and made to represent the popular TWO-PIECE STYLE, with light top and dark knickers. White belt at waist and available in Royal/Black, Green/Black, Red/Black, Orange/Black, also in Black or Navy. PRICE, each Post Free. **3/11**

Bargain Basement, Aisle 19B.

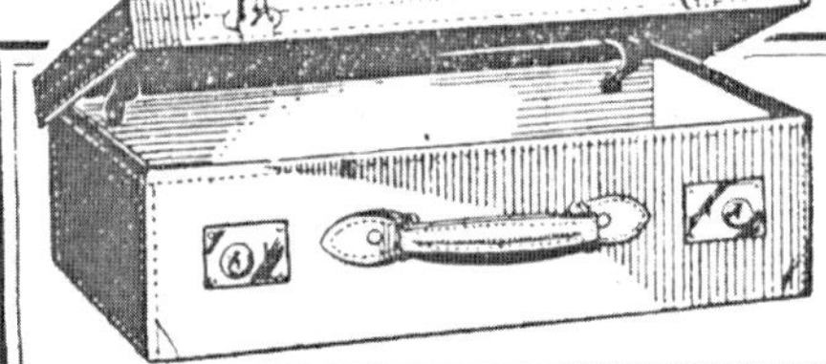

The "Traveller" Suitcase

will endure hard wear, though it is quite light to carry. Made of Cowhide on fibre foundation, steel frame, strongly sewn edges. Each fitted with two strong double action locks, and lined with a cotton material. Size, 24 × 13½ × 6 inches. Post Free. PRICE, each **25/-**

Trunk Department, First Floor.

COOKERY SERVICE
NOTES No. 66

JULY, 1945

THE GOSPEL
ACCORDING TO
ST. MARK

ACTIVE SERVICE EDITION

VICTORY IN EUROPE
CAKES AND ICINGS

R.B.1
16
MINISTRY OF FOOD
1953-1954
SERIAL NO.
BH 926640
RATION BOOK

A
Personal Message
from
General DWIGHT D. EISENHOWER
November 8, 1943

FIRST ARMY
THANKSGIVING SERVICE

for the Victory granted to

THE ALLIES
in
NORTH AFRICA

What the compass and instruments are to the aeroplane in flight, so the Bible is to us in our passage through life.

This Gospel will give you guidance and help for each day's journey.

When this Gospel has been read, you will find yet more help and guidance in the complete New Testament, a special copy of which is bound for the Royal Air Force, and your chaplain will tell you how to obtain a copy.

A MESSAGE FROM
HIS MAJESTY THE KING

"To all serving in my Forces by sea or land, or in the air, and indeed, to all my people engaged in the defence of the Realm, I commend the reading of this book. For centuries the Bible has been a wholesome and strengthening influence in our national life, and it behoves us in these momentous days to turn with renewed faith to this Divine source of comfort and inspiration."

September 15, 1939

'CHOCOHOLIC'
NOSTALGIA

(Courtesy of Cadbury's)

1922

Bournville biscuit
assortment

1 lb. Tin 3/-

1/2lb Fruit & Nut
Chocolate block 1/6.

Assorted chocolate
creams 2/6 per lb.

Vanilla chocolate
drops 2/6 per lb.

1926

Milk Tray and Bournville
chocolates 3/- per lb.

Milk chocolate covered
biscuits 2/6 per lb.
(In 4lb. Tins)

1929

Milk chocolate neapolitans
3/- per lb.

Brazil nut chocolate bar
2/6 per lb.

Milk Tray Turkish Delight
2/4 per lb.

Milk chocolate covered
almond whirls
3/4 per lb.

The Doddington Institute was for many years the focal point of community activities. The picture below shows it looking very sad and in an advanced state of dereliction prior to it's demolition. No trace of the Institute now remains on the site it formerly occupied.

Lower pictures show the power of steam, a cider mill at the Colliers Arms and threshing at Arthur Breakwells.

Coreley post office and stores (Goodman's) was for many years a well known local amenity which served the community.

DODDINGTON WEDDINGS

Copy of the certificate relating to the first marriage to be solemnised at St. John's, Doddington in 1849. From that date to the end of 1998 no less than 228 weddings have been conducted at Doddington.

Below left - Daniel Claverley and Margaret Morgan 1937.
Below right - Horace Key and Clarice Dolphin 1939.

1849. Marriage solemnized at the District Church in the parish of Cleobury Mortimer in the County of Salop.

No.	When Married.	Name and Surname.	Age.	Condition.	Rank or Profession.	Residence at the Time of Marriage.	Father's Name and Surname.	Rank or Profession of Father.
1	Nov. 22nd	Edward Morris	20.	Bachelor	Carter.	Cornbrook		
		Anna Maria Smith	19	Spinster		Doddington.	Silence Smith	Carter.

Married in the District Church of Doddington according to the Rites and Ceremonies of the Established Church, by .... or after banns by me, Henry Browne

This Marriage was solemnized between us, Edward Morris his mark, Anna Maria Smith her mark X, in the Presence of us, Lydia George (her mark) X, George Davison.

CERTIFIED to be a true copy of an entry in the certified copy of a register of Marriages in the Registration District of Cleobury Mortimer
Given at the GENERAL REGISTER OFFICE, under the Seal of the said Office, the 9th day of November 1998

MXA 368841

This certificate is issued in pursuance of section 65 of the Marriage Act 1949. Sub-section 3 of that section provides that any certified copy of an entry purporting to be sealed or stamped with the seal of the General Register Office shall be received as evidence of the marriage to which it relates without any further or other proof of the entry, and no certified copy purporting to have been given in the said Office shall be of any force or effect unless it is sealed or stamped as aforesaid.

CAUTION.—It is an offence to falsify a certificate or to make or knowingly use a false certificate or a copy of a false certificate intending it to be accepted as genuine to the prejudice of any person, or to possess a certificate knowing it to be false without lawful authority.

WARNING: THIS CERTIFICATE IS NOT EVIDENCE OF THE IDENTITY OF THE PERSON PRESENTING IT.

Form A513MX

Form MXA Dd 0080 100M 3/98 Mcr(203253)

GENERAL REGISTER OFFICE ENGLAND

Left-Cyril Key & Elizabeth Millman
1957.

Below-Tony Breeze & Eileen Bytheway
1967.

Bottom left-Philip Pearsall &
Sonia Webb - 1970.

Bottom Right-Timothy Evans &
Kerry Hall - 1998.
(The first wedding at Doddington
after an interval of eleven years).

Revd. Frank Peers with St. John's choir 1949.   The 'Local Lads' cricket team.

THE SECOND WORLD WAR - 1939/1945

No communities in our land were unaffected by the war. Whilst the rural communities of South Shropshire escaped the bombing that was endured by their neighbours in the industrial towns and cities of the West Midlands, daily life did change. There was rationing which had an effect on every man, woman and child. The population of the area grew dramatically with the influx of evacuee children who were moved from the bomb ravaged industrial areas to the comparative safety of the country. Many hundreds of military personnel had temporary homes in the area, particularly the RAF & WAAF personnel who manned the RAF Clee Hill radar station, and later in the war American army personnel who were gathered together in vast tented camps in readiness for the D Day invasion of the mainland of Europe. In addition to the groups already mentioned many young women of the Women's Land Army (WLA) came to live and work in South Shropshire. These ladies, most of whom had no knowledge of agriculture prior to joining the WLA, worked alongside the established labour force which had been depleted due to many young men being conscripted into the armed services. Many books have been written that go into great detail on various aspects of the war. I make mention of the war, purely as an introduction to the personal stories of some of the above groups of people. In the case of the former members of the WLA, and it's sister organisation `The Women's Timber Corps", I feel that the establishment has for many years failed to give them their deserved recognition. It gives me particular pleasure and satisfaction to be able to put a few of their stories into print.

RATIONING

Rationing was in force throughout the war, indeed it continued well beyond the war with some items remaining on ration until 1954.

The basic weekly ration mid-war per person was -

2 ounces tea.
2 ounces butter.
2 ounces margarine.
4 ounces bacon.
4 ounces Jam.
1 ounce powdered egg.
8 ounces sugar.
2 ounces lard.
12 ounces meat.
4 ounces cheese.
1 egg (sometimes).
3 ounces chocolate or sweets.
3 1/2 pints milk.

Tinned food was allocated on a points system, with each person having a given number of points. Families often combined points to buy luxuries (such as salmon) for weddings and other special occasions.
Clothes & textiles were rationed from June 1941, with adults receiving 66 points per year.
A mans cotton vest cost 2/3d (11p) plus 4 points. A nightdress cost 12/11d (65p) plus 6 points.
Fresh vegetables and offal were never rationed. It was reported at the time that the general health of the population (particularly in some of the poorer industrial areas) improved during rationing due to an improved diet with the increase in the use of vegetables.
During the period of food rationing the allowance of certain foods was increased in rural areas to permit the feeding of extra workers at hay making and harvest time.

Following Recipe taken from - 'We'll Eat Again', a collection of war years recipes selected by Marguerite Pattern. (Permission of Imperial War Museum).

FOOD FACTS

preparing for Christmas

Christmas begins in the kitchen and it isn't too soon to begin planning the best use of the Christmas rations now. So here are advance recipes for Christmas fare, all of them tested by practical cooks in the Ministry of Food kitchens.

CHRISTMAS PUDDING WITHOUT EGGS

Mix together 1 cup of flour, 1 cup of breadcrumbs, 1 cup of sugar, half a cup of suet, 1 cup of mixed dried fruit, and, if you like, 1 teaspoon of mixed sweet spice. Then add 1 cup of grated potato, 1 cup of grated raw carrot and finally 1 level teaspoon of bicarbonate of soda dissolved in 2 tablespoons hot milk. Mix all together (no further moisture is necessary) turn into a well-greased pudding basin. Boil or steam for 4 hours.

A GOOD DARK CHRISTMAS PUDDING

Cooking time: 4 hours then 2–3 hours *Quantity:* 6 helpings

2 oz plain flour
½ teaspoon baking powder
¼ teaspoon salt
½ teaspoon grated nutmeg
¼ teaspoon ground cinnamon
1 teaspoon mixed spice
3 oz sugar
½–1 lb mixed dried fruit
4 oz breadcrumbs
2–4 oz grated suet or melted fat
1 oz marmalade
2 eggs or 2 reconstituted dried eggs
¼ pint brandy, rum, ale, stout or milk

METHOD: Sift the flour, baking powder, salt and spices together. Add the sugar, fruit and breadcrumbs and suet or fat. Mix with the marmalade, eggs and brandy, rum or other liquid. Mix very thoroughly. Put in a greased 2 pint basin, cover with greased paper and steam for 4 hours. Remove the paper and cover with a fresh piece and a clean cloth. Store in a cool place. Steam for 2–3 hours before serving.
Note: If the smaller quantities of suet or fat and fruit are used, the pudding should not be made more than 10 days before it is to be used. With the larger quantities you can make it a month before it is to be used.

APPLE MINCEMEAT

Make mincemeat go further by blending it with grated or finely diced raw apples or with thick apple pulp.
If you have not been able to make, or obtain, mincemeat then flavour grated apple with plenty of spices and add a little mixed dried fruit or chopped cooked prunes or chopped raw dates. You then have a pleasant filling for the traditional Christmas tarts.

Those who lived through the trauma of the war, whether man, woman or child, would be hard pressed not to think of and make mention of Mr Churchill, later Sir Winston Churchill. A politician, who during the dark days of the early 1940's became our leader and inspiration. He put his party politics aside to lead a coalition government, perhaps the finest government that this land of ours has ever experienced. His leadership combined with his fine use of the English language guaranteed that his speeches would inspire our Nation and the free world. I quote a few passages from his speeches as a small tribute to a man that many consider the Greatest man of his time.

WINSTON LEONARD SPENCER CHURCHILL. NOVEMBER 1874-JANUARY 1965

Photographed on the occasion of his broadcast from Downing Street at 3.00P.M. on May 8th 1945. He concluded the broadcast with the words - "Advance Britannia, long live the cause of freedom, God save the King". Photograph courtesy Imperial War Museum

"We are fighting to save the whole world from the pestilence of Nazi tyranny and in defence of all that is most sacred to man".

"This wicked man, the repository and embodiment of many forms of soul-destroying hatred, this monstrous product of former wrongs and shame, has now resolved to try to break our famous Island race by a process of indiscriminate slaughter and destruction. What he has done is kindle a fire in British hearts, here and all over the world, which will glow long after all traces of the conflagration he has caused in London has been removed. He has lighted a fire which will burn with a steady and consuming flame until the last vestiges of Nazi tyranny have been burnt out of Europe, and until the Old World - and the New - can join hands to rebuild the temples of man's freedom and man's honour, upon foundations which will not soon or easily be overthrown".

"The battle of France is over, the Battle of Britain is about to begin. Upon this battle depends the survival of Christian civilisation, upon it depends our own British life and the long continuity of our constitutions and our Empire. The whole fury and might of the enemy must very soon be turned on us. Hitler knows that he will have to break us in this island, or lose the war. If we can stand up to him, Europe may be free, the life of the world may move forward in broad sunlit uplands, but if we fail; then the whole world, including the United States , all that we have known and care for, will sink into the abyss of a new dark age made more sinister and perhaps more protracted by the lights of perverted science.
Let us therefore brace ourselves to our duties and so bear ourselves that if the British Empire last for a thousand years, men will still say - this was their finest hour".

THE WOMEN'S LAND ARMY

During the war, farming was to change dramatically. From being a nation that imported much of its basic foods, it became necessary to produce enough to be more self sufficient. With a growing population of military personnel to feed, both at home and overseas, and with the added losses of merchant shipping to enemy U Boats at an alarming rate, the need for agricultural expansion became a matter of national survival. To help in this task the Women's Land Army was formed and was made up mostly of young women with little or no previous experience of the work that they would undertake. In spite of these handicaps, they worked along side the established labour force and earned respect by their efforts.

What follows are the experiences of a few former WLA members, but their stories reflect the dedication of the many.

NORA WALLS (NEE LEWIS), was a young nursery nurse, who in July 1944 joined the WLA at Shrewsbury, and remained as a member until September 1948.

She reported to the local HQ at Abbey Foregate to be kitted out. At that time the HQ was under the control of Lady Boyne

Next came a period of six weeks training on a dairy farm at Wentnor. During this time she learned to milk by hand, use a scythe and become familiar with some of the ways of a farm workers life. She particularly mentioned that this was a good farm, with good food and treatment.

After training she was posted to various farms, six in Shropshire and one in Wales.

"On some postings land girls seemed to be considered on a par with the beasts of the field. At one such posting my best friend was an Italian prisoner. I milked 20 cows morning and night, spent endless hours whitewashing cow sheds, plus time in the fields in all weathers. The compensation was Sunday tea with fruit and cream, all served on the best china".

"Next was a farm near Bridgnorth, a bad posting. Very hard work with poor food and a farmer who was a `pig'. Dinners mostly of bread, gravy and turnips. The other girl and myself applied for a transfer and on our last night at this farm we went to a local dance, when we returned to the farm the farmer wouldn't let us in. An adjoining farmer gave us a bed for the night and remarked that he was surprised that we had stuck it out so long".

"We were next posted to Mr Peake's at Stoke St. Milborough. A super farm where we were treated as family, as were the cowman and his wife. I was trained as a waggoner with Captain & Major, both shire horses, and Bessie, a Clydesdale as trace horse. I'm only five foot tall, so had to stand in the manger to put their collars on. I loved working with the gentle shires. I was also milking cows by machine and milking goats. It was hard work, but a great place and at times when Mr Peake booked for the family to go to the cinema, we all went. We also worked with sheep and whilst we were learning the ropes, were a source of amusement to the farmer. The Peake's sold up and moved to a farm on the Welsh coast near Aberystwyth and I went with them. I had some happy times at Pengarreg".

Nora was then posted to a farm near Oswestry, following that she had her final posting to Radbrook College.

"I spent over a year at the college doing back up work with the horse and in the dairy in support of the two teachers. The WLA then offered me a years scholarship at the college to study domestic science, dairy and poultry work; as far as I know I was the only land girl in the county to be offered such a chance, and I jumped at it".

Nora and her husband now live in `busy' retirement at Whitchurch.

LOIS BRISBOURNE (NEE HAZELDINE)

In 1942 the young Lois lived with her parents in her native town of Chester, aged 16 1/2 she longed to be in uniform serving her country. The Navy turned her down as maths were her weak subject. The ATS and WAAF's had vacancies for cooks, but she couldn't cook and she had no particular desire to be trained to do so. They also had vacancies for drivers, but she was too young to even be considered. Next door was the recruitment office for the WLA, where she was welcomed, given an immediate medical, accepted and informed that she would be called for service when she was seventeen.

"1941-1942 was a bad winter, I got my orders to report to Stockport Parks Department for training. I enjoyed the work and the company of the other girls. I eventually lodged at a house in the town and was put onto food production work. The regular staff played cards at lunch time, for money. Girls were barred from this gambling activity; just as well as our wage was £3.00 per week of which £2.00 was taken for board and lodgings".

"My next posting was to a market garden near Alsager, with accommodation provided in a hostel that catered for munition workers from Radway Green.. The food was terrible and I existed on a diet of fish &chips, obtained enroute whilst cycling the three miles from work to the hostel".

After another couple of postings, the war ended and Lois had her final posting to Cleobury Mortimer.

"My final posting was to an estate at Neen Savage belonging to the Tompkinson family. This was a good and interesting place. I was first billeted at a remote farmhouse (Cold Comfort farm!!!). I quickly moved to The Fox Inn, sadly no longer in business. As with my previous posting, I had access to horses. I had a great time with Moonrise who was well over 17 hands, in spite of being thrown on occasions, nothing got broken. I was eventually offered a permanent job at the farm, but with my father being ill and having a young man back home, I opted to leave the service and eventually married".

Lois goes on to write that she is grateful for the experience of the WLA, but wonders what happened to the `Benevolent Fund' of which she never saw any. I feel I must make a note of one of her quotes. "There was a small herd of forty cows and one bull, no test tube nonsense here: thank you!!!".

Lois now lives in Shrewsbury.

AUTHORS NOTE - During July of 1998 whilst working on the Second World War chapter of this book, I suffered a heart attack. The effect of the work was that it slowed to a "tick over" during my recovery period. One day during this period the doorbell rang and on going to the door, Mary was greeted by two ladies who said "If Eric lives here tell him two Land Girls have come to see him". These ladies introduced themselves as Sally and Muriel. They told me they had been close friends since their service in the Women's Land Army. Sally had a very outgoing personality and in spite of living for almost fifty years in Shropshire, her Liverpool origins were betrayed by her accent. The lively conversation of my visitors cheered me up and I persuaded Sally to write down a little of her wartime story. What follows is that story to which I have done a minimum of editing as it's original content is so human and warm!!.

"My name is Sarah Handley, known as Sally. A Liverpool lass by birth, a Salopian by adoption. At the start of the war I was first evacuated to Bangor in North Wales. I hated it and was so homesick that I was allowed to return home after a few weeks. Shortly afterwards I reached the age of fourteen and started work in a tobacco factory. My task was to strip the stems out of tobacco leaves. I became very popular with the boys, as when they asked what my job was, I told them I was a stripper. At eighteen I enlisted in the Women's Land Army and was duly kitted out with hat, overalls, breeches, wellingtons etc., and of course my treasured badge which I was advised to always wear. I was posted to Shifnal and lived in a hostel with other girls, it was great. Next day I was sent to work on a farm three miles away, no transport provided, so I had to walk both ways. I often returned to the hostel so tired that I fell asleep in a chair. I was eventually allotted a bicycle. I'd never had one before, so got a few bruises whilst learning to ride.

Winters on the farm were so cold, I got a bit of comfort from putting a hot water bottle down my breeches. On one occasion I didn't tighten the stopper enough, and as I cycled to the farm, the water trickled out. No one believed the bottle had leaked and I got dubbed with the nickname Sally Wet Legs. One weekend when I was due to go home for a break I was in a hurry to finish milking so that I could get away . We had some new heifers who had never been machine milked. One of them kicked out and caught me in the mouth causing me injury and the loss of a tooth. I went home looking like a prize fighter. I soon got the hang of controlling their kicking by pushing my shoulder into their hip. Living in the hostel with so many girls had a few disadvantages, some had the habit of `borrowing' anything that was left about. One girl in particular always used my toothpaste. On one occasion the Doctor gave me some cream to treat my cystitis. I left it on the shelf with my toiletries and after about a week my borrowing friend remarked that she didn't like the flavour of my new toothpaste. When I told her what she had been putting in her mouth, she almost threw up. She never borrowed again.

The hostel had a flat roof which in summer was a favourite spot for girls to sunbathe. During these brief spells we saw many curtains twitch in local houses, this movement was not a result of the breeze. I must relate an unfortunate incident involving Muriel. The farmer asked her to walk behind a machine to check that it was working. The farmer was on the tractor and she shouted to him that the machine was moving, but too late she realised it was a muck spreader. She was in such a state that we had to hose her down before she was allowed into the hostel. We regularly attended dances at a local hall, the cost was 1/= and music was provided by records. We got on well with the local lads, but some of the girls resented the attention they paid us. Some of the young men used to climb up the drain pipe at the hostel and try to peep in at the windows. This practice stopped when one of the girls poured a bucket of water over a would be Peeping Tom. I bet he had a job explaining to his mother how he came to be we through on a fine sunny evening.

I eventually married a local lad, he was a builder by trade and we built our first home together. I loved my years in the Land Army and have so many memories of those years which I shall forever cherish. Muriel and I have remained close friends and meet regularly".

GRACIE SKEVINGTON (NEE FARMER)

Gracie was born in 1918 at Knapp Farm, Neen Sollars. She enrolled in the WLA at the start of the war and was employed on the farm of Mr Wilfred Barrett at Reaside Manor, Cleobury Mortimer. In 1961 together with their three sons, Gracie and her husband Robert Ske79
vington emigrated to New Zealand to farm. Gracie died in 1991.The delightful picture of Gracie was taken in 1942 and was loaned by her sister, Jean Hollis of Knowbury.

Sheila Sally Muriel

THE WOMEN'S TIMBER CORPS.

Mrs. Mercy Vaughan, now living in Bridgnorth spent her early years with her family at their home in Wheathill. In 1940 Mercy together with several other young women was interviewed by Lady Boyne who was recruiting personnel for the Women's Timber Corps. This organisation was in parallel with the Women's Land Army. It's members being employed in forestry as opposed to agriculture. The work in both branches of the service was arduous and at times thankless.

Mercy passed the interview and was duly kitted out with her uniform, a uniform which varied slightly form that of the WLA. Timber Corps members wore a green beret and had a brass badge of crossed axes on the sleeve of their overcoat and a cotton badge of similar design on their jersey.

"I was put to work with several other girls at Nine Springs above Bitterley. We were picked up each morning in an old Ford lorry driven by Mr Arthur Whitefoot. Trees felled by the timber fellers were hauled out of the wooded area by two teams of horses. The teams were operated by Mr William Clent with his son John and Mr Tom Gatehouse assisted by his son Tom. Most of us girls were aged 19 - 25 and often thought that the lads (teenagers at that time) only came to work with their fathers in the hope of clicking with the girls. Some of the RAF men from Doddington were also frequent visitors. I quite liked a flight sergeant but found he was married. It was a happy time at Nine Springs with much singing and joking. At break times we went to the Dhustone Inn where Mrs Jenkins kindly made us tea and sandwiches. We adjusted to life in the woods, including the total absence of toilets. When nature called we selected a quiet area of trees, but as a precaution left a girl on lookout. When work at Nine Springs was completed, we split into groups and moved on. I was one of a group of six that went to Hereford and together with several WLA and WTC members lived in the Redhill Hostel. Shortly after this I passed my driving test and was allocated to an Austin Lorry. My first task of the day was to transport girls from the hostel to various work sites. My main task of the day was to transport pit props from various sites to the railway sidings for their forward transportation to the collieries.

The work of the WTC was hard, we chopped down trees, cut them to length and stacked them, plus numerous other tasks".

"At the appropriate season of the year, I would stop my lorry on the way back to the hostel and keep watch whilst some of my passengers scrumped apples and pears. It was in many ways a sad day in 1945 when I resigned from the service. I have some very happy memories of the times I had and the people I knew during those now long gone days of my wartime youth".

LEFT - Mercy Vaughan (Nee Green) pictured in 1942 wearing her WTC uniform.

BELOW - 'Winter Warmers',
Mercy and WTC colleagues in a 'risque' pose outside their hostel.

EVACUEE'S

During the war many thousands of school age children were evacuated from the densely populated and industrial areas of our land. The nightly bombing of these areas took a heavy toll on the residents and industry. South Shropshire became a sanctuary for many young evacuees, most of them from the Midlands and industrial Lancashire. I was not evacuated, but many of my friends were. To most it was a totally alien environment, but like children normally do, the majority adapted well to the country and it's ways. The following are the stories of a few of the evacuee's who had their first experiences of country life in South Shropshire.

Mr. T. Blackwell, now of Ramsgate was a child living in Birmingham during the war. His father was overseas in the army, so at weekends his mother and aunt's would travel with him to Clee Hill, to spend a couple of quiet day's away from the air raids.

"The Midland Red single deck buses on which we travelled to Clee Hill didn't seem very mechanically reliable, with most of them appearing to be overdue for replacement. The journey from Birmingham took about three hours and we often had to change at Kidderminster. Some of the buses were powered by gas which was contained in a huge tank on the roof. It was quite common to have to get off the bus near Far Forest and walk up a steep hill that the bus couldn't manage when full of passengers. I was told about the sheep on the hills and wanted to keep a lamb for myself. In the early 1940's we used to stay at a big house with the Jordan family, I think Mr. Jordan worked in the quarry and one of his daughters was named Violet. The house had no gas or electric, coming from a city house I found this exciting, particularly the oil lamps and going to bed by candlelight. We always seemed to have good meals, in spite of rationing. One of my favourite walks was to Coreley, over the common and Fairy Glen. I recall picking water cress from the stream and a small farm that had several Bantam fowl. A lot of houses had old hand operated water pumps outside and people didn't mind us helping ourselves to a drink. I remember vividly one beautiful summer day (I now know that this was the lead up to the Arnham airborne assault) standing watching waves of bombers with gliders in tow passing overhead. There was often a dance in the village hall on Saturday evenings. Music was provided by a small live band, but my main interest was a glass of pop and a packet of crisps. After Sunday dinner we had to walk to Ludlow to secure a place in the queue to get the bus back to home. We often had to wait for several hours, as so many people had come to the country to get a brief respite from the nightly bombing in the industrial areas. It was normal for extra buses to be used to get everyone home".

There is no doubt from his letter, that Mr. Blackwell has a deep affection for South Shropshire, the area that over fifty years ago offered him a brief respite from war and it's associated discomforts.

Howard Croston was one of the eight children of a Liverpool publican. The families' standing in the community meant that he enjoyed a reasonable high standard of living in the late 1930's. When the air raids started on Liverpool, Howard and his younger brother were evacuated to Chester. They didn't adapt well to the harsh discipline of the lady they were billeted with. They rebelled, and after an incident when a chamber pot was thrown down the stairs, they arrived back in Liverpool within hours. Some days later they were put on a train with other children and told to get off at a place called Highley, where they would be met and taken care of. Highley and other places along the Severn Valley were to become home to hundreds of evacuee's, as at that time the railway had direct links to the Midlands and North West. Young Howard and his kid brother were destined to spend the remainder of the war as reluctant country dwellers at Highley.

In later years, Howard started writing poetry for pleasure, the following are examples of some of his works which relate to his time as an evacuee in South Shropshire.

`EVACUEES' (1941 - 1945)

Being evacuated when you are eight years old,
Is not hard to comprehend,
Just rethink the memories,
From the beginning to end.

Two young lads from Liverpool,
Heading out of town,
Gas masks and a bar of chocolate,
Not knowing where your bound.

We ended up in `Highley',
A village near Bridgnorth,
To escape the German bombers,
And the Atrocities of war.

Not knowing our fate or destiny,
We had to stand our ground,
And wait until selected,
By a local female hand.

Her name was Mrs. Walker,
She said you call me Nan,
But this lady was no substitute,
For the person we called `Mam'.

Life was a game of survival,
Competing with the rest,
The local village children,
The countryside and all it's pests.

We didn't have many comforts,
Or solace when in pain,
Especially when potato picking,
In the `B!!!!!` rain.

We survived the mumps and whooping cough,
And goose grease on our chest,
But scabies between your fingers,
That really was the test.

A boil on the bum was something else,
That no one could explain,
And then a Kaolin poultice,
Just to relieve the pain.

When the war ended in 1945,
I can look back in retrospect now I'm 65,
We have lots of happy memories, my kid brother and me,
It wasn't all bad, being an evacuee.

`GOING TO CHURCH'

To go to church on Sunday,
Really was quite a treat,
With no jobs to be done,
Only hymns to be sung,
And the occasional treat or sweet,

I still have my presentation prayer book,
Awarded when I was eleven,
The message it told,
Was very bold,
Your reward will be in Heaven.

`QUIET MOMENTS'

The view from our bedroom window,
Was tranquil and serene,
The golden corn,
On a summer's morn,
And the changing patterns of green.

The Clee Hills in the distance,
They seemed so far away,
With your thought's of home,
You were never alone,
And the war would end one day.

COAL DELIVERY

Coal was delivered to the garden gate,
The work was then begun,
To get it to the cellar,
Took two little fellas,
More than an hour to shift a bloody ton,
You would carry each bucket, more than twenty yards,
Each step engrossed in pain,
No use complaining, even when raining,
For the next load would be the same.

Howard Croston has remained in contact with the granddaughter of his Highley `host' family. During his youth he made many return visits by either hitch hiking or cycling. He now retains his contact with occasional visits by car, and regular telephone conversations.

Norman Painting, although a few years younger then me, was also born in Small Heath. Our careers have followed similar courses. We both trained as apprentices with the former Morris Commercial Cars and remained with that company for the early years of our careers. In later years we both became historians and authors. Although Norman was evacuated to Bewdley, a few miles short of Shropshire, I decided to tell his story as it allows me to use the photograph of `Grandad Birch'.

"Dad decided to evacuate us to Bewdley in Worcestershire where he had spent part of his childhood, his parents at one time had kept The Angel Hotel. The local folk were reluctant to put up Birmingham people, especially a family with two boys aged six and two. After walking round the town all day, with me in a pushchair, accommodation was eventually found with the White family who lived in the old town hall building up Sandy Bank. This was a cobbled lane on a 1 in 5 incline, so I proved to be quite a burden in my pushchair during trips to the shops. My brother being of school age attended the little school close to the railway bridge on the Wribbenhall side of the river. Dad continued to work at Wimbush's bakery throughout the war. He travelled daily (six days a week) to and from work by Midland Red bus, a journey of over two hours per day. It was at Bewdley that my curiosity nearly cost my life. On the White's smallholding was an old bath tub of water for the pigs. One day I managed to hoist myself up to the rim and reached a point at which my bottom became heavier than my top, with the inevitable result that I plunged into the water, head first. Luckily I was spotted, lifted out and had the water unceremoniously beaten out of me. I developed pneumonia which caused the family concern for several weeks. I remember helping to feed the chickens which were kept in tent shaped netting runs that could be moved about. I used to go and watch Grandad Birch, a relative of the White family, he made all sorts of woven baskets in his workshop. He had a talking magpie in a cage on his wall, but I never once heard it utter a word".

"Following the war we had occasional family holidays at Bewdley. Sometimes spent in a B & B establishment on Severnside North. The owner of this establishment took pride in pointing out the tide marks on the walls, which indicated that the premises had on occasions been flooded to a depth of about four feet".

"On other occasions we stopped in a rented chalet on the opposite side of the river, by Northwood Halt. I recall that the chalet seemed to be riddled with spiders, and I lay in bed for hours (it seemed hours) watching them".

Authors note - Norman and his family lived close to the BSA armament factory (see elsewhere in the book), and I can well understand their need to get away from home to the relative safety of Bewdley.

Down in the country far away, Little evacuee.
My thoughts are with you every day,
Hope you still think of me:
Hope that you' re doing your best to please,
Hope you are not putting on airs,
Hope you remember to wash your knees,
Hope you still say your prayers;
Write to me soon, dear, don't forget,
I miss you, I confess,
Take good care of yourself, my pet,
Good-night dear, and God bless!.

AN ASPECT OF THE BLITZ ON THE CIVILIAN POPULATION - THE TRAUMA OF AIR WARFARE.

Whilst researching in the archives of the former BSA (Birmingham Small Arms Co.) during 1996; I came across a very poignant document, the content of which has since haunted me. It was a verbatim account by a BSA worker following the terrible night of 19th November 1940. As an historian I consider this document to be of tremendous importance because of the way it describes the suffering of the innocent in time of war. Although the BSA factory was a mere forty odd miles from Doddington, on the 19th November 1940 it could have been on a different planet. What follows is an edited extract from the above mentioned document. I make no mention of names that may serve to identify the original narrator, whom I have been assured died peacefully some years ago.

It is the night of 19th November 1940. The nightshift has commenced at the BSA munition works, men & women totalling over 1,000 are busy at the task of making Browning Colt machine guns for Spitfires, A vital part of the war effort.

Work swings along merrily, machines sing out their ceaseless tune, joined from time to time by strains of the latest dance tune from some budding crooner. All are intent on producing guns for the defence of our country. Whilst the machines continue working, I pause to look round. Some of my colleagues look happy, cracking jokes with their neighbours, others look troubled, some even sad, perhaps bad news received of some loved one, I will enquire later as the night is young, only 7-15p.m, all night to go. But listen, there goes the siren, the signal that Jerry planes are within striking distance.

Colleagues look at each other, some chaff, some sneer, others look troubled about it. Hundreds of workers immediately headed for the shelters, others like myself carry on working, it's the same siren we have heard on scores of other nights, perhaps they will be driven off before they reach us, perhaps this, perhaps that. There's work to do and money to be earned, so we carry on. Some workers shout remarks, one saying "Come early tonight to see us", another more serious says, "Looks like a bad night coming this early". We see a steady stream of workers heading towards shelters, with coats & gas masks in their hands. Some go slowly, others hurry as there are four flights of stone steps to descend before making the four minute journey to the outside shelters. We chaff some as they pass with such remarks as "Yellow", or "Mind you don't get hurt", but they pass into the night with one thought, personal safety.

After they have gone, we settle to work, but not for long, the danger signal sounds, the clock shows 7.30p.m. Enemy planes are overhead dropping incendiary bombs and flares around the factory, time for us all to make a dash for it. Some wait for nothing and dash for the stairs, I collect my coat and mask. All the lights have by now been switched off, so we must escape in total darkness. I find my flashlight, my companion during several raids, it's light is enough for me and my mate Charlie to safely get down the stairs. Charlie is a grand old warrior of 65 and can't see in the dark, so relies on me for guidance.

He was inwardly afraid of the raids, but showed pluck and fortitude. With a slight limp and snow white hair, he was affectionately known to us all as Old Charlie. We reached the foot of the stairs, but too late to go to the outside shelter for we could hear the planes circling overhead and the thud of anti-aircraft guns. We go into the basement, a place we have often sheltered in. A very long building that ran the length of four workshop floors above, each of which contained hundreds of tons of machinery. Round the basement and down the sides of gangways, wooden forms had been placed for us to sit on. The hurricane lamps gave out a glimmer of light, just enough to let us get seated without knocking too much skin off our shins. Strange, everyone seemed to go to the same seat on every raid night, same faces in the same places. There was a strange hush in the semi-darkness, we all talk about a long or short raid tonight. We hear thuds from outside, is it bombs or guns?. Women can be heard to say that they hope their children will be all right, the men hope their wives and families will be safe and sound. Some laugh, some talk, some are quiet, having a hunch that anything can happen on such a night as this. Some eat, some sing as an accordion starts to play.

I sit and talk to old Charlie and the man next to me on our seat, over and above everything, there is a strange tone that you can almost feel. Someone calls out to ask the time, he is told it's five minutes to eight. Some settle down to sleep, others sit and think, old Charlie does that. I settle on the form and listen to the accordion, guns are still going, planes still rumbling overhead. Then comes a dull thud, bright lights stab the darkness for a second, then a rumbling noise, as though the whole building is being crushed in a pair of huge pincers. The one thing I had always said would never happen, had happened, a bomb hit the outside wall and the whole building had collapsed like a pack of cards. Hundreds of tons of machinery and brickwork had descended on us. What happened next I hardly know, for I must have been knocked out by a blow on the head. How long I was unconscious I do not know, perhaps not long, I came round to find that my two companions had been killed and crushed beside me. I took stock of myself, and was surprised to find I had nothing broke, but one foot was held fast by something. I began to wonder if it was crushed and made frantic efforts to get it free, it must have taken best part of an hour to do so, for I was hemmed in on all sides and above by a solid wall and roof of machinery, concrete and brickwork that had come from floors and roof above. Having got my foot free and finding it only a little strained, I wriggled and twisted to a small space on the floor that looked similar to a fireplace and about as large. How this small space came to be left clear near me, must have been the hand of providence. Men and women were shouting out in agony for help, I started to shout by loudest with them. I now noticed that a curved girder had come down and crushed my two companions, but the curve is just clear of me, and held up the debris from crushing me, what an escape, but escape from what I wonder, for I'm in a living tomb. Fear takes hold of me and I join in the shouting again with the poor wounded and dying, but little did we realise the depth of the ruins above us. No one on the outside could hear our cries. I then noticed that a fire had started near my feet and was starting to burn fiercely. This increased my fright and fear. No escape now I thought, while the cries of the injured and dying were all round me. Some were offering up prayers for their wives and children in the future, for they knew they would never see the outside world again, neither did I expect to at that time. I still shouted, louder and louder, but got no reply. I lay watching the fire wondering how long it would be before everything around me that would burn would be alight. How long?. I noticed that a machine that had crashed down was stood up on end, forming a small arch under which I wriggled and twisted, so that I felt safe from anything that may slip and fall from above me. But that fire, I see now that it is burning the form I had sat on, and that my two companions were starting to burn. The sight sickened me and caused me to increase my frantic shouts for help, by now there were few shouts from the others. Dead by now I thought, how long shall I last?. The smoke begins to get down my throat. Then I feel a trickle of water coming from above, I realise they are trying to put out the fires above us. What shall I do?. I think of my wife, and wonder what she well do when they tell her I am gone?.

I now offer up prayers as hard as I can pray for my wife and myself. My boot now catches fire for I can't get my legs back far enough from the fire, but by scraping bits of ruin round me, I get it away from the fire and put it out. What's the use I ask shall I bang my head on something and let the fire see me off, at least I shall not feel it then. Other parts of my clothes catch fire, and I become frantic in my efforts to put them out, for I have no room to turn about. Then I decide I must keep calm and use my head, for I notice the smoke from the fire is commencing to blow away from me and the air gets a bit clearer, so I think if I can keep under the machine, the fire will keep burning away from me. This calms me a bit and I decide to have a smoke if I can. I still have my pipe and after a lot of twisting I get my tobacco and matches from my pocket. The tobacco is fairly dry, although by now I'm soaked through by the water from above. I fill my pipe, but my matches are damp, so I have to hold two by a hot cinder until they flicker up and I manage to light my pipe. Ah, that was better, one bit of comfort.

Water is now beginning to collect on the floor on which I am half sitting, half lying. I pulled two pieces of flat concrete towards me and wriggled then underneath to sit on although water was running out of my trousers. I now see my two companions burning up and the form we were on has become dust, poor chaps, but they could not feel it, thank God.

I now became conscious of a voice talking to me, although I could see no one, I felt the presence of my Dad around me. My Dad who had passed from this earth some months earlier. Something seemed to comfort me in a way I can't describe, but his presence was there. Although never a believer in spiritualism, I would have believed anything just then. I began to believe I would be saved, although how, I could not see. I again began to shout, help, help, but no response. I realised I must lie there and wait, but for how long?. Could I keep my senses until someone got to me, yes!, I made up my mind I would. So I reclined there, thinking of hundreds of things. Mostly my wife and home. The unseen voice was still near me, and I felt I had company. The silence was terrifying, but my main concern was the fire. It seemed I had been down there for hours, so I resumed shouting, anything to break the awful silence, but I got no response. I say my prayers again. At this time I can't keep a limb still, shivering from cold and wet, although I can feel heat from the fire on one side. Time drags, so I start shouting again. After a while I fancy I can hear an answer to my cries. I become frantic and shout louder. I listen and faintly hear an answer, but it sounds miles away. After a while I hear a voice asking where I was before the collapse. I shout out my position, they shout back telling me to hang on and keep up. My prayers are answered, I'm in touch with the outside. I hear rumbling above and realise they are moving wreckage to get to me, I wait, it seems hours. Why don't they hurry?. I didn't know until afterwards how much debris had to be moved. I was excited and kept shouting and could hear them shouting down a small hole, almost over me. They ask if I'm injured or crushed, I tell them I'm all right except for the fire. They say that's the first they know about the fire. They burn away metal and machinery until they see the light from my torch. After a while they get a large hole over me and ask if I can get up to it, I tell them I can't stand, I'm pinned in. They burn more metal away and drop me a rope, I hold on to it and am pulled up and up, until my head is through the hole. They grab my arms and I'm dragged through the hole to freedom.

Never did freedom and safety seem so sweet as at that moment. They patted my back and congratulated me on my escape. I shook their hands and found myself crying with joy and felt my rescuers were also crying. They had won a victory over death, I thank them with all my heart. Planes are still overhead, and bombs continue to drop as I'm placed on a stretcher and carried to a dressing station. I was in a bad state, shaking from shock and exposure. The doctor and nurses ripped my remaining rags off, give me a hot drink and rub life into me with hot towels. I ask the time and am told it's quarter to six, I had been down there for nine hours. Seemed more like ninety nine to me. The doctor says I'm to be taken to hospital, but I have enough life in me to tell him there was no hospital or nurse could look after me better than my wife. I was going home. We heard the All Clear going and we all breathed a sigh of relief, they could now look for other survivors. Would they find any? I thought doubtful. Then they bring in another man, the poor devil is out of his mind, I'm later told he had to go into a mental home. Finally I'm put into an ambulance, for my back had been hit and I couldn't walk. We reached my home and the ambulance man informed me that my house had been bombed. In spite of my injury, I got from the ambulance and saw the broken door and windows of my home. I got inside and called for my wife, my fear increased when I got no reply. She had been taken next door, and hearing my cries ran to me. We clung tightly to each other, we had both been through and endured a terrible night. Two souls with a single thought, thank God your are safe. The fire was lit, she attended to my cuts and dressed me, quite forgetting her own ordeal. What a nurse, what a spirit, a true Britain with true English pluck. I thank her for all she did for me. We sat and told each other of our experiences of the night, we thanked God for sparing us to each other. So ended a night we shall never forget. To anyone who reads this little story, I would say "Never Give Up Hope, You Die With Despair". What of my fellow workers?. Of the eighty three who were sheltering in that basement, eighty one passed out of this world. Poor Souls. What saved me? Perhaps my prayers, perhaps that spirit around me. Here I am, although carrying on with a crippled spine and one eye, often thinking of the night which has given me the nickname, among all who know about it of - "THE LUCKIEST MAN IN BIRMINGHAM".

AUTHORS NOTE: I have several extracts from a book entitled 'The Other Battle'.

It tells the story of the BSA war effort.

The extracts can be looked at on request.

THE NATURAL HISTORY OF TITTERSTONE CLEE

If one stands on the Hoar Edge and looks across the summit of Titterstone, one can still see the scars of long abandoned quarries, and also how nature has regenerated a landscape that was once alive with men, machinery, noise and dust. It is now quiet and peaceful, with only the 'mew' of a buzzard or the 'baa' of a sheep disturbing the tranquillity. Stonecrops and Wall peppers now grow where stone was once blasted from the cliff face and the many ledges form nesting places for ravens and falcons. The entrance to mining tunnels are hidden by brambles, which in their season yield food for insects, birds and small mammals. Bracken abounds, the fern which is responsible for the glorious changing colours of the hill, from the bright new green of springtime to the darker emerald of summer, through the yellow and reds of autumn, to the brown covering of winter. Among the scattered dhustones grow other ferns, including the rare oak fern, and in grassier places, the little known Adder's Tongue.

There are many habitats for wildlife on the hill, which explains the large variety of species to be found. Perhaps the most obvious is the moorland, where in summer the carpet of heather looks and smells wonderful. Other little plants bloom unnoticed under the bushes, flowers such as tormentil, cinquefoil, lousewort and heath spotted orchid. In some years, thousands of ladybirds are found, on occasions one will see a slow worm or lizard taking the sun on a rock. One can see many birds, (often rare in other areas) such as the meadow pipit, yellow hammer, wheatear and snipe. Skylarks still sing above the moors, but their numbers have declined over the past few years. In spring and autumn, many parts of Titterstone are ablaze with yellow European gorse and observant folk may spot a stonechat atop the highest branch, or hear the 'tsak, tsak' of it's warning call. Buzzards can often be seen soaring overhead, sometimes eight or nine together, searching with their marvellously keen eyesight for an unwary rabbit, or voles and mice as they move in the undergrowth. Rabbits keep the high growing grasses in check, giving space for other species of plants to bloom. Little easily missed flowers such as the yellow forgetmenot, wild thyme, speedwells and bedstraws. In the wet flushes there are exciting flowers like bog aspodel, bogbean, ivy leafed bellflower, lesser skullcap and insect eating butterwort and sundew. In the ponds are water crowfoot, pondweeds, bur-reeds, water milfoil and others. Plants and animals are inextricably intertwined in the web of life. Remove one species and the web collapses. For example, dragon flies with their wonderful flight patterns and glowing colours will only be seen where there are insects for them to catch in their leg baskets, and where there are tadpoles etc., for their ugly underwater larvae to feed on. If the pond is drained, a whole 'world' is destroyed. Similarly, butterflies are only found where suitable food plants for their caterpillars exist. One can sometimes see meadow browns (grasses), orangetips (crucifers), holly blues (holly & ivy),painted ladies (thistles), red admirals and tortoiseshells (nettles), but they are becoming rarer as their food plants disappear under cultivation and modern intensive farming. As well as the loss of traditional food plants, butterflies are under threat from insecticides meant for garden and agricultural pests.

For those who can walk quietly, early or late, there are foxes, badgers, squirrels in the wooded areas, and if you are very lucky, dormice. You may hear the yaffle of a great green woodpecker, or see the flash of red, white and black, which is the great spotted of the family. Tawny owls can be glimpsed winging over hedges of sitting in a tree at dusk. The barn owl is now rarely seen, it's decline can be partly blamed on the conversion of barns to dwellings for humans, in effect robbing it of it's traditional nesting places.

Whilst considering the wildlife of the area, we need to take account of the many streams, so easily polluted by thoughtless and reckless human behaviour. The Cornbrook, Colleybrook and Benson's Brook, all used to contain a wealth of species, such as mayfly, stonefly, and caddisfly larvae, which provide food for dippers, trout and many other species. Sadly in recent years, effluents such as quarry waste, slurry overflows, pesticides and overuse of fertilisers, have wiped them out, and with them the dippers etc. They will hopefully return at some time in the not too distant future. A similar fate has befallen many of the hay meadow, where glorious arrays of wildflowers once abounded. Traditional summer meadow flowers such as green winged orchids, devil's bit, moon daisies, cowslips, ladies smock etc., with their attendant butterflies, birds and insects that fed on them. The meadow habitat of the above has been devastated by rural development, altering of water courses and changes in agricultural practices, such as the alteration from hay to silage production.

Titterstone Clee is still a splendid place for wild life. As we come to a new Millennium with it's challenges, let us resolve to endeavour to preserve the unique environment in which we are privileged to live, so that it may be enjoyed and hopefully appreciated by future generations.

Patricia H. Waite

There is a spot, 'mid barren hills,
Where winter hours and driving rain;
But, if the dreary tempest chills,
There is light that warms again.

The mute bird sitting on the stone,
The dark moss dripping from the wall,
The thorn-trees gaunt, the walls o'ergrown,
I love them - how I love them all.

Emily Bronte.

SCHOOL

For several generations many Doddington children had their first experience of formal education as pupils at Hopton Wafers Church of England School. Many changes have taken place at the school in recent years, however when viewed from a distance many of the buildings must still appear as they did to pupils of yesteryear. In spite of outward appearances the interior of the older buildings have changed dramatically and are now in keeping with the concept of a modern teaching environment. When one sees the present volume of traffic on Hopton Bank and reads almost daily of the actions of evil people, it is very difficult to imagine that not so many years ago, the children of Doddington walked to and from school in total safety. The prospect of any child now having to walk this route is frightening. Older members of the community speak with great affection, not only of Hopton Wafers school, but of the staff who taught them and helped to shape their lives during their early years.

What follows are the recollections of a few of those former pupils, together with some of their treasured pictures.

SAM GUMBLEY spoke of his happy school days at Hopton and of his harmless boyhood pranks. One of those pranks involved the local road lengthsman, Chris Cole. Chris was responsible for the upkeep of the verge, ditches etc., along the A4117 from Clee Hill common to Hollywaste, the main tools of his trade being a wheel barrow, bill hook, broom and assorted shovels; plus a pair of red flags to warn traffic of his whereabouts as he worked. It was customary for Chris to poke his flags into the hedge a hundred yards or so each side of where he was currently working. It was the custom of young Sam, and no doubt others of his age to move the flags if they had to pass them during their walk to or from school. It was quite a harmless prank at that time due to the low volume of traffic.

EILEEN BREEZE (Nee Bytheway) was a pupil at Hopton Wafers School during the early 1950's. Eileen has written the following very vivid and human account of those days. Her account is printed in it's entirety with no editing. It's content can't fail to evoke memories for many of us, irrespective of where we attended school.

"I walked a mile to Hopton Bank before catching a bus with my class mates which took us to school.

There were 3 classes, Junior, Infants & the third class which was used solely for dinners which all the children took for just a few pence.

In each class was an open fire which in the winter burned brightly, stoked by the 2 teachers & surrounded by heavy cast iron fire guards. Today modern storage heaters take their place and turned on by a flick of a switch.

Each child had a wooden desk with a lid, where we kept our books, any undesirables, & the odd piece of chewing gum stuck to the lid for later. On top were the ink wells, wooden handled ink pens with replaceable nibs & of course the inevitable blotting paper. On the back of every exercise book were the multiplication tables which we had to learn parrot fashion. I still remember the daily chant.

There we sat while the teacher chuntered on until break when we would get our third of a pint of milk with a straw. Today the classes are open plan with tables & children are able to move around freely (within reason).

The teachers were strict & the ruler available for misbehaviour. I remember being on the receiving end of this once, but do not recall for what reason.

There were large blackboards on one wall & the chalk screeched across the surface. Today they still have blackboards, but much more scaled down.

"Go and wash your hands for dinner" the teacher says today & off they trot to the modern toilet block with hot & cold water, but where did WE go. We took our little metal bowls with the wooden handles outside to the pump under the window. There the handle was pumped furiously for the water to fall into the stone sink below. You had to be quick, because when the handle stopped being pumped the water stopped. Often in the winter it froze.

"Please may I go to the toilet" they ask today & off they trot to the toilet block with flushing toilets, but where did WE go, you've guessed it, outside & up to the top of the playground to the toilet sheds with the earth toilets. The boys had an outdoor walled round urinal. Pretty cold in winter I might add when the snow drifts crept in under the doors. Needless to say a trip to the toilet took a very short time.

The playground was divided into two by a stone wall which sprouted strange little clover like plants which we picked as part of a game. Boys played on one side and girls on the other.

The wall is now demolished and is now one big playground.

We had gardens round the school, where quite often the children went outside to do a spot of gardening. Today the gardens have gone to be replaced by tarmac & now part of the playground.

We often went for nature walks up Stockhall Lane & Ditton Lane & picked primroses and bluebells.

We used the old village hall for our nativity plays & odd dramas. One of the teachers being very keen on dancing. We would cover half a playing hoop with crepe flowers & paper and incorporate the hoops into the dance. I remember the tune vividly .

When we became 11, we took what was then the 11 plus exam to ascertain which school we would transfer to. Those that passed went to the grammar and high schools at Ludlow and us other little dears would go to Lacon Childe at Cleobury Mortimer. We no longer have this exam and all children transfer to Lacon Childe.

I am now in my 50's & have worked at the school for the past 27 years doing clerical duties. I have seen my own children pass through the school & now my grandchildren.

The school is now all modern with computers being common place. A new demountable being erected in 1997 for extra space.

Yes I have happy memories & to me yes those were the days"

JANE MEREDITH (Nee Williams) arrived at Hopton Wafers as a young woman of twenty years old to become a teacher at the village school. She remained at the school for several years, leaving in 1931 to get married. In 1992 she wrote the following for the publication, 'Shropshire Within Living Memory'.

"At the age of 20 I took up a teaching post at Hopton Wafers. Then I really knew what it was like to live in the country. There was very little transport and of course no school buses. A bus ran to Ludlow once a week and one to Cleobury Mortimer. When I went to Hopton I went by train to Ludlow, caught a bus to Clee Hill and was met by the vicar's son with a pony and trap.

Lodgings had been arranged for me at a farmhouse which to me seemed so cold and bare after living at home in a small town house in Shrewsbury. When I was shown the lavatory I had my first surprise. It was the little house at the end of the garden and on entering, there it was in all it's glory, a three seater. One of the spaces was smaller, which I presumed was for a child. I thought it must have been built for Father, Mother and Baby Bear. I never tarried there in case someone decided to join me.

The children walked a long way to school with no school dinners or milk. Sometimes they were caught in storms and arrived in very wet clothes. We had large fires in the classroom so the coats were draped around them but it was a very steamy atmosphere. If there came a sudden fall of snow the fathers would come to school to take them home, often having to carry the little ones.

We had some bad winters when the water in the jugs in the bedroom would freeze. No electric blanket, not even a hot water bottle so when undressed I would get into bed and put my feet in my fleecy lined knickers - so much for hygiene!

The children seemed to get on well at school. One or two managed to pass the exam for the grammar school but most of the left school at the age of 14, the boys to work on farms and the girls having to move further afield to find domestic work in the town houses where they 'lived in' and did not get home very often. Whist drives and dances were held in the village hall and if there was one at another village several of us would walk there together.

There was a good attendance at church, I think people looked forward to meeting friends there after the service. It was a place to hear and pass on any news. It was at Hopton Wafers that I heard my first Wireless. The vicar's son made a crystal set, we wore head phones and by moving the small wire (known as a cats whisker) we could faintly hear music or someone reading the news, but not very clearly.

I met my husband to be at the village hall and in 1931 gave up my job at Hopton Wafers to get married. We married at the Abbey Church Shrewsbury, and I recall we had to pay an extra half crown to have the Great West Door opened at the ceremony".

To me, fair friend, you can never be old,
For as you were when first your eye I ey'd
Such seems your beauty still.

Sonnet, 104.
William Shakespeare.

Programme.

HOPTON WAFERS C. of E. SCHOOL

PRESENTS

"THE WHISPERING WOOD"

by *Rodney Bennett*

Music by *Martin Shaw.*

IN THE VICTORY ROOM

HOPTON WAFERS

— ON —

FRIDAY & SATURDAY,

28th & 29th APRIL, 1950

at 7 p.m.

ADMISSION 2/- 1/6 & 1/-

PROCEEDS FOR CHURCH AND SCHOOL FUNDS.

3d.

WHISPERING WOOD

CHARACTERS.

Snow White	RUBY JACKS.
Queen...	SHIRLEY WOODHOUSE.
Spirit of the Wood ...	MARGARET MACKEMSLEY.
Light	HILDA RYDER.
First Flower	SHEILA BARKER.
Prince...	JEAN CROWTHER.
Puck	EILEEN MACKEMSLEY.
Unus	JOHN HALL
Secundus	RAYMOND HARRINGTON.
Tertius	DAVID EVANS.
Quartus	JOHN CLEETON.
Quintus	BRYAN CHINN.
Sextus...	DEREK TURNER
Septimus	DOUGLAS HALL.

Flowers :—	Sally Evans,	Dilys Wiseman,
	Eileen Chinn,	Sandra Hall,
	Glen Wiseman,	Frances Breakwell.
Butterflies :—	Janet Ryder,	Angela Pendrous,
	Eileen Link,	Margaret Day,
	Julia Pain,	Beryl Woodhouse.
Puck's Men :—	Desmond Key,	Reuben Evans,
	John Pain,	Barry Harrington,
	John Evans,	Colin Dolphin.

Top picture 1919 - lower picture 1923

The following poem, WHAT IS A SENIOR CITIZEN?, is reproduced by kind permission of 'Rock Cottage Crafts', Nantwich, Cheshire.

It shows how things used to be. To those of similar 'mature years' to the author, and with memories that have not become fogged by the years, it is pure nostalgia.

WHAT IS A SENIOR CITIZEN?

A Senior Citizen
is one who was here before;
the pill, television, frozen food,
contact lenses, credit cards.....
and before man walked on the moon.

For us "Time Sharing" meant
togetherness, not holiday homes,
and a "chip" meant a piece of wood.
"Hardware" meant nuts and bolts,
and "Software" wasn't even a word.

We got married first, then lived together,
and thought cleavage was something
butchers did.
A "Stud" was something that fastened a
collar to a shirt, and "going all the way"
meant staying on a double decker
to the bus depot.

We thought "fast food" was what you ate
in Lent; a "Big Mac" was an oversized
raincoat and "crumpet" we had for tea.
In our day "grass" was mown,
"pot" was something you cooked in,
"coke" was kept in the coal house and
a "joint" was cooked on Sundays.

We are today's Senior Citizens.
A hard bunch when you think
how the world has changed!

ST. JOHN'S PCC MEMBERS AND VISITORS ENJOYING THE 1998 CHRISTMAS FAYRE

ON TOP OF THE CLEE

When ever I want to feel free,
I take a walk on top of the Clee
Where the view is SO WIDE
`As far as the eye can see'.

The fields and the mountain ranges
The blue sky and the clouds above
Which forever changes
The colour and the pattern
Of the landscape I love

The patchwork fields in the valley below,
Where here and there little cottages grow,
Like mushrooms out of the ground
Where many streams can be found
Running like a silver band
Down the hillside onto the land
To make it so beautiful and green
To feed the cattle which can be seen.

All this beautiful view is FREE !!!
for those who walk on top of the Clee.

ON Top of The Clee is the third poem in this book to be dedicated to Titterstone Clee Hill. Each in their own way demonstrates the hypnotic effect of Titterstone Clee on the writers.

This final poem of the three was written by Erika Rollinson,
German by birth,
British by marriage,
Salopian by choice.

ornbrook Bridge, Clee Hill near Ludlow.

ACKNOWLEDGEMENTS

I'm indebted to the companies, organisations and numerous private individuals, who in response to my pleas/requests for assistance have responded so positively. It is their response with data, stories and pictures, coupled with their kind permission to use that material, which has been a major factor in the compilation of this Millennium souvenir book. I offer my most sincere thanks to each and every one of them. I have attempted to make mention of them all by name. If I have omitted any from the following list, it is as a result of human failing (possibly coupled with my age), for which I offer my humble apologies.

Extracts from 'We'll Eat Again' and Winston Churchill picture courtesy of The Imperial War Museum.

Extracts from 'A History of Shropshire' by Barrie S. Trinder (1998 revised edition) courtesy of Phillimores & Co Ltd., (Publishers), Shopwyke Manor Barn, Chichester, West Sussex.

'Rock' by Robert D. Thompson, published by Kenneth Tompkinson Ltd., Kidderminster.
'Shropshire within Living Memory', published by Countryside Books, Newbury.
Eileen Breeze, M. A. (Mac) Harrington, Dunlop Tyres, AGCO Ltd., Norman Painting, Alan Webb, Sam Gumbley, Nora Walls, T. Blackwell, Howard Croston, Mrs Anne Woodward, Mr Christopher Woodward, Mrs Lois Brisbourne, Royal Air Force Shawbury, Sheila Goode, May Jordon, David Jones (Aerial photography), Mr A.G. Cave (BSA archives), The National Library Of Wales, Sarah (Sally) Handley, Desmond Key, This England, ARC (Clee Hill Quarry), Mercy Vaughan, Jean Hollis, Sheila Gabb, Jean Gittens, Kay Grainger, Pat Waite, Jean Meredith, Jessie & Chester Davison (USA), Rock Cottage Crafts (Nantwich), Rt. Revd. Dr. John Saxbee. Ken & Stella Butcher, Erika Rollinson, Linda Clayton, Sonia Pearsall, Doug Hall, Kerry Evans, Revd Mark Burgess, Dennis Crowther, 'Jock' MacPherson, Norman Goodman, Sheila Barker, Jim Tennant, Bruce Astbury, Peter Bartlett (Photographer), 'Dot' Shorthouse, The British Commonwealth War Graves Commission, Ford Motor Company.

Mr Geoffrey Heath of 'Box Of Tricks' for his graphic work on the front cover and family tree pages, Cadbury Schweppes, Ted Edwards, Crid Webb, Alf Jenkins.

I must make special mention of three ladies who have given me valuable support and assistance in bringing this project to fruition.

Mrs Joan White for going into the 'field' (between showers) to obtain specific photographs for inclusion in this book.

Mrs Dorothy Aston who has laboured long and hard over her computer to give a 'professional' appearance to my original manuscript and layout sketches.

My dear wife Mary, who has given me support and encouragement throughout the duration of this very worthwhile enterprise. In addition to her normal support (which includes tea making and proof reading), she spent several months nursing me back to health when illness threatened to terminate the entire project.

To all who contributed in any way, I offer my
sincere, heartfelt and unreserved thanks.

THANK YOU

The objective of the Doddington Millennium Project was to secure and preserve interesting and entertaining data (both local and national) for posterity.

Much of what has been gathered is now contained in the Doddington Community Scrapbook, which during the project has expanded into a second volume. In parallel with the Scrapbook, this Millennium Souvenir Book has been produced. I sincerely hope that this book will etch the name of our small rural community in the pages of our nations history.

The entire project has benefited by financial sponsorship with a substantial Millennium Grant from the Help The Aged Millennium Award Scheme. This grant, together with the financial support of the following persons who have made advance subscriptions for this book, have made it's publication possible.

Eileen & Tony Breeze - Hopton Bank
Terry & Dorothy Edwards - Kimbolton
Sylvia & Robert Sutton - Hopton Bank
Mr & Mrs Michael Middleton - Yardley
Bruce & Margaret Astbury - Hollywaste
Brian & Owen Bytheway - South Africa
Margaret Whitehouse - Staunton On Wye
Derek & Peggy Bytheway - Hopton Wafers
Shirley & Chris Elliott - Balsall Common
Ronald Frederick Perry - Newport Pagnell
Mrs A Woodward - Hopton Court - 3 copies
Avondale Park Homes - Atherstone - 2 copies
Elaine Ball - Copper Kettle Tea Rooms - Ludlow
Michael & Barbara Harrison - Weston Super Mare
Annie Pearsall & Andy MacKellar - Kidderminster
Shropshire County Libraries - Shrewsbury - 6 copies
Worcestershire County Libraries - Worcester - 2 copies
Howard Croston - Liverpool - dedicated to all former evacuees.
Nora M Walls - Whitchurch and Lois Brisbourne - Shrewsbury
Both former members of The Women's Land Army

Kate & Sarah Lovedee - Thurlaston
Mary Watkins - Newport
Muriel Ferriday - Priorslee
Dawn Hawker - Crackley Bank
Sophie & Luke Ryder - Priorslee
Sally Handley - Snedshill
Carol Handley - Snedshill
Antony Handley - Snedshill

The above eight books have been purchased and dedicated by Sally and Muriel, both former members of The Women's Land Army
Mercy Vaughan - Bridgnorth - former member of The Women's Timber Corps.

STATISTICS ARE LIKE A BIKINI,
THINGS THEY REVEAL ARE PROVOCATIVE,
THINGS THEY CONCEAL ARE VITAL.

Clifford Smout - Upper Hayton
Mark Williams - Telford
Joyce & Roy Holmes - Hall Green
Stuart Murray - Kings Norton
John Cleverley - Northfield
Geraldine Brown - Mirfield, Yorks.
Bruce Waite - Knowbury
Mr Percy Folkes - Bromyard
Vera Heard - Shenstone
Jaquie Newby - Kelso
Howard Astbury - Devon
Revd. Ian Williams - Lichfield
Hollie Isley - Coreley
Mr & Mrs Ted Edwards - Coreley
Naomi S J Vail - Hopton Bank
John A Vail - Hopton Bank
Mr C R D Woodward - Hopton Court
John Parry - Severnside, Dowles
W D 'Jock' MacPherson - Ludlow
Amy Rose Heath - Wythall
Louisa Jayne Udall - Pensham
Victoria Ann Udall - Pensham
Terry Blackwell - Ramsgate
Lucy Griffiths - Neen Savage
Mary & Norman Goodman - Hints
Mr & Mrs T A Vickers - Priorslee
Mrs Elsie Hotchkiss - Highley
Mr & Mrs L Chaffe - Walsall
Richard Chaffe - Little Stretton
Mr C Bullock - Little Stretton
Mrs Gwen Lloyd - Knowbury
Mr John Aston - Henfield
Mr H S F Rogers - Shirley
Vera Ladds (nee Bradford) - Radlett
John Brindley - Birmingham
Frances Chinn - Oreton
Marion James - Kinlet
Penny & Chris Hand - Bewdley
Pat Radnor - Knowbury
Robert Skevington - New Zealand
Judith Roele - Knowbury
Pat & Harold Deane - Hopton Bank
Martin & Brenda Cramp - Coreley
Mr & Mrs Bernard Cramp - Weymouth
Elizabeth Jones Lucas - Ludlow
Kathleen & Ernie Bishop - Norfolk
Ray Flaherty - Birmingham
Mathew Flaherty - Birmingham
Norah Phillips - Birmingham
T. J. - Birmingham
Karen & John Banford - Bewdley
William Edward Perry - Chesham
Jean & Ken Dalby - Pershore
Alf Jenkins - Orleton
Kay Grainger - Kings Norton
Paul Murray - Kings Norton
Valerie Ostick - Rawdon, Yorks.
Norman Painting - Small Heath
Erica Waite - Knowbury
Diana Humphries - Farlow
Margaret Fullman - Langton Green
Jeanetta Maxwell - Oreton
Pat & Ken Abell - Yarpole
Mrs M West - Oldbury
Gladys Hows - Foxwood
Emma Birch - Malvern
Andrew M Vail - Hopton Bank
Jan Vail - Hopton Bank
Mrs J R Perry - Hillocks Farm
Duncan Dormer - Tenbury Wells
Nathan Mark Foulgar - Hollywood
Lucy Charlotte Heath - Wythall
Rebecca Dawn Udall - Pensham
Roy Tomlin - Llanelen
Pat & Terence Walsh - Foxwood
Mr Christopher Gill MP - Ludlow
Mrs M E A Vail - Wellington
Desmond & Rosemary Key - Ludlow
Dot Shorthouse - Hopton Bank
Graham Chaffe - Cornwall
Mrs Iris Parks - Rowley Regis
Mrs J Welch - Marshbrook
Mark & Rose Green - Foxwood
Mr & Mrs B Hall - Hopton Castle
Mr & Mrs B Johnson - Derbyshire
Betty Millman - Kidderminster
The Wolseley Register - Birmingham
Frances Bentley - Kinlet
Nick Evans - Canada
Frank Jenkins - Ludlow
Jean Hollis - Knowbury
David & Mary Rogers - Dursley
R D Jordan - Crumpsbrook
Marina Clent - Knowbury
Richard Owen Stinton - Devon
Karen & Phil Perks - Coreley
Dean & Sharon Hall - Coreley
Steven Gardener - Birmingham
Andrew Gardener - Birmingham
James Gardener - Birmingham
Louis Anthony Meeson - Birmingham
Patricia Hume - Birmingham
Ann Whittaker - Leeds
Elizabeth Louise Penfold - Selsey

I do love
My country's good with respect more tender,
More holy and profound, than mine own life.

Coriolanus, Act 3.

DODDINGTON

Jean Cheadle
Leigh Latham
Joan & Gordon White - 2 copies
Freda & John Childs
Stan & Phyllis Edwards
Stella & Ken Butcher
Hilda & Tony Farmer
Mary & Eric Russell - 4 copies
Geoffrey Barratt
Iris & Andy Anderson
Sylvia & Ian Potts
Barbara & Gordon Mutlow
Joan & Douglas Owen
Stuart & Tracy Evans
Phillip Pearsall
Keith Jones
Mary James - in Memory of Don
Sheila & Meg Gabb
Joyce & John Round
Patricia Ann Ludlam
Ted Collins
Pat & Les Davies
Fred Lynch
Beryl & Derek Edwards
Tracy Clayton
Steven Clayton
Adrian & Lynne Clifford
Beryl & Alan Evans
Mr & Mrs Farrand
Gordon & Dorothy Stanyer
Sue & Terry Prince
Dave & Doreen King
Norman & Gill Goodwin
Joe & Violet Kirrage
Crid & Alan Webb
Tim & Kerry Evans
Mark & Gordon
Luke Latham
Heather Stark
Joan & Harold Kirk
Mo & Derek Field
Erika Rollinson
Betty Clark
Ken Newby
Gwen & Harry Pearce
Clive & Beryl
Diane & Duncan McDougall
Justine Dingley
Stuart Barker
Carol & Maurice Evans
Sonia Pearsall
Alex Pearsall
Sam & Mary - 'NI SAN HI'
Sheila Elizabeth Barker
Rose & Gilbert Bond - 2 copies
Marion & Harold Raithby
Susan Patchett
Maurice & Dorothy Aston
Jean & Fred Gittens
Eileen & Michael Mapp
Linda & Richard Clayton
Natalie Clayton
Rob & Lynne Pinner
Karla & Dennis Onions
Mr M MacDonald
Marjorie & Allan Bush
Doug & Doris Hall
Shirley Annable
Valerie & David Clifford
Matthew Clifford
James Clifford
Hannah Clifford
Walter & Alice Dolphin

CLEOBURY MORTIMER

May Jordon
Ronald & Brenda Hall
Amanda & Mark Pugh
Sarah Astbury
Beryl & Ted Cartwright
Kath Grove
Mark & Myfanwy Baldwin
Kate Morris
John Morgan
Les Martin
Eileen & Bert Clegg
Rosemary & Alfred Clark

CLEE HILL

Nesta Boden
W Jordan
Janet Yapp
R & J Tennant
Ken Hall
Dennis Crowther
Betty & John Varnish
Graham & Pam Edwards
Marlene & Ken Lockett
Elizabeth & Charles King
Hanson Aggregates - The Quarry
Mr & Mrs Jim Tennant
Mr & Mrs Jack Tennant
Mr & Mrs G Pugh
Mona & Roy Clent

At first glance the following poem may well have been specially written to commemorate the Battle of Britain!!

A look at the writer's name and the date of the work shows that this is not the case.

The time will come when thou shalt lift thine eyes
To watch a long drawn battle in the skies.
While aged peasants, too amazed for words,
Stare at the flying fleets of wondrous birds.
England so long mistress of the sea,
Where wind and waves caress her sovereignty,
Her ancient triumphs yet on high shall bear,
and reign, the sovereign of the conquered air.

Thomas Gray 1716 - 1771.

Was Thomas Gray blessed with the gift of foresight, which permitted him to view things of the future so graphically; or did he have an imagination that was two centuries ahead of his time?

We shall never Know

EPILOGUE

As the new century and Millennium dawns, it is surely the right time for us to take a long and thoughtful retrospective look at the now fast fading Millennium; with particular thought for those whom we held dear and are sadly no longer with us. From the conquest of 1066 to the present day, our Nation has grown and prospered as a result of the work and wisdom of our ancestors and leaders. There have certainly been some bad times and grave injustices, mostly as a result of human behaviour, but a few can be attributed to factors over which mankind had no control.

Let us hope and pray that our politicians and future leaders will strive and show wisdom during the difficult years ahead and maintain all that we and previous generations held and hold dear.

Let us also hope that mankind will show compassion and understanding in his treatment and behaviour towards his fellow beings.

Not the King's crown nor the deputed sword,
The marshal's truncheon nor the judge's robe,
Become them with one half so good a grace
As mercy does.

Measure for Measure, Act 2.
William Shakespeare.